CHILDREN AND TELEVISION

For my mother and father

Children and Television

CEDRIC CULLINGFORD
Dean of Educational Studies,
Oxford Polytechnic

Gower

Published by
Gower Publishing Company Limited,
Gower House, Croft Road, Aldershot,
Hampshire GU11 3HR, England

Reprinted 1984

British Library Cataloguing in Publication Data

Children and Television.
    1. Television and Children development
    2. Child
    I. Title
    155.4'18   HQ784.T4

    ISBN 0-566-00655-3

Printed and bound in Great Britain by
Biddles Ltd, Guildford and King's Lynn

Contents

Introduction

'When I survey this countless multitude of beings, shaped in each other's likenesses, among whom nothing rises and nothing falls, the sight of such universal uniformity saddens and chills me, and I am tempted to regret that form of (aristocratic) society which has ceased to be . . .'

De Tocqueville — *Democracy in America*

Television has been the subject of a great deal of debate at a variety of different levels. From the point of view of social psychologists with their particular interest in violence, or the sociologists with their concern for the organisations that control the mass media, to the critics who analyse the content or journalists who set out to demonstrate harmful social results, television arouses heated interest. But this concern with television, supported by large amounts of government money, contrasts with the absence of interest in studying the ways in which children learn.

The content of television is far easier to analyse than what goes on inside people's heads. And yet any study of the nature of response must be concerned with discovering how the individual approaches and reacts to what he sees, rather than setting out to prove an assumption or hypothesis that depends on guesswork. To say that research on the effects of television has proved disappointing, because its methods and conclusions have demonstrated an absence of curiosity and open-mindedness, is a donnée so often repeated (e.g. Tracey, 1977; Bruner,

1978; Eysenck and Nias, 1978; Williams, 1979; Hornick, 1981) that it does not need reiteration here. But the fundamental reason is the lack of attention paid to the nature of actual 'effect' or 'response'.

This book does not seek to prove one simple hypothesis, for example that violence seen on television is copied or that a children's picture of the world is imprinted by the stereotype of men as heroes. It attempts to discover, from children, what the truth is, from the attitudes that children bring to bear when watching television to their understanding of the distinctions between the true and the false. The nature of response is a complex subject and although the book approaches it from a number of different angles, the truth lies in the complex whole. The aim is to uncover something about the ways in which children learn, to give insight into the inner worlds of children, and not only into the obvious images of television. For this reason it is not a critique of all the work that has been done before, but puts forward positive evidence by using fresh material and relating it to some of the interesting work that has been carried out in areas such as imaging, perception and opinion change. Most of the experiments that show insight into the nature of response are carried out in complete isolation from each other because of the academic barriers set up by the tradition of scientific experiments, but many throw light on the reasons underlying the primary evidence given here. Thus the book is designed to give a clear insight into the ways in which children learn from television (and from other stimuli), and does not rely on analysis of the content of television. The programmes are ephemeral; children's learning is not.

Since the subject of television is of such interest, a well-known danger in this kind of topic is that everyone thinks he is the expert. The first thought that many people have about television often remains their last. In the face of any evidence they stick to their own hypothesis. But as research on opinion change shows (q.v. Chapter 13) it is a human characteristic to stick to an opinion once it is established, even in the face of massive evidence. This human characteristic applies equally to researchers, many of whom have set out, or been paid, to prove by experiment or correlations that there is a connection between television and violence. What we need, however, is an open mind and fresh evidence and a genuine curiosity about the nature of response.

This survey of children's response to television is based on more than five thousand children. Since there were no assumptions made before starting, about differences in family or temperament, they come from a wide variety of backgrounds. The majority were from northern England, from rural and urban areas, from Manchester and from different parts of Cumbria, large or small industrial towns — some suffering severely from economic depression — farming areas or rural areas dominated by tourism. In addition a group of children came from Birmingham, especially those parts which are distinctive for having a sizeable majority of first- or second-generation immigrants. To make the survey even more 'cross-cultural' some research was also carried out in North America, concentrating particularly on an area in Texas which included a variety of different ethnic backgrounds. The social variety of children in this survey is therefore very wide, and covers as large a spectrum as possible in a work that does not set out to make assumptions about such distinctions by selecting particular groups. But the most important fact about the children is that (some difference of age and sex apart: see Chapter 19) there were *no* differences in response in the findings due to class, ethnic origin, domestic circumstances or the style of television programme shown in different countries. One of the most important facts about the survey is the general consistency of the findings despite the wide variety of circumstances and experiences.

Rather than a series of small-scale experiments, this book provides primary material from children to illuminate the nature of response. This derives from open questions and from written material provided by the children. Not only were the answers given by children consistent but they showed a great deal of accuracy when their answers were tested. Naturally there is no point in asking questions like 'Are you affected by violence on television?', or 'How much time do you spend watching television?', however large the survey. A basic mistake, like a transferred question which is actually about defensive perception (vide Belson, 1978), is the worse compounded for being repeated. Children were therefore asked questions, often the same one more than once, which did *not* depend on a pre-judged hypothesis. There were therefore no expectations about their answers that might have affected them, like a researcher obviously relishing evidence about sex and violence being given what he wants (since children can be very polite and seek to please, vide Chapter 8). Instead of being asked a question like 'How many programmes did you watch last night?' children would be asked to say *what* they had watched, so that their answers would be both more revealing and capable of being tested against the schedules. The same type of questions, implicit in the different chapters, were used on a number of different occasions to check the consistency of the response, to make sure that, for example, their favourite programmes were not just a matter of a passing fad, a trend amongst their friends, or that they were not replying out of false bravado or any attempt to show off to the questioner.

Children are usually better at answering questions honestly than adults; they are less determined about the impression that they wish to make and much less self-deceiving. Naturally, some of their answers smacked of parody of their parents, as in the case where they brought out all of the moral strictures about those very programmes they insisted on watching themselves, thereby allying themselves to the universal voice which says 'All people are affected by what they see on television, except *me*' (see Chapter 15). Children's characteristics of honesty in answering questions created their own difficulties. One example is the way they would try to answer all questions literally. When questioned about matters such as identification or truth and falsehood they showed that they did not share some of the assumptions that the questioner might have expected; their answers were revealing at a different level (cf. Chapter 6 and 14). Children also showed that they did not consider that many of the programmes were worth thinking about. They were used to undergoing comprehension tests. They were quick to adapt to the use of television as a comprehension test, for their approach is quite different if they *know* they are going to be questioned. But they were unaccustomed to thinking in the same way about the content of their favourite programmes. Thus many of the assumptions that have been made by researchers — cathartic reactions, modelling, stereotyping, hero-worship — simply pass over the children.

The emphasis throughout the book is on the children, and their response to television. It might be thought that their reactions are not in fact, very different from those of adults. Their tastes after all, are very similar. But the point is that they reveal subtle styles of learning, far removed from the primitive notion that they are empty vessels into which material is poured. Their answers show a consistency of response that lies below the superficial differences between programmes. The details of the programmes themselves are not particularly important since they are soon dated. Although American television is taken into account (many of the favourite programmes in Great Britain come from the United States) children's answers about programming styles, especially the 'routining' of advertisements are based on British television. But the difference between styles of presentation, like the difference between children, is superficial compared to the consistencies of response which children reveal, from what they expect from television to what they take from it, whether this is seen in terms of information or violence, advertising or education.

PART I
WHAT CHILDREN EXPECT FROM TELEVISION

'A taste for poetry . . . is apt, if too much indulged, to engender a fastidious contempt for the ordinary business of the world, and gradually to unfit us for the exercise of the useful and domestic virtues which depend on our not exalting our feelings above the temper of well-ordered and well-educated society.'

Sir Walter Scott, *Letters*, vol.II, p.278

1 Children's tastes on television

'I like watching the television; if we did not have one I would be bored stiff.' (boy, 11)

A small but significant proportion of programmes are designed specifically for children. The producers take great care about the style and content and are sensitive about their audience, both in terms of the viewing figures and in terms of the expected, or possible, response. They wish their audience to imbibe all that is best in television by being entertained and instructed. To the producers of children's television popularity is a necessary step towards success.

Children are very clear about their preferences. From an early age they show themselves to be knowledgeable, accurate about what is offered on television, and consistent in their tastes. When asked to cite their favourite programmes, either on a particular day of the week or overall, they show an almost unanimous indifference to children's programmes. This does not mean that children do not watch children's programmes or that they will not be able to give interesting opinions about them when asked, but their overwhelming preference, from the age of six, is for programmes designed for adults. To some extent their preference is due to children's growing sophistication towards television although there have always been signs of this preference since its early days (Himmelweit et al. 1958).

The most popular programmes on television are those that are designed purely for entertainment. Even if producers explain their intentions in terms of subtle social messages, and even if they suggest pro-

3

found insights into personal relationships, these ambitions are not perceived as significant by the majority of the audience. Television is linked in children's minds with the undemanding pleasure of watching serials or being entertained by advertisements. With a few exceptions, such as cartoons, children's programmes do not offer the type of pleasure, in terms of style or content, that is manifested by programmes designed for their parents.

Children state clear preferences for certain types of programme, knowing exactly what to expect, and wishing this expectation to be met consistently. One girl of twelve, uniquely, showed a more subtle sense of discrimination saying that she would watch programmes 'only if it is about something I like'. All the others not only knew what they liked but which programmes would provide it. Their tastes read like a reflection of the Neilsen ratings, for they welcome what is most on offer. Children reflect a taste which has not changed to any significant degree over the last thirty years. In 1951 Smythe and Campbell demonstrated how much time was taken up with some form of drama, from thrillers to medical shows and comedies. In the three years from 1951 to 1953 Smythe discovered that drama of one kind or another accounted for virtually three-quarters of the programmes. This dominance of drama over documentaries is equally true of programming in Great Britain and the United States today. Gerbner et al. (1969) underline the general popularity of drama and light comedy. Even on days which Open University and the BBC Schools Service broadcast their programmes, the proportion of all 'cultural' programmes — news, discussions and opera — as well as education, is small.

Children welcome what is generally on offer. They reflect the ability to adapt to the overall style of television. But in their adaptation they also show clear preferences. From the age of seven thrillers such as *Starsky and Hutch* or *The Professionals* are clear favourites. The consistency of tastes among different groups of children, from a wide variety of backgrounds, makes it clear that their tastes are not expressions of complex individual needs. Instead, they show a thirst for entertainment met by drama thrillers which were cited by about half of all children, and by situation comedies, such as *Are you being served?* or *Open All Hours*, which were the favourite programmes of about a third of the children. Other favourites cited included football and other sports, and *Top of the Pops*. Very few gave soap operas such as *Crossroads* or *Coronation Street* as their favourites; even fewer gave a children's programme such as *Blue Peter*.

Children's preferences for particular programmes naturally reflected what was available. When asked to cite their favourites on particular days they showed detailed knowledge as well as distinct tastes. Thus it was clear that while the overwhelming preference on Saturdays was for drama, a rather larger number of boys than usual preferred the sport. On Sundays an unusually large proportion of children preferred to watch some form of comedy. On an evening when the thrillers on offer were rather less attractive, or the comedies like *Fawlty Towers*, (especially for boys) rather more so, their preferences would divide more equally between the two. On its particular night *Top of the Pops* would win more support; occasionally children would find themselves forced to cite a documentary such as *Tomorrow's World* which they would genuinely enjoy if there were nothing on television closer to their normal tastes.

The fact that children prefer certain types of programme, and do so quite distinctly, does not imply that they do not watch many others. Nor does it imply that they derive no pleasure from the others. *Tomorrow's World* is liked by a high proportion of those few who actually watch it. On special occasions boys would prefer to watch a football match or boxing rather than their overall favourite serial. Children had clear preferences for each day of the week, although the types of programme they liked were nearly always consistent with their favourite overall. It is as if they followed the analysis of the contents of television as given by Gerbner (1972) and Goodhardt et al. (1975). Apart from a tendency for girls of six to enjoy *Blue Peter*, there is little indication of fundamental changes according to age although some boys turn to football instead of programmes such as *Dr Who* or *Cannon*. Girls show a greater tendency to like some comedies (cf. Chapter 19).

The liking of thrillers, especially American serials, such as *Starsky and Hutch, Kojak, Six Million Dollar Man* and *Charlie's Angels*, is a significant constant with children from the age of six. This preference prevailed even while boys were expressing an additional interest in football, and girls in domestic comedies. In terms of comedy, children's tastes show different tendencies according to sex. Girls consistently demonstrate a liking for adult situation comedy, especially those concerned with domesticities such as *Some Mothers do 'ave 'em* and *The Good Life*. Boys are more interested in 'live' comedians such as Benny Hill, the Two Ronnies and Morecambe and Wise. Cartoons such as *Tom and Jerry* are also of interest to younger children. Younger boys of five and six prefer the knock-about cartoons; older boys the stand-up comedians, including those who parody well-known personalities.

Apart from cartoons, children's interest in comedy is in tune with adult tastes. There is little evidence that they prefer those programmes ostensibly designed for them. Their favourite thrillers, and their other favourites from comedy to football, are already close to the viewing preferences of adults. Children seem to develop their viewing habits early. Of all the offerings during the time when children return from school until 7.30pm less than 18 per cent of all the children said they liked any of the programmes designed with them in mind. Of this small proportion most were children of five and six who liked cartoons. These preferences are the most distinct because it is clear that their experience of many programmes is extensive; they watch a great deal that they do not particularly like.

The reason that children like certain programmes is both simple and complex. The simple reason is that children, like adults, view television as a source of entertainment. They do not seek intellectual stimulation or emotional demands. Thrillers, with their ritual of fulfilled expectations in which the heroes will always survive, and comedies in which the situation is always the same, offer entertainment that can be relied upon not to vary. Serials which combine a great deal of action without changes in character offer that blend of familiarity and 'safe' excitement that children soon grow to like. But the reasons that children derive pleasure from television programmes are also more complex. On the one hand they suggested that their favourite programmes fulfilled definite expectations — 'lots of fighting', 'very funny', or 'I like adventure programmes'. On the other hand they gave pragmatic reasons for liking distinct programmes — 'I like the dogs in it', 'I am football crazy' or 'I like animals'. Occasionally they would cite a specific reason, having learned something new or different. Thus they are *capable* of liking the unexpected even if they generally preferred to have their well-tested expectations fulfilled.

Children like thrillers because of their tone and style, but even programmes that they do not particularly like can interest them because of a particular event, as in the case of *Blue Peter* when there is a programme about animals. Thus the more varied magazine programmes can be interesting for personal reasons: 'Because some actors from a children's programme were there. They did some nice acting' (girl, 7), or 'Because it had a quiet little tiger cub on it' (girl, 8, of *Beasts on the Street*). A boy of seven liked *A Question of Sport* 'because it has my best sport players on and it had a funny football on'. *Top of the Pops* was liked, naturally enough, for the music but also because 'it has got punk on it and I like to see their hair styles and I like sexy pistols' (boy, 11).

Some of the reasons that children give for liking programmes are not surprising. Boys referred to 'lots of fighting' or the 'murders and detectives'. But many children, when asked about what they had enjoyed the night before, referred to a programme they liked best 'Because there was nothing better on'. This sense of watching because it is there pervades many of the statements the children make: 'It's a habit to watch *Crossroads*', 'It is on every week', 'There's nothing better to do' reveal more about their expectations than about their distinct pleasures.

No programme on television fulfils children's expectations of entertainment better than advertisements (cf. Chapter 14). Nearly all children like advertisements, and their awareness of what advertisements are for does not diminish their enjoyment. The entertainment value of advertisements is significant as it suggests that they are seen as minor programmes in their own right and that the very repetition is a form of pleasure. The reasons that children like advertisements do not depend upon the product being advertised. As in their favourite programmes, children appreciate the humour or the characters depicted. Eighty per cent of children from the age of ten like advertisements because of the way they are presented, whatever the advertisement is for:

'I like it because it has some humour in it.' (girl, 9, of Home Insulation)
'I like the little green man and you get a good laugh.' (girl, 10, of Butlins Holiday Camps)
'I liked the way the cans walked.' (girl, 11, of McEwans Lager)
'I like the song and it rhymes.' (boy, 10, of Peanut Butter)
'It shows action and I like the music.' (boy, 10, of Striker football game)
'He always does funny tricks.' (boy, 11, of British Telecom)
'I know it off by heart.' (boy, 12, of Nightnurse)
'It was football and I like football.' (boy, 11, of Gillette razors)
'I like the boy when he runs.' (girl, 10, of Weetabix)
'I like it because it is funny.' (girl, 11, of British Telecom)
'With its green man; I like it when one is playing a guitar.' (boy, 8, of Butlins Holiday Camps)

If children are clear about what they like on television they are even clearer about what they dislike. Children dislike those programmes that make the most demands of them. Although children of seven take almost a moral stance and suggest that they dislike programmes that deal with war or horror as much as *Blue Peter*, they later become quite clear that it is the news or documentaries that least interest them. More than a third of all children pointed out that although they would watch the news since it was unavoidable they were bored by it. Some children took sharp exception to *Crossroads* or *Coronation Street*; quite a number rated children's programmes as the least interesting on television. They dislike those programmes that make demands on them either in terms of the levels of expected attention or in the reliance on words rather than images. They dislike those programmes that make demands on them not because of the level of presentation (they dislike

John Craven's Newsround, designed especially for them, as much as other documentaries) nor because programmes like *Blue Peter* are too young for them, but because the programmes which demand close involvement from the audience contrast sharply with the more familiar satisfaction to be gained from a regular thriller like *Starsky and Hutch*. A programme like *Blue Peter* can make a strong appeal to those children who watch it, and it is an appeal that varies considerably from one programme to the next. But it is not an appeal to which children look forward in happy anticipation.

Quite a number of children who watch *Crossroads* or *Coronation Street* appear to enjoy disliking them. Both fall between the categories of detective thriller and situation comedy. The response they seem to elicit is a kind of familiar contempt. Whereas boys tend to dislike domestic drama, younger girls do not rate football programmes very highly. But children's dislikes are dominated by programmes that rely on the direct spoken word. Halloran (1970) pointed out that delinquents particularly dislike programmes that make educational demands on them. Himmelweit et al. (1958) reported that 'Only the Election broadcasts and *Panorama*, which tend to rely on verbal rather than pictorial presentation, obtained really low reaction indices' (p. 135). Even those advertisements which draw attention to their message and rely on the clarity of rational argument are the most disliked, and the least effective (Cox, 1961; Janis and Feshbach, 1953). Thus the lowest-rated personalities on television are those who contrast most strongly with the silent action-packed heroes of thrillers. Children's least-favourite personalities are those whose fame depends upon their talk rather than their actions. The more attention to distinctions of character (i.e. Clement Freud, Magnus Pike or Mohammed Ali) the more likely is a reaction *against* that character. Three-quarters of the children said that they dislike those who talk and draw attention to themselves, like politicians:

> 'She is always talking.'   (boy, 8, of Margaret Thatcher)
> 'He never smiles when I have seen him; he's boring.'   (boy, 10, of Richard Baker)
> 'His arms confuse me.'   (boy, 11, of Magnus Pike)
> 'He always talks about politics.'   (girl, 11, of Harold Wilson)
> 'He is a big head.'   (girl, 9, of Edward Heath)

The real distinction between pleasure and boredom is the level of demand; the heroes *do*, and the villains *talk* (q.v. Heroes and heroines, Chapter 5).

The way in which children talk about their favourite or least-favourite programmes suggest that they have come to terms with the medium as a source of entertainment rather than a major source of stimulation. The fact that they have clear favourites does not imply that these are the only programmes, or types of programmes, that they watch. Children watch numerous programmes they do not particularly care for, but continue to watch in the absence of anything better. Loyalty to a particular programme or a particular channel is mitigated by the habit of watching for its own sake. The scheduling on Sundays, for example, gives children a problem since there are not as many of their favourite types of programme from which to choose. But children still watch, even if they cite the programmes as 'all middling'. Children's responses to the question of their favourite programme on Sundays show a balance between their consistent preference for programmes with the highest immediate entertainment value, and their ability to adapt to the offerings of a particular evening. Children watch even when there is little they really like.

Some children have large numbers of favourite programmes, and can cite them all:

> 'I like watching television on my holidays like *Dennis the Menace, Bionic Man, the Munsters, Frankenstein, Mr Ed, Charlie's Angels, Tom and Jerry, Crackerjack, Starsky and Hutch, Bugs Bunny, the Muppets, Seaside Special, Man about the House, Benny Hill, Laurel and Hardy* and *Carry On* films, I sometimes play on my bike and go to the pictures.'
>
> (boy, 9)

> 'The things that interest me are mostly watching TV. My favourite programmes are *Starsky and Hutch* and *Charlie's Angels, Mr Ed, Top of the Pops, Bionic Man, Bionic Woman* and the *Addams Family*.' (girl, 10)

The sheer number of favourites implies that there is no particular 'station loyalty'. Although there is a marked tendency to avoid BBC2, and, subsequently, Channel 4, and a preference for ITV rather than BBC1, most children switch readily from one channel to another. But if there is no strong loyalty evinced towards channels, there is a considerable degree of loyalty towards their favourite programmes. Over 90 per cent of all children from the age of seven said that they would, in a week's time, watch the same programme that they had enjoyed most on the previous evening; furthermore, they actually did so. The minority who did not were mostly those who pointed out that the ending of a particular series prevented their watching it in a week's time. As Bailyn discovered as early as 1959, children want to see more of the kinds of material of which they already see a great deal.

Children's distinct preference for certain types of entertainment is clear. Those who do not watch television so much make sure that they see their favourite thriller; heavier viewers combine their favourites with everything else that is on. Children accept the distinction between the most typical offerings on television, designed to entertain rather than to give information or extend sensibilities, and the rarer programmes that would be deemed 'high culture'. Children show a consistent liking for entertainment rather than instruction. Coupled with a suspicion of those programmes that make explicit demands, this shows a ready adaptation to a set of standard expectations of television that soon become norms.

2 Children's viewing habits

'It's a habit to watch *Crossroads*.'   (girl, 11)

Television offers children a great deal of what they want to see, and children spend a great deal of their time responding to this offer. Although there will always be a few exceptions, the sheer amount of time that the majority of children spend watching television is a constant surprise. It is also a significant factor in understanding their response to television.

Early research on the impact of the medium on children was dominated by the question of how much time children spent watching television. Since it contrasted so strongly with other means of spending time and other media such as comics. Himmelweit, Oppenheim and Vince (1958) and Schramm, Lyle and Parker (1961) were particularly interested in the changing habits of children and the difference television made to the amount of time they spent with their parents and friends. This early research had the strength of its own pragmatism. While it did not explore the consequences of viewing behaviour, it did help establish the fact that a surprisingly large proportion of children's lives is spent watching television. This finding is an important first step in understanding the formation of attitudes through watching television.

After their commercial introduction, after the second world war, television sets were brought into the majority of households too quickly for researchers to set up studies using 'control' groups without television. It is now rare to find any child that does not watch regularly, let alone one who does not possess a television set. Among all the five thousand children interviewed for this study, only six did not have a television set in their homes. Four of these lived in a rural area without electricity. Even this did not prevent them having some access to television in their friends' houses. Lyle and Hoffman, in a survey of American homes in 1972, found that less than 2 per cent of households did not own at least one television. The days when television was a rare and excitingly unusual entertainment are long past.

Television is now a natural part of children's lives, accepted with a degree of sophistication that derives from familiarity. The existence of television sets in houses does not automatically indicate that they are switched on, nor if they are switched on that they are watched. But many surveys have confirmed that television is watched for an average of hours, not minutes, every evening. Diamond (1975) found that 66 per cent of the American population had their television sets on for six hours every evening during the summer, and for seven hours every evening in the winter. Goodhardt et al. (1975) confirmed similar habits in the United Kingdom. Belson (1960) showed that the acquisition of a television set meant that much more time would be spent at home. But while the family as a whole was affected by this change of habit, children very quickly grew up accustomed to it. It is not only adults who spend many hours in front of the small screen (BBC, 1978; Bailyn, 1959). Liebert, Neale and Davidson (1973) discovered that children under the age of thirteen watched television for at least two hours every day. Greenberg (1976) measured the amount of time children watched as three hours every day in winter, and two hours and ten minutes on average during the summer. Gilbert (1978) confirmed that children under the age of twelve spent two hours per day watching television. Bush (1978) suggests that the amount of time spent viewing increases after the age of twelve.

This overall figure of between two and three hours per evening is an *average* one; and covers a whole range of habits that includes some very lengthy sessions. It is significant, however, that children tend to watch television every evening; and one only needs to question them about what they have seen to understand the extent of their viewing. In this survey over 93 per cent of children had watched television the previous night, whether they were questioned in the summer or the winter, during term time or in the holidays. They were not asked how many hours they had watched, for there was always the danger of minimising the amount of time the television was on. But the details of their replies about *what* they had seen indicated that the average of two hours per evening, even if it contains periods, like holidays in Spain, when children cannot get to a television set, is a low average. Children are consistent in their viewing habits, not only consistent in taste, but in the amounts they see. Even those few children who had not seen any television the previous evening had invariably seen some during the evening before that. The break in the television habit did not last long.

The fact that children watch so much television implies that they watch a significant proportion of what they do not particularly like. They do not watch only their favourites; other programmes, such as the news or *Blue Peter*, inevitably intrude into an evening's entertainment. Their knowledge of what is on offer is detailed and extensive, not only about the times when their favourite programmes appear or about when their favourite programme for each evening is scheduled, but about those programmes they do not like and might prefer to ignore. Their very regularity means that they become familiar with diurnal routines. They do not wait until the right time for their favourite programme before turning on the television, and do not subsequently turn the television off. When they were asked to cite the programmes that they had seen, the amounts that they appeared to have watched varied considerably. Only 3 per cent had watched just one programme; 13 per cent had watched at least two, 19 per cent had watched at least three programmes and 21 per cent had watched at least four. The other 44 per cent of children had watched at least five programmes during the previous evening; some of which might have been fairly short, but others substantially lengthier. Younger children up to the age of eight watched only slightly less than older ones.

There were a few 'heavy viewers' who followed the programmes through virtually from the moment they came home from school to the time they went to bed. One girl of eleven, for an example, only began looking at the television at 5.45pm (the news) but then saw *Crossroads*, the *Kenny Everett Show. Coronation Street, A Sharp Intake of Breath, The World in Action*, the *News*, a feature film *(The Prime of Miss Jean Brodie)* and then the horror film which started at 11.30pm. This included switching from ITV to BBC1 and back. Some children stayed with a particular channel for an evening, like a boy of eleven who watched ITV; from *Enid Blyton's Famous Five* at 4.45pm. through *University Challenge, Lookaround, Crossroads*, the *Kenny Everett Show, Coronation Street*, to *George and Mildred* which began at 8pm. Some occasionally watched nothing but BBC1, like a girl of ten who began with *Jackanory* at 4.25pm and ended, taking in *Top of the Pops*, and *Blankety Blank* on the way with the feature film *(The African Queen)* which ended at around 11pm.

When children cite how many programmes they see on television they do not only reveal the large amounts of time they have spent in such an activity but also give evidence of an accurate knowledge of the schedules of television. Naturally, the more they watch the more likely they are to see those programmes that appear to them to have designs upon them, programmes designed to make them think. Children cite not only drama and comedy as programmes they have seen but news and documentaries. They might not like the news but are aware of the programme. Thus although few children particularly *like* to watch *Blue Peter*, few will deliberately go out of their way to avoid watching it. When children cite the programme they have seen it sometimes reads as if they were repeating the schedules of the *Radio Times* or the *TV Times*. This is in itself quite a remarkable achievement, clearly demonstrated whenever one tries to repeat it. It is as if all the energy of memory had been given to a knowledge of what programmes appeared, rather than what was in them (q.v. Chapter 10).

Children's detailed and comprehensive knowledge of what is on television, which develops rapidly from the age of six, includes awareness of the pleasures to be gained on particular days. Thus Saturday is associated with thrillers; or, for boys, with football and other sport. Sundays are not particularly looked forward to although Sunday afternoons are considered to be 'prime' time by some. But children's knowledge of what is on is helped by the consistency of the scheduling. There is a regularity in the appearance of certain types of programme, even if the details vary, a regularity made the more significant by the permanence of series such as *Crossroads* and *Coronation Street*. Certain serials are watched regularly by very large numbers of children. All but 3 per cent of all children have regularly seen *Dr Who*; and three-quarters or more are or have been regular viewers of thriller serials such as *Starsky and Hutch, Kojak, Wonder Woman, The Bionic Woman, Charlie's Angels* and *The Rockford Files*. Those who watch any one of these series, who have a distinct favourite amongst them, will almost invariably watch all the others in the same genre as well.

Most of the children's favourite programmes are screened in the later part of the evening. While the television set might be switched on from the moment they arrive home after school, or, during the vacations, from the moment there is anything to see, children make sure they watch their favourite programmes which appear generally after 7.30pm, and sometimes much later. Their favourite programmes on Saturdays, for example, tended to appear later in the evenings; more than one-third of the children regularly watched their preferred programme after 9pm. This prevalence of late night viewing and this taste for adult programmes is exhibited as much by children of eight and nine as by children of ten and eleven. Saturday nights might be a special case for some children, but late-night viewing is one of the distinct pleasures that often seems to take place throughout the week, although the coming of the video might make a change in this pattern. This expression of preference for 'adult' programmes was not only an expression of desire; even the younger children actually *watched* their favourite programmes week by week. Even in the case of comedy programmes children much prefer to, and do, watch situation comedies, or comedians appearing after 7.30pm rather than children's cartoons that appear in the late afternoon. Himmelweit et al. (1958) and Maccoby (1951) suggested that television made little difference to the time children went to bed. Children's habits must have changed since the 1950s.

Late night viewing can be defined, from the point of view of seven- and eight-year-olds, as being anything after 7.30pm by which time many children will have been watching for several hours. Children continually discuss programmes in 'prime' viewing time from 7.30pm to 9.30pm. But to the children themselves 'late' implies those films that go on after midnight, as in 'late night movies'. All children of eleven had stayed up after midnight to watch particular programmes; more than half of the children aged eight had done so. A few of them had stayed up longest to watch a special occasion such as the Apollo 5 rocket launching, or the Eurovision Song Contest. But most had stayed up late to see horror films. One of the general complaints about television is that programmes unsuitable for children are put on too early in the evening. For this reason horror films are scheduled very late. But this does not prevent the children seeing them (let alone buying their own videos). Series such as *Appointment with Fear* or *For Adults Only* gain a significant regular audience of children from the age of eight. Most children have seen films such as *Dracula, Frankenstein, King Kong, The Devil Rides Out, The Earth Dies Screaming, Werewolf versus Frankenstein, Horror in the Opera House* and *Island of Terror.* All these films were scheduled late to avoid the possibility of children watching them, on the grounds that such horror, unlike Grimm's fairy tales, might disturb or frighten them.

Even the most popular thrillers, like *The Professionals,* full of deaths and car chases, are not generally thought particularly suitable for children. Every six months or so newspapers carry articles complaining about the amount of violence in these programmes. The fact that children nevertheless watch them raised the question of the role of parents. Greenberg (1976) suggests that from the age of seven or eight children begin to be allowed to watch television late. This survey indicates that all children are generally free to watch whatever they wish to, whenever they wish. There are some parents who do retain strict control. They choose which programmes their children watch, and sometimes watch *with* their children. But although children are aware of their parents' choices it is more like an awareness of a difference in taste, or a question of convenience rather than a sense of strict control. Only about a quarter of the children from the age of eight actually said that their parents allowed them to see anything they wished to; they were aware of some form of parental control. But the reasons for this control showed distinctions of taste rather than censorship; 'I can't watch Tom and Jerry when my dad wants the news on' (girl, 8); 'It all depends if they are in a good or bad mood' (boy, 10); 'Good films which she has seen and I haven't; that's what she stops me watching' (boy, 11). Even when children were aware that their parents did not want them to watch thrillers, they did not feel actually prevented from doing so. And even if they *felt* prevented, the fact remains that children actually watch, as well as prefer, adult programmes and satisfy their taste for horror movies. When parents are asked about what they allow their children to see they give conventional answers, and suggest that they are strict in their choice, discriminating in their judgements and modest in their rationing of amount. Children themselves, in a parody of their parents, say that they, too, would support strict censorship, and prevent younger brothers or sisters or friends watching certain programmes. But the gap between what they say and what they do is very wide. The programmes that children say they would *not* allow their younger siblings to experience are almost invariably their own favourites. What is right for them is not right for others. Thus children parody their parents not only in viewing habits but in the ways in which they talk about them. Just as parents make generalised judgements based on their own experiences, so do children. Just as parents try to give the impression they feel they *ought* to give, but in fact act in a different way, so do their children. Children reveal the distinction between their own tastes and their attitudes to other people's.

On the one hand they are pragmatic about what television offers, but on the other hand suggest the dangers of viewing violence as if they were parodying the conventional stance of commentators and critics. Children even express a tendency to be slightly more censorious than their parents. Apart from suggesting that others should not watch a programme such as *Crossroads* — 'because it's rubbish' — they give concern that other children should not be frightened — 'I wouldn't let them watch a thriller; it would frighten them' (girl, 10); 'Anything with murders and things' (girl, 11); 'A programme when they were shooting birds' (boy, 10); 'One of those with lots of blood and that' (boy, 9). But they make certain that they have seen the programmes themselves, or they would not be in a position to know what they should prevent others.

Children's pragmatism about television is not just expressed in the amount that they watch, or when they watch, but the way in which it becomes part of the texture of their lives. Some children watch whatever is on, with varying degrees of boredom. Others time their lives according to what is on. Their habits are expressed in a complex interaction between programmes and other events:

'The things I like doing are woodwork and riding my bike and when I go inside I like watching TV and my favourite programme is *Tarzan*.' (boy, 7)

'I watch *Starsky and Hutch* and I play in the back street and *Star Trek* then I went into the park to play.' (boy, 7)

'When I watch television I like to watch *Playschool* and I like to watch *Stop, Look and Listen* and I like to watch *Words and Pictures* and other programmes. I like to play with my friends and I like to ride my bike.' (girl, 6)

'Every Friday after school I come home and watch television because I don't like playing outside. I watch it 'till about five o'clock and then it is my tea. After tea I watch *Crossroads*. After *Crossroads* there is a knock on the door and it is Alison so I have to play with her. We play until about half past six and then I go in and watch *Dennis the Menace*.' (girl, 10)

'When I come home from school I sit down and watch *Emmerdale Farm* or *The Cedar Tree*. Then I look in the paper to see what is on next. It is *Playschool* so I switch off the television and go play with Tracey and Helen my next door neighbours. The best programmes I like are the *Muppets* and *Starsky and Hutch*. On Saturday afternoons it is very boring because all it is, is football and wrestling and other boring things so I go and play out . . .' (girl, 9)

Examples of this adaptation to television abound; for television is one of children's central interests. They express distinct tastes and work out their lives around the schedules, whether they stay in and do other things at the same time, or whether they feel forced to go outside during the summer. Their knowledge of what is on, and their programme loyalty, remain as strong as their habits of watching. Television is therefore a central part of their lives both in terms of the time spent watching and in the way in which it is part of the normal texture of their lives.

3 Children's viewing styles

'I did not concentrate on this programme to tell the truth;
I ate my tea.' (boy, 12).

On the advent of television the most clearly voiced concern was that it would alter the habits of domestic life. The two early surveys of the impact of television (Himmelweit et al. 1958, Schramm et al. 1961) stressed not only the difference that television programmes could make to the knowledge or opinions of the audience, but the difference that the presence of a television set could make to the domestic behaviour of children and their attitudes towards work and play:

'Thus, as 150 million people rearranged their lives in the 1950's, to accommodate the picture tube in the living room, the rearrangement was most striking in the homes with children.' (Schramm et al. p.11)

One of the major points they made was that instead of listening to the radio, children would spend an equal amount of time, or more, in watching television. They argued that television would change children's habits of entertainment by displacing the role of comics, and by increasing the amount of absorption in such habits, since television provides a rich combination of visual and auditory stimulation. Their great fear of television stemmed from its very attractiveness; it was seen as a viable alternative to the 'normal' pattern of home life revolving around the sharing of conversation, games and interests. Television was seen to destroy more active human relationships by taking away the time spent in maintaining them.

The amount of time spent in watching television is well established although the significance of the amount has rarely been fully analysed, since more attention has been paid to what children watch than to their experience of watching television. The fact that a home possesses a television set does not mean that the set is necessarily switched on. The fact that a television set is switched on does not necessarily imply that it is being watched. When television was first introduced it carried a certain amount of prestige; it was unusual enough to be special. It was taken seriously as a medium that could be trusted more than news-papers in its presentation of the news. This sense of its importance was exhibited not only by children and their parents but by researchers and commentators. But television is nowadays taken for granted to a far greater extent, and therefore the more easily ignored. Far from being watched with close attention it is more likely to be left switched on while other activities take place. A survey of forty-two homes showed that the television in the living room was switched on permanently during the period that children returned from school in all but two of the homes. But less than half the families were making any effort to watch with anything more than the occasional casual glance. It was only later in the evening that the whole family might stop their individual tasks and pay attention to a programme.

The habit of watching television contrasts with tasks that demand close attention and necessitate learning. While the television set can be ignored as a background noise, it can also be watched as if it were no more than a background effect. Television presents information of all kinds but this does not mean that those who watch actually pay attention to the information. One of the most significant devices in the study of viewing habits has been the Bechtel technique (Bechtel et al. 1972). This instrument records the eye movements of viewers to see how much of the time they are actually watching the screen. Although the audiences ostensibly fix their eyes on the screen, they actually only watch for a proportion of the time. Rather like the saccadic movements of reading, when the eye, instead of following a steady movement from left to right, actually jumps around in an almost random restlessness, so the television screen elicits only passing glances. With a moving image, as opposed to the stillness of print, it might be thought that all the necessary perceptual motion was being taken up in the flickering, changing images of the screen. But most viewers actually look away from the screen even when watching their favourite programmes, not only to take more visual information from elsewhere but to receive less from the movements before them.

As the Bechtel technique makes clear, children do not closely watch every part of the programme. They combine viewing with other activities, whether these be playing with toys or eating their tea (Lorch et al. 1979). Television can be a background to many other activities, but it can appear as little more than a background even at its most intense moments. Even when watching an exciting film the audience tends to look at the set for only about 76 per cent of the time (Diamond, 1975). Children's visual attention is not particularly high (Yussen, 1974). The process of television viewing does not depend upon a complex analysis of information; the very variety of stimuli makes the act of response,

that of gaining a minimum amount of necessary or required information, relatively easy. Thus children learn to pay attention to certain
recognisable clues, and do so without too much difficulty. The fact that
they do not keep their eyes focused on the screen is not only a physiological fact but an insight into the nature of the entertainment offered,
and the way in which they approach it. Children bring their own
attitudes to television and, as many have pointed out (for example
Brown, 1976) what they bring to television is as important as what
they receive from it. It would be surprising, given the amount of television that children see, if they could fully concentrate for such a
length of time. The Bechtel technique establishes that the attention
paid is limited, even physically, let alone at the level of mental activity
brought to bear.

The ways in which children watch television are themselves significant in the formation of their overall response. The fact that television
is both taken for granted and often ignored, coupled with the fact that
it is seen as a medium for light entertainment, creates the conditions in
which any analysis of effect must be based. Children's approach to
television is different from their approach to material on which they
expect to be tested. They will scrutinise a programme on which they
know a teacher will ask questions quite differently from one they
watch out of their own choice. The very fact that other tasks are
carried out while viewing (Atkin et al. 1972; Lorch, Anderson and
Levin, 1979) means that a certain type of selective attention can be
established in such a way that it becomes a habitual approach. It is as
if children assume that television does not demand nor deserve the
closest concentration or complete involvement (Robinson, 1969). The
irony of this is that the medium itself becomes more important as a
constant, more important in itself than in the information it presents.
Television is seen as a style of entertainment in which the act of
watching is more important than the distinctions between types of
content. It is in this sense that Himmelweit et al. (1958) suggested that
the 'effect' of television was cumulative.

The experience of television is unlike any other partly because the
audience finds it possible, even easy, to ignore what is potentially completely absorbing. Watching television is not just a different way of
spending time but a particular way of doing so. The regularity of the
habit and the extent to which children take it for granted in their lives
results in a laconic indifference to particular moments, but a greater
attention to the pleasures to be derived from the act of viewing. One
result is that children know more about the schedules than about the
individual programmes, more about what can be anticipated than what
can be recollected. Their distinct programme loyalty reveals an inevit-

able awareness of regular series. Over 90 per cent of the children expressed, and acted upon, their intention of watching the same programmes at the same time the following week; over 80 per cent pointed out that they were regular viewers and always watched the same series. They had formed a distinct habit in viewing the familiar and the expected.

The sheer amount of television which children watch and the conditions in which they do so are in sharp contrast to the atmosphere of the classroom, or the artificiality of the experimental laboratory. Television does not elicit the strenuous involvement which is associated with the testing of recall; the very conditions of viewing make any learning that is derived the more complex. One cannot assume that the conditions of the classroom, complex as they are in themselves, can be likened to the conditions of viewing in the home. The testing of memory, in all the classical experiments from Ebbinghaus (1902) onwards, suppose carefully controlled conditions. These are in marked contrast to the way in which children actually view the screen; they do not carefully learn what is presented to them, study with concentration and then imitate or regurgitate what they have seen. Even in experimental conditions Cronbach and Snow (1977) point out the importance of general influences in their 'Learning Environment Inventory'. In watching television these background influences prevail. That children are *capable* of looking closely at a programme, with a view to remembering what took place, or particular details on which they can be tested is clear. But children do not normally approach television in such a way. The distinction between their competence and their actual performance is marked not only in terms of the outcome but in terms of their approach. The capacity of children to remember large quantities of information is well established (Miller, 1977; Tulving, 1972), but this capacity is not always used (Birnbaum, 1969). There is a touch of bewilderment in children when they are asked to recall material they do not think is worth remembering or upon which they have not bothered to concentrate. They do not approach television to *learn* anything, or to remember anything. The pleasure lies in the atmosphere and in the fulfillment of the anticipation. Children feel they need to remember the time the programme is on, or, in the case of a long running soap opera, the roles that various characters play. Even details of plot are not as important as the recognition of relationships, for the story-line is subsumed within the roles. As Sperling (1960) demonstrated, people see much more than they report; when children watch television they do not approach it with the idea of reporting what they see. They actually learn to disregard many features as they grow older (Hale et al. 1968).

The very idea of trying to recall features of programmes that they have seen seems rather odd to children. They are surprised at the idea of approaching television educationally, and make a clear distinction between material they are supposed to learn and material which is for their entertainment. They do not expect their favourite programmes to provide anything memorable, apart, perhaps, from the experience of watching. Children learn to 'tune-in' to the level of entertainment offered on television, and acquire the awareness of what to expect. They adapt themselves to the craft of watching television (Shute, 1976) before they learn to discriminate between different possible, or required reactions. Rather than modelling the 'message' of programmes children respond at a more emotional level (Schachter, 1964). They do not react to the mood of a particular character or a particular programme as much as imbibe the mood of television as a whole, and rely on its underlying uniformity. There are many ways of providing entertainment, from murder to comedy routines, but the provision of entertainment for its own sake is the most important factor. Just as Anderson and Bower (1973) found that people would respond to those things to which they were expected to respond, and recall what they were told to, so it is possible for television programmes to create a condition in which the act of viewing for entertainment is the 'required' response in itself. Children do not become intensely caught up in the traumas of *Starsky and Hutch* or *The Professionals*; they are supposed to enjoy the programmes, to be entertained. Children have the ability to select certain elements from an overall context, and to exclude other elements (Bates, 1976). The underlying expectation of television, the selected element for children, is that of entertainment without demands. Herriot (1974) pointed out the important distinction between 'nominal' and 'functional' stimuli; those most appropriate to television are not so much the signs seen within the context, but the context as a whole.

Although the level of attention given to different programmes can vary, children who watch a large amount of television and have many regular favourites become accustomed to a constant state of indifferent attention. To children entertainment on television suggests ease, not great excitement ot stimulating new ideas. Entertainment in emotional security is expected by the audience and provided by the majority of programmes. Thus even the moments of great danger for the hero of a popular thriller are recognised as being in the context of ultimate safety and a happy ending. The amount that children see creates a condition in which an intense experience is rare, and difficult to achieve. To fit 'types' of children to different tastes in programmes (Bailyn, 1959; Belson, 1978) is to ignore the influence of the audience's pre-set expectations of all programmes, and the variety of different attitudes within one programme. Children can, for example, attend the least demanding programmes with great assiduity if they wish, and ignore those that make clear demands on them. When, for a quiz show, they are asked to remember distinct visual details seen only as a small part of a few frames of film, they reveal great powers of concentration and immediate recall. But for most of the time children watch all programmes, including the news, without any real awareness, or concern for what is going on. As Halloran (1978, p.62) found, children react either weakly or not at all to what they see on the television screen.

Children therefore learn the conventions of television as a popular form of entertainment. Seeing the medium generally as a 'pleasant way to spend an evening' (Bowers, 1975) they become used to an habitual ease of response that does not vary much according to the type of content being presented. Adolescents also show a low level of expectation, viewing television as 'just a way of relaxing' or 'enjoyable entertainment' (BBC, 1978), but little more. These findings are all confirmed by the work of researchers in Japan (Furu, 1971). Children are, in fact, very open about this aspect of television viewing; they actually associate the pleasures of television with a mild form of boredom. A large number of children said they were tired after watching a lot of television, and a significant number said they were bored. Although they show determination to see a familiar programme again only one or two children said they felt like watching more at one time. The love of an organised ritual, once undergone, is quickly past, just as it quickly returns. Thus we find in children's statements about television a combination of two attitudes; pleasure and boredom. The audience seems to have become accustomed to the pleasure it also despises. Boredom is so little trouble. Many children associate television with having nothing better to do.

'I sometimes watch TV when I am bored. I like watching the *New Avengers, Charlie's Angels, Starsky and Hutch* and the *Bionic Woman*.' (girl, 9)

'I like watching telly when there is nothing to do.' (boy, 9)

'I sometimes watch *Charlie's Angels* on the TV when I am bored and I also watch the *Six Million Dollar Man* and Woman, *Starsky and Hutch, Come Dancing* and *Mr Ed*.' (girl, 10)

The sense of boredom is not a positive distaste; they watch their favourite programmes just the same. But their favourite programmes make few demands on them, and it is this consistency that children seem to like.

Children's favourite series can be watched without undue attention. The Bechtel technique reveals that television elicits less than full physical, let alone mental, involvement. Obviously this general attitude in children is not in itself consistent; their pragmatism makes them capable of extracting whatever information they want. If they have a love of animals, for example, they will be more prone to watch *Tarzan* or an advertisement that includes monkeys or a bear. They can, in Schramm's phrase, 'reach out for a particular experience on television' (1961 p.2). But the overall attitude children bring is more significant than the distinct items that appear at odd times. Children view television with a great deal of sophistication tempered by indifference. There are few signs of their being closely caught up in a significant experience that they might go and imitate; the very amount and the variety they see would make imitation difficult. One of the conventional wisdoms about television is summed up by a girl of nine:

> 'I like watching television as well because you can learn a
> lot of things watching television.'

Another donnée expressed by a girl of twelve (as part of a story), is that 'You can't believe everything you see on television'. Both are in their different ways parodies of conventional clichés which actually have little to do with the general style of children's viewing. Far from seeking out learning, or judging what to believe, most children expect the television not to instruct but to entertain.

4 Children's attention to television

'I like Starsky because he is like my brother who is older
than I am.' (girl, 11)

Children's responses to television cannot be understood by applying
models of information processing. Those who draw attention to the
style of the medium (such as Baggeley and Duck, 1976), to the individual needs of children (such as Noble, 1975) or to the limitation of
many studies that apply straightforward assumptions about imitation
(Howitt and Cumberbatch, 1975) all accept that television is more than
just a matter of conveying information in a particular way. It cannot be
assumed that children are constant in their attention or that they will
make continual discriminations between the important and the unim-
portant, between the main message and the peripheral information.
Children's favourite programmes show no particular clarity of purpose,
and do not present information in such a way that it can be more easily
learned. Children find the idea of paying close attention to a situation
comedy, or thriller, or a cartoon, absurd.

Children's expectations of television mean that they adapt to what is
offered; they do not only reflect what is offered. They do not automatically attune themselves to the news because it demands more
cerebral attention. Children have difficulty in learning to distinguish
between the significant clue and the insignificant. On television 'significance' is of a different order than a set of ideas or numbers; it is a
matter of knowing what to look for in a pattern made the more complex by the quantity of heterogeneous material, visual and musical as

well as verbal. The very richness of the medium, compared to print or the radio, makes significant clues become embedded in a mass of detail. There are many distinctions of style such as contrasts between pictures taken in the studio and those taken outside (Lyle and Hoffman, 1972), between those which are real or those which are make-believe, those 'live' and those carefully rehearsed. These are all parts of a pattern that contrasts with classical models of learning. In school children learn to concentrate upon the important central messages, on what Maccoby and Hagen (1965) in their experiments on the effects of distraction on central and incidental recall terms 'task-relevant material' (p.280). But it is difficult to know what is relevant material on popular television programmes. Hale et al. (1968) found that children under the age of twelve had great difficulty in discriminating between essential and 'non-essential' features when viewing a film even when they were looking for 'correct responses' (p.72). Children find it difficult to define the 'coherent' matter to be learnt (Baggeley and Duck, 1976). They learn a kind of selective attention, but do not select information in terms of verbal messages. Krull and Husson (1979) in their exploration of children's attention to television programmes discovered that children spent more time exploring more complicated stimuli, and that they were attracted to the most visually active and novel parts of television programmes. They were led to expect that these higher levels of complexity would cause children to pay more attention rather than less, but they then found that there was no correlation between attractiveness of display and children's subsequent recall. They came to the conclusion that programmes such as *Sesame Street*, based on complex visual attention-demanding sequences designed to promote learning, would actually fail to do that, and that the *more* stimulation that was presented the less actual learning took place (cf. G. Lesser, 1974; H. Lesser, 1977). Krull and Husson suggest that the expectations of a programme would be highest when the levels of attention were moderate rather than high because at high levels of attention children would realise that the materials of the programme would be likely to change, and become less interesting.

> 'If attention is low, expectancy is low because there is no information on which to build expectations. At moderate levels of attention, expectancy would be high because children would know that the interesting material presented would continue for a short period at least. When attention is very high, expectancy would again drop because children would know the programme material is soon likely to change to a different, and probably less interesting form.' (p.107)

This assumes that children anticipate what will appear. What it does show is the fact that children cannot sustain attention over a length of time, especially when every sequence is designed to exploit every device possible to create interest and excitement. While Wright and Huston (1981) point out that attention can be influenced by the associations viewers have with previously experienced attention-worthy content, it is clear that previous experience can also influence them to apply even less attention.

Even when children ostensibly pay close attention to television programmes, and this is not often, there is no direct correlation between attention and learning. Some (such as Yussen, 1974) suggest that children's recall is highly correlated to visual attention, but much depends on the nature of the material and the reasons for which children are being tested, as well as the convictions with which children change their normal viewing habits for the sake of the test. In Yussen's case he was looking for a form of 'demonstrated behaviour'. Salomon et al. (1972) found that attention to *Sesame Street* did *not* increase as children became older, in contrast to other set learning tasks. Lorch, Anderson and Levin (1979) found no difference in comprehension between two groups of five-year-olds, one of which was distracted by having toys to play with and the other which was supposed to be paying undivided attention. Friedrich and Stein (1973) found visual attention unrelated to knowledge of 'programme content'. All these reports show different levels of attention and expectation, and all show the difficulties in creating close attention to television. For children soon learn to look more casually, to predict the outline of what is presented. As Wright and Vletstra (1975) show, children learn first to 'explore' what they see, and then, as they get older, to 'search' out what is significant to them. This is why younger viewers seem to prefer more perceptually stimulating material in conditions of close attention; but later they learn to disregard material that is irrelevant to their needs.

The distinction between children's capacity to pay close attention and their actual performance show a wide range of different levels of response. On one level is the comparatively well explored matter of cognitive understanding, including the awareness of hierarchies of concepts and semantics. But the less well explored levels of attention normally evinced in viewing television are less easy to test. They are nearer to the concept of 'habit' or 'set', the selective response to stimuli in a subconscious expectation of what these stimuli should be like. Rather than responding with the consciously formed realisation that there is to be an addition to the store of information, the subject responds by fitting any new stimulus into what is already there in such a way that the new stimulus is unlike itself, is no longer complete, cannot be crisply determined as a definite 'fact'. Additional material, is re-interpreted in terms of pre-existing expectations. Postman and Egan (1949) defined set as 'a readiness to respond to stimulus objects in a selective way . . . By its set, the organism is selectively tuned to events in the environment' (p.327). Baggeley and Duck (1976) stressed that 'the lasting effects on the viewer are likely to be those of the non-verbal elements exclusively, the imagery of television that stems from the presentation techniques producers use' (p.78), but although they were trying to discover the distinctions between different types of presentation they were actually uncovering the importance of the gradual accumulation of a habit of attention through the similarity of various presentations rather than the difference in style. With most television programmes the central unvarying constant as far as the audience is concerned is not the verbal message or even the plot but the details or images that make up the repeated actions or gestures. If 'set' denotes the readiness to respond to selected stimuli it is likely, given the amount of repeated material, that the easiest to accumulate will be those which fit a preconceived pattern. Much of the material of television's most popular programmes is enjoyed because it is expected, and satisfies the sense of the familiar. The audience's 'set' is undisturbed. As Ornstein (1977) points out, viewers learn to acquire an 'habituation' of attention.

Many experiments have shown the ability of subjects to concentrate on particular items. It is a donnée of perception that most stimuli are automatically ignored at the level of consciousness, whether they are background noises or visual elements that are peripheral or out of focus. The ears can switch attention from one source of sound to another, and choose to listen to what is already there. But although concentration on one subject implies ignoring another, it does not follow that the object concentrated upon will be the most obvious one. African natives, for example, on being shown a film with a specific message about health education only remembered a glimpse of two hens which were seen in the background of one frame for such a short time that the makers and the presenters of the film had not themselves been aware that they appeared at all (cf. Klapper, 1960, p.22). While different audiences attend to different things, and attention can be given to unattended, unusual or idiosyncratic material, unattended items can themselves make a significant impact. Out of the ability of subjects to concentrate on particular items comes the fact that much material that is seen is actually ignored, or at least ignored to the extent that it cannot be recalled. Moray (1959) demonstrated that the ability to concentrate on a specified passage of prose led to the almost immediate discarding of other information. Norman (1969) reiterated this point when he showed that subjects do not remember unattended items when asked to concentrate on a particular passage. Glucksberg and Cowan (1970) explored not only the ability of subjects to attend to particular items, but to impose such a structure on their minds that certain tracts of material were deliberately ignored. Davis and Smith (1972) drew the connection between people's deliberate ignoring of unattended messages and the subsequent inability to recall them. Thus the experimental literature reveals the inability of people to attend easily to more than one item or a small sequence of items at one time. It also shows how concentration upon particular events implies the exclusion of others. Selective attention is inevitable in approaching any material. When selective attention is applied to television, when there is no clear verbal message to be learned, the selection can be made from the anticipated details of the plot or behaviour of the character, or those elements that fit more easily into pleasant expectations (Berelson and Steiner, 1964). The 'relevant' material of television includes the archetypal as well as the distinctive, the 'non-essential' like the hero's typical actions or gimmicks, as well as the structure of the plot. The dominance of the inessential is especially marked because it is children's habit to view television with less than fully concentrated attention.

The phenomenon of 'set', therefore, denotes not just selective attention but the fitting of what is perceived into a pre-existing pattern (Janis, 1963). The audience with a desire not to be disturbed by the unexpected (it is 'tuned' into sudden twists of plot in a thriller or a horror film) sees what it wishes and expects to see, and accepts ostensible contrasts as minor variations. The dominance of 'habit' over 'drive' (in terms of deliberate motivation) is at the heart of children's perception of television. Vernon (1962) points out that 'the direction of attention . . . causes an observer to perceive what he expected to see rather than what is actually presented' (p.162). The work of Bruner (1974, Bruner and Goodman, 1947) explores an earlier dictum of Woodworth about selective attention, and can apply to any of the mass media (Klapper, 1960). Armed, as it were, with what Festinger (1957) terms 'cognitive dissonance', the reaction against and rejection of material that does not fit expectations, children's perception of television lies very close to their pre-set expectations. As Bruner (1974) suggests, there is a distinction between behaviour that copes with the requirements of a problem (as in a test) and behaviour that is designed to *defend* against entry into a problem (pp.7–42). Children learn not only to select contemporaneously from the complex material presented to them, but learn to select sequentially between different levels of attention. They learn to ignore some of the stimuli to concentrate on others, according to need and preference. They can ignore what would seem in semantic terms to be the important message or *raison d'être* of a programme.

To some extent the images on television (cf. Chapter 17) relieve their audience of the need to work at the job of attention. Moving pictures create their own 'rhythmic process' (Krugman and Hartley, 1960, p.186) which helps develop the perceptual response that Vernon (1962, p.184) call 'marginal awareness'. The capacity to pay close attention remains but is rarely applied. The different levels of attention are easy to demonstrate by asking adults to scrutinise material such as a woman's magazine with close critical analysis. Like children, they become aware that they are looking critically at something normally taken for granted and will almost resent the idea of applying such intensity to a magazine that does not suggest or warrant such levels of attention. Both children and adults are aware of different levels of attention and like to give what seem to them appropriate responses. The more 'peripheral' the information, the easier it is to glance rather than study. The very process of reading a comic, for example, once the important clues are recognised, is 'easier' than reading a book. Television, in its very presentation, illustrates the conditions of entertainment in embodying Weber's law that constantly increasing differentials are required to maintain a sense of discrimination (see Gregory, 1974). The loudness, the exaggeration of imagery, the blood or the fast cars, the dancing or the cartoons, do not in themselves increase attention, but vie with each other in such a way that attention begins to become, as it were, lazy and indiscriminate. Instead of concentrating for the sake of learning, the viewer knows that there will be enough liveliness on the screen to enable him to project less liveliness from himself. One violent act described in print reads far more horribly than one more, among many, seen on the screen. A description of *Starsky and Hutch* seems genuinely brutal when written down or explained after the event and yet the audience finds the same actions innocuous when projected on the screen, and when understood in their own ritualistic terms. The very liveliness, the very exaggerations of the television presentation make it easy for children to see it as entertainment which does not demand close attention.

Television does not always demand concentration but this does not mean that it demands no attention at all. Bruner (1974, p.76), in applying Weber's law to unfamiliar material, shows that all sensory systems require changes in stimulation in order to maintain perception. The constant juxtaposition of television creates a fairly constant perceptual state. The differences between changing images are so extreme that they are not easily detected *in situ*. It is as if Weber's law of perceptual differences were being constantly demonstrated. When one remembers the difficulty of receiving information in two different ways at the same time (Stroop, 1935), it is easy to see how children can fixate on particular clues in the imagery, and not necessarily on the rational message. It is for this reason that researchers have had such difficulty in finding out what children comprehend from watching television programmes. Even when they try to apply the same tests that are normally applied to a passage of prose it is clear that there are other levels of attention being applied, apart from the capacity to prepare themselves for whatever test will be inflicted on them. As Broadbent (1958) demonstrated in some of his work on word associations, the senses go on reacting even under conditions of severe distraction. Children, for instance, respond to other things while ostensibly attending to television (Atkin et al. 1972). Thus it is possible, even perceptually necessary, to select information for attention. This information is of a particular type.

One of the phenomena of television is that peripheral information itself sustains the audience. The very activity of the television screen creates a sensation of movement which makes for a far easier response than the need to concentrate upon one thing, or the need to focus the eyes on a picture. The simplest visual perception is the response to movement (Gregory, 1970). Children need to learn how to look at a photograph or any still picture but the movement on television is far easier to see despite the fact that the eye converts a series of dots and lines into an image. The reason that a television picture is viewed in such a casual way is not just to the inappropriateness of undivided attention, but a result of television's perceptual demands. Children adapt easily to a medium that lends itself to distraction as Baggeley and Duck (1976) and Howitt and Cumberbatch (1975) point out. Hull (1943) had already demonstrated that when two stimuli act together the result is quite distinct from each individual stimulus. The most automatic responses are caused not only by exaggerated or varied items but by the irregular and heterogeneous (Berlyne, 1958). Novel and changing stimuli command attention (Berelson and Steiner 1964), but it is attention of a particular kind, that Bruner defines as 'the tendency for perceptual hypotheses to fixate after receiving a minimum of confirmation' (1974, p.81).

The distinction, first made by James (1890), between voluntary and involuntary attention is crucial in understanding television. Voluntary attention is the deliberate storage of ideas, remembered over long intervals. Involuntary attention consists of holding onto preceived material until attention is directed towards it (cf. Underwood, 1976, p.206). When children learn to perceive elements in television that are significant to them, these are more likely to be repeated actions or patterns than the rationale or plot. Content as such, in terms of meaning or information, is not as significant as the way in which it is approached and attended by the child. For this reason Schramm's (1955) dictum about the importance of what a child brings to television is often cited (e.g. in Collins, 1979, p.74; Brown R, 1976), even if it is cited to support the notion of individual differences rather than that of the different types of use children make of the medium. Salomon (1979) points out that 'The child's perception of the viewing . . . task determines what information and how much of it is to be extracted. Thus, it determines what symbolic elements will be dealt with' (p.79). But even when children try to recall an outline of a plot they find it difficult to apply such an approach to television. Even when specifically asked for information children show how small an amount that they see is subsequently understood. Collins (1979) writes:

> '. . . Younger children's difficulties in comprehending complex audio-visual narratives seem to involve not only poor memory for explicitly portrayed content; they also involve relatively little likelihood that remembered information will be integrated to relate these explicit events across time.' (p.33)

He found that older children are more capable of explicit recall when they applied their minds, but that none of the children had paid any attention to elements beyond those to which he had directed their attention.

Much of what children see on television passes them by. The more they see, the less likely it is that they will pay close attention. That children are *capable* of exerting great powers of concentration is clear, but as the experiments that try to elicit this capacity themselves reveal, children find it difficult to pay such attention to television, especially over any length of time. The very nature of their styles of viewing and the very conditions of viewing in the home, make it even less likely that they will approach television in any other way but with the minimum of attention. Research on visual and auditory perception makes it clear that television, by the nature of its own style of presentation, does not make complex demands. The very juxtaposition between moving image and sound makes the perceptual response it elicits one of the most basic and most easily maintained. Before one can analyse what children see in television, or what they learn from television, it is important to note that they bring with them clear expectations of what television offers, and distinct styles of viewing. Nothing could be more different from formal experiments or from comprehension exercises in the classroom than the television set in the corner of the room, half-ignored, half-watched over long periods of time, sought out for entertainment without great demands, made into a convenient form of entertainment, and providing the expected. Children do, through involuntary attention, through distraction, or through peripheral perception, imbibe a great deal of information from television, but this information is of a particular type. What children actually perceive in television is itself complex, for it is not simply the material that is presented to them.

PART II
WHAT CHILDREN SEE
IN TELEVISION

'Plenty of people will try to give the masses, as they call them, an intellectual food prepared and adapted in the way they think proper for the actual condition of the masses.'

M. Arnold, *Culture and Anarchy*

5 Heroes and heroines

'I like Dracula because of the way he sucks the blood
of women.' (boy, 9)

The world of television is peopled by a rich variety of characters, playing an almost infinite number of different roles. They not only depict
different characteristics but approach the audience in a number of
different ways. Some convey information, while others preach, some
act as themselves in front of the cameras, while others act their parts.
To make sense of such variety entails a sophisticated series of reactions,
and an innate sense of difference between the theatrical and the real.
Despite this complexity there has been a tendency amongst some commentators to assume that television gives a unified and consistent
picture of the world from which children learn to delineate their own
attitudes. By analysing certain aspects of the content of programmes
researchers have suggested that children imbibe stereotypes of people's
roles, either of sex or occupation. De Fleur (1964), analysing a Mid-
western American community's viewing for six months, came to the
conclusion that they were learning that no women worked, that pro-
fessional people had all the power, and that each profession had a clear
stereotype: doctors were handsome, policemen brutal, artists tempera-
mental and lawyers clever. Content analysts take up the assumption
first made by Himmelweit et al. (1958): 'It is . . . the similarity of views
and values conveyed in television programmes, particularly in plays,
(that) make the cumulative impact' (p.37). By pointing out the ways
in which heroes behave, their age, their sex and their professions, they

suggest that children learn to pick out of all the details generalised assumptions about people, growing into respect for the professions and despising women for their role as housewives. As the De Fleurs wrote in 1967:

> 'It seems safe to conclude that, within the limits of the present sample of children and occupations, television is a more potent source of occupational status knowledge than either personal contact or the general community culture.' (p.787)

They went on:

> '(It) can be suggested that TV provides children with much superficial and misleading information about the labour force of their society. From this they acquire stereotyped beliefs about the world of work.' (p.789)

Although such analysis presupposes at once a simple notion of modelling, together with a complex level of analysis by the audience, it has continued to be popular. Seggar and Wheeler (1973), by counting instances of sex and job, concluded that men were shown as having 'better' jobs than women. Dominick and Rauch (1972) described how often women portrayed in advertisements were depicted in the role of housewife and mother. Manstead and McCullogh (1981) found that two-thirds of commercials were 'voiced over' by men. Six different studies have been made counting the percentages of male domination of the leading roles in popular television drama, placing the percentage between sixty-eight and eighty. Busby (1975) showed that 75 per cent of advertisements with women in them were for kitchen and bathroom utensils. Lemon (1978) concluded that 'on television, class (as indicated by relevant occupational status) predicts dominance better than sex'. (p.64).

The analysis of content rests on the assumption that children model themselves on what they see; that they choose to imitate certain characteristics and take attitudes conveyed through the depictions on the screen. Children are supposed in particular to imitate their heroes and heroines. It is much easier to analyse the content of television than the nature of children's responses, but it is clear from the latter that their reactions are far more complex than a matter of simple modelling or even identification with the characters they see. One of the outcomes of the hypothesis of modelling is that children are supposed to identify themselves with certain heroes, to respond to the behaviour of their favourites with emulation. Maccoby and Wilson (1957), although they discovered that their subjects did not instantly reproduce the action of the heroes on the screen, nevertheless went on to assume that emotions are covertly reproduced through a close personal identification with the character. They felt that learning came about through children's need for identification, and that fantasy characters would become of such emotional importance to children that they would pattern their own behaviour on that of the hero. Maccoby et al. (1958) went onto suggest that children would identify with characters of their own sex by placing themselves imaginatively inside the fantasies they were watching. Some researchers have suggested that children are constantly reinforced for imitating same-sex models (Fruch and McGhee,1975), and that stereotyped sex roles are taught because girls identify with heroines and boys with heroes (Sprafkin and Liebert, 1978). Ruble et al. (1981) assume that children pick up sex-roles from commercials that they seek out information that is appropriate to their own sex.

The hypothesis that children model their behaviour on their favourite characters is not borne out by the evidence. It would be very difficult for children to do so, given the nature of their favourites, and the impossibility of their copying many of the gestures that they see. There are, after all, so many different characteristics to choose from. The question remains whether children's attitudes are formed through watching particular characters, and whether they closely identify with certain characters. The phenomenon of the reader being emotionally caught up in the eponymous heroine of *Emma* is as well known as the manifestations of enthusiasm by fans of pop groups who copy a particular style of clothing. Television does help convey *knowledge* of these styles; the question is whether children are emotionally wrapped up in the characters that they like to see regularly, and whether the fan has something of the mimetic in terms of attitude as well as clothes.When it comes to children's favourite programmes, and their enthusiasm for particular heroes, it is clear that their attitudes are extremely equivocal. One fan of Starsky and Hutch described them thus: 'They go after girls, play totally ignorant jokes on each other and catch crooks' (girl, 12). Like many others she associates them with their actions, and does so not altogether approvingly. To most children, given the variety of different heroes, and the sheer number of programmes to choose from, the 'hero' is at best the person who is the lead in a thriller, who acts more than he talks. Any attitude learned is not one that is expressed, or easily copied, apart from the catch phrase. The hero or heroine fulfils certain expectations of pleasure; they maintain a standard image in a variety of similar circumstances. They have high recognition value but are essentially part of the pattern of the thriller. One response to the generic mode was given by a ten-year-old boy: 'Petrocelli is a person like Charlie's Angels who investigates crimes and goes to see people in jail and lives in a caravan'. The last detail actually refers to a different detective called Rockford but this mix-up is itself telling. Children are nearly always fully aware of the differences between popular characters but are also strongly aware of the importance of the *roles* they play.

Children's interest in the action is such that they have no particular concern about the sex of the main protagonists. Many popular television series like *Charlie's Angels* or *Wonder Woman*, are as popular with boys as with girls. Both sexes equally enjoy *Starsky and Hutch*. Attempts to prove that children relate to particular characters through personal involvement have often been based on the idea of identification with personalities of their own sex. Maccoby et al. (1958) suggested that viewers concentrate their attention on their own sex, not looking at the opposite sex even in a love scene. While Edgar (1977) points out the differences in taste according to sex. (Hobson (1980) also showed that women prefer programmes such as *Crossroads* to the news), and he goes onto suggest that this follows the audience's liking for protagonists like themselves. When we analyse the particular favourite characters of children we find, however, not a reflection of their own sex but a domination of male heroes, despite the existence of *Bionic Woman* and others. Nearly all boys citing their favourite characters cited men; three-quarters of all girls cited men. But there are few indications that the sex of the hero really *matters*, let alone evidence to support the notion of emotional identification. The fact that thriller heroes (those by far the most cited by all children as their favourite characters) are part of a continuous series seems like an advantage in gaining recognition value, but actually makes them the more associated with a style of plot. Although no simple copying has been proved (apart from a detail of dress or gesture) the tradition of exploring the emulation of well-known personalities (Horton and Wohl, 1956) has continued (Adler and Douglas, 1976). But an analysis of children's favourite characters that appear on television reveals how ambiguous is the relationship between them and the stars they recognise. The 'personality', be it Kojak or Wonder Woman, *is* the programme and creates the entertainment's momentum by taking part in a series of actions and providing recognisable characteristics to help sustain them. Three-quarters of the children's favourite characters were part of their favourite programmes. As children become older they gradually make a greater distinction between their favourite programme and their favourite character. Far from becoming *more* emotionally tied, children tend to become even less so.

Children's television heroes are important for what they do. There is a tendency for children to remember a whole series in terms of the repeated actions of the heroes. In this they are, in a sense, correct, for the

40

ability of Wonder Woman to spin round like a hoop until she reappears in a swimming costume and tiara, and with superhuman strength, is crucial to every plot. Children's pleasure in the programmes depends on the presentation of the expected; part of the expected is the unvarying actions or gimmicks of the hero. Children have a close knowledge of the characteristics of their favourites. They can cite the appearance and style, and sometimes the real name, of their hero. They recognise certain traits which make each series unique; they have knowledge of looks and actions that places each character firmly within its serial. Even after not seeing *Kojak* for some time children were able to give all the central characteristics of the hero, not with any sense of admiration for heroic looks or magnificent achievements but as a kind of recognisable mark of identity. They know that Kojak says 'Who loves ya, baby', that he is bald, that he wears sunglasses and sucks a lollipop. They identify these characteristics closely with the personality himself, without needing to imitate them. For the recognition factor of the series as a whole depends upon the distinguishing characteristics of its hero. Many of the popular American serials strive for a sense of individuality rather than fulfilling typecast ideas of the usual perfect hero, in an urge to help the immediate identification of their programmes (Adler and Cater, 1976). The series' success lies in sustaining automatic associations and fulfilling expectations from one week to the next. In the case of Kojak it was clear that there was a great deal of overlap between his appearance and his behavioural characteristics. That he sucks a lollipop seems to most children far more significant than the fact that he 'shoots people' or 'fights crime'. That he says 'Who loves ya, baby' is a more interesting characteristic than his car chases because it marks him out as a distinctive character. But it is nevertheless because of the car chases that they watch the programme.

Part of the marketing of a series depends on the publicity given to the distinction of the 'hero'. This 'brand image' is a mixture of the clues that distinguish the appearance of the leading personality and the actions he undergoes. The very power of the hero's characteristics makes them the more difficult to separate from individual episodes. Children perceive the personal marks of the hero as a glue that holds different parts of the action together. This ease of recognition makes it possible for children to remain a ready market even if a series has been off the air for a year or more. Kojak is known for his lack of hair, Starsky and Hutch are known for their two contrasting shades of hair; it is the contrast between the pair that most stands out in children's minds, for the series depends as much on the characters' interaction as on the popularity of each individual (although there is a slight preference for Starsky over Hutch despite the latter's fame as a singer). Whereas the appearance of Kojak is distinct from the kinds of gestures he makes, Starsky and Hutch suggest even more strongly the fact that their image depends upon certain types of action. It is the 'stunts', as children characterise them, that are at the heart of the programme. The behavioural characteristics of Starsky and Hutch include 'shooting people', killing people', 'catching criminals', 'driving fast in cars', 'gun fights', 'jumping on car roofs', 'smashing doors and windows', and 'bashing people's noses'. The largest proportion of children cited 'killing people' but without any sense of moral stricture, and no indication of deep emotional involvement, let alone emulation. They laconically recognise it as one of the main things that Starsky and Hutch do: they are as aware of that, or of jumping on car roofs, as they are aware of Kojak's baldness or lollipop. The programme's appeal depends upon this action rather than on the particular 'mystery' that the heroes are supposed to resolve. The heroes themselves are, after all, a structural rather than a moral feature. Children are aware of the underlying ritual of the programme as they are of the names of the two actors. This is one of the reasons that makes Adler and Douglas (1976) stress the importance of characters in television series, when the leading role merges with the play of which it is part. Conrad (1982) goes so far as to suggest that the star of a television show is the 'victim' of his own stereotype.

The close association of the 'hero' with the role he plays is illustrated by the way in which children acknowledge the characteristics of their favourite characters and the way in which they delineate, quite objectively, the salient facts about a number of heroes and heroines. Each popular series confirms the recognition of the leading actor and the performance he or she gives. The gimmicks vary, but the recognition factors remain constant. In the case of *Wonder Woman* the children give due importance to the change in appearance, from the wearing of spectacles as 'Diana Prince' to the useful results of her spinning round. The power of such a change and its consequences themselves replace the underlying motives for such action. For the actions themselves dominate: children see her as someone who 'spins round and changes clothes', or as someone who 'jumps high over obstacles'. The unifying element in all the plots is the change from a secretary who wears glasses to a woman of fantastic powers dressed in a distinctive uniform. Against this the variations from one episode to the next are comparatively minor. While it could be suggested that the association of wearing glasses with being a secretary is the fulfilment of a social stereotype, children see this merely as a necessary, simple pre-requisite for a change in appearance. If children like to watch the power manifested by Wonder Woman, they are even more fond of the idea of 'bionic' powers; it is, in fact, the kind of 'quality' they would like to possess themselves (see conclusion). Both 'superheroine' series have a clear brand image. The contrasts with the more hazy set of clues associated with programmes such as the *Rockford Files*, where there are no such obvious characteristics of behaviour or style as 'jumping high' or 'running fast'. More than half the children could indicate they would recognise James Garner (the actor), but they could not think of any particular gimmick to associate him with. They knew he 'fights, shoots people, knocks people out, solves cases and catches criminals', but these are characteristics that apply to others as well. Just as the plots in the *Rockford Files* tend to be more complex, so is the image of the hero. When it comes to less popular series such as *Petrocelli* or 'one-off' dramas, this recognition factor naturally disappears. In a popular series such as *Charlie's Angels* the main device is that there should be three heroines, 'one a blond, another with short dark hair and the third with long brown hair'. Children readily note that their *raison d'etre* is to 'use guns', 'shoot people' and 'catch criminals'.

Children's awareness of the characteristics of the 'heroes' of television shows an objective realisation of repeated images. They do not give any indication of uncomplicated identification or emulation; they are, after all, perfectly aware that they do not themselves possess bionic powers. Content analysts have tended to assume that the repeated sight of heroes would gradually cause imitation through the substantiation of behavioural norms. Balázs (1970) suggested that an audience watching famous film stars would be playing out their fantasy roles while watching. Bailyn (1959) attempted to connect aggressive children (boys in particular) with a preference for aggressive heroes. Halloran (1970) attested that aggressive boys would always identify with their aggressive heroes, like Starsky and Hutch. Maccoby and Wilson (1957) suggested that children covertly reproduce many of the elements of behaviour enacted by their heroes on the screen, although they did not make a distinction between the recognition of such actions and the difficulty in reproducing them, such as 'jumping on car roofs' or 'shooting people'. Indeed, when Maccoby and Wilson tried to prove that a child would recall more if he was the same social class as the hero, they were unable to do so. They then hypothesised that some form of 'need relevance' rather than identification would take place. But even in children's attitudes to popular heroes we find the picture more complex; too complex to be explained in terms of simple imitation or personal identification. Children's recognition of heroes is more pragmatic. Even with novels, which might be thought to have a stronger chance of personal identification. Harless (1972) could not show any simple cathexis (pattern of identification) or sweeping attitudinal change. Winkley (1975) found that even children's ability to associate does not lead to a close, uncritical identification with a character in a story. When Lyle and Hoffman (1976) attempted to prove that children imitate the actions of their heroes, they failed to do so.

Ever since the 1950s, and underlying the influential work of Berkowitz (1964) there have been many attempts to prove that the influence of television lies in the example it gives in the behaviour of the 'stars'. Zajonc (1952) characteristically came to the conclusion that children were amoral when he asked them which character they most liked in a popular space serial, and they invariably came up with the one who had the most power and who survived. What children were indicating was not a Machiavellian assessment of the realities of survival in a harsh world, but a realistic indication that they know the rituals of action thrillers. The leading figures exhibit the most power; it is the hero who survives to the end. It is inevitable that the hero must, through guns or unnatural abilities survive until the next week. This does not then lead to personal identification with either sex or aggression; it makes little difference whether the hero is the same or the opposite sex, or whether he or she is rather more or less involved in violence. Children recognise that the heroes of television have distinct parts to play. Their characteristics are their roles. The plots derive from these characteristics. Children do not describe, let alone become involved with, personalities as such. They describe those facets that make their heroes individual in terms of the action; those characteristics that are easily recognised.

The reasons children give for liking their favourite characters show how varied and complex, and how far from simple adulation, is their response. The very ways in which children phrase their reasons show a wide variety of attitudes. Some children reveal clear pragmatism — 'because he is the star of the show' (girl, 8), 'because he is the hero' (girl, 11), 'he is a star' (boy, 10) or 'because he is the only one on the show' (girl, 10). Sometimes children refer to the 'niceness' of character; 'he always helps people' (girl, 8), 'I like her because she has a kind face' (girl, 9), 'she is nice to her patients' (girl, 10), 'he's calm and you can understand what he's saying' (boy, 10) or 'she solves problems' (boy, 11). But they are just as likely to take a more equivocal view, like 'he is a laugh' (boy, 11), 'he is daft' (boy, 10) or 'he is a millionaire' (boy, 10), 'he is stupid and daft' (girl, 11) or 'he is a good advertiser' (girl, 10, of Steve Austin). Boys are particularly likely to say, with a superior affection, that their favourite actor is 'stupid' (as in the case of Manuel in *Fawlty Towers*), but they are also more likely, especially when younger, to admire physical prowess or action; whether this is 'bionic' or 'he has lots of secret weapons' (boy, 9), 'he is fast on guns' (boy, 10), or 'he is a good fighter' (boy, 11). They give no indication of close personal association. Even those who mention 'kindness' often cite a particular deed that they admired in one episode such as 'because she saved her baby brother's life by going in front of a falling tree by throwing her brother out of the way so that the tree falls on her instead' (girl, 11). Those that mention good looks talk of details such as 'big blue eyes'. The tone with which children talk of their favourites as 'daft' or 'silly' is rather akin to their sense of those personalities that go *too* far, that 'get on my nerves'. Children are also aware of acting ability. Girls go for 'looks'; and are more aware of 'kindness'. Boys are more impressed by 'strength'.

Children learn to develop a laconic attitude to their favourite personalities (cf. Cullingford, 1982 a and b). As they get older they are more apt to like 'good acting' or 'daftness' than 'niceness' or 'kindness'. The importance of the role played in a thriller is, however, matched by the importance of humour in personalities appearing in shows. Personalities who appear in their own right must not make serious demands; instead they must be 'happy'; 'he had short hair and he has nice clothes and he does not get angry' (boy, 7). This air of amusement extends to the sheer 'lunacy' of characters such as Kenny Everett, or Terry Wogan. They approve of those who are 'completely lunatic', 'a complete idiot' (girls, 12) or 'comical and absolutely stupid' (boy, 12). Constant cheerfulness is important; 'looking cheerful', 'funny and sometimes daft' (boy, 10) or 'daft as usual' (of Terry Wogan). The prevailing sense of humour is obviously an important part of the pleasant personality: 'he is very funny and I think he always smiles on television' (girl, 12) or 'he made everybody laugh an awful lot' (girl, 10, also of Terry Wogan). This sense of fun even extends to Rockford: 'I like the way he fights because he makes me laugh' (boy, 8).

Children watch so many programmes of different types that it is very difficult for them to develop any awareness of the underlying characteristics of certain personalities, like film stars. Nevertheless, more than two-thirds said that they would like to be like their favourite personalities, not out of admiration as much as pragmatism. Their reasons were very instructive. Many would like to be able to do what their heroes do: 'make funny faces' (boy, 10), 'have a good sense of humour' (girl, 11) or 'I'd like to be cool' (boy, 11). Many more would like to possess some of their advantages: 'she is beautiful and so are the other men' (boy, 11), 'he is a good looking lad' (boy, 10), 'he is strong, fights well and looks good', 'she is beautiful' (boys, 12), 'she had nice clothes and nice hair' (girl, 9), 'they had a lot of good hair styles and punk outfits on' (boy, 11), or 'he is good looking and all the girls like him; so do I' (girl, 11). Children naturally would like to possess the qualities of their heroes, but most of all would like to be rich and famous and appear on television:

'he is well known and has lots of money' (boy, 10)
'getting all his money' (boy, 10)
'he is very rich' (boy, 11)
'he's a millionaire' (boy, 12)

'she's famous' (girl, 10)
'rich and handsome' (girl, 12)   etc.

If they learn anything from the personalities it is the advantages of fame and money. But children also like their heroes' ability to do what they call 'stunts':

'I like to drive fast' (girl, 12)
'I could do everything faster and be stronger' (girl, 12)
'he can handle a gun' (girl, 11)
'jump, run fast and lift objects' (girl, 11)
'I would be able to run at 60 mph' (girl, 9)
'I like his car and he hardly hides from someone when he is shooting' (boy, 13)
'I would be able to win every race' (boy, 12)
'he does a lot of stunts and gets lots of money' (boy, 11)
'he does lots of exciting action' (boy, 11)

Children enjoy the stunts their heroes undergo, but the idea that they take them seriously strikes children as funny. They are aware of the fantasy involved, and aware of the money. Their heroes are people who carry out their roles in the favourite programmes and get well paid for it. The ways in which they fight or do stunts are part of the individual style and tone of a series. Heroes are part of a context, and admired for their success off the screen as well as their entertainment value on it. But most of all they are seen pragmatically. The following example illustrates the importance to children of the mixture of the roles their favourites play and the rewards they get.

'He is well known and has lots of money; he acts in films.' (Steve McQueen)
'Because of the action she does as a private investigator.' (F. Majors)
'He has plenty of style as an undercover detective.' (D. Soul)
'He is very rich and he can run and fire and shoot.' (P. Glaser)
'He stars in exciting films.' (Clint Eastwood)
'She is a very good actor and I like the way she gets out of everything.' (Joan Crawford)
'He batters folk up.' (Lee Majors)
'Lots of exciting action, driving around and getting mucked up. And saving people at the last minute.' (P. Glaser)
'I like him when he shoots bad men down dead.' (John Wayne) '
'The way he acts and doesn't take things seriously.' (Tom Baker)

'He wins.' (Brendan Foster)
'Makes money.' (Clint Eastwood)
'He's always fooling around and that's what I want to do when
I grow up.' (Bill Oddie)

These are just a few examples from ten-eleven-and twelve-year-olds that show the variety of attitudes towards their heroes; their objective assessment and the sense that what makes them interesting is the role they play. As a boy of thirteen expresses it 'he can do many things an ordinary man cannot do' (of Steve Austin). Children like to have their expectations satisfied; the particular actions, whether it is 'tap dancing' or 'running fast', 'bionics' or 'lots of exciting things' are all appreciated when distinctions of personality are not. Sometimes children are specific about certain gestures, like a girl of ten saying of Starsky that he 'jumps around corners and shouts "freeze you bum"', or an eleven-year-old, of Henry Winkler, 'he says "hey" and I like his hair style'. The mixture of attitudes and the fact that there is an easy rather than intense emotional attachment can be seen in reflections on Starsky:

'He can sometimes be funny. He is brave.'
'He makes me laugh.'
'The way he drives and shoots his gun.'
'Acts and makes me laugh.'
'He speaks funny and eats funny and is always eating.'
'He chooses the best cars I've ever seen.'
'The way he drives his car.'
'He does his own stunts.'

They refer to his role, his acting ability and only sometimes to his personality. There is the sense of the ingenuous in a remark about Noel Edmonds, 'He always seems happy and tells terrible jokes' (girl, 11) or about Hutch: 'Bending people's arms back and holding up a gun and when he stands there and sulks' (girl, 12).

Children's objective assessment of their heroes does not prevent them being fans, nor does it prevent them liking the kinds of clothes that are worn, or wishing they could have similar attributes, especially money. A few children reveal what it is to express pleasure in being a fan: 'If I was him I would not be able to go mad over myself like the way I go mad over him the way I do now. He's extremely good looking and very calm and casual about most things and when he sings . . . I wish he was here' (girl, 10, about David Soul). The vagaries of taste do not prevent temporary fixations, encouraged by magazines. But these are more a matter of collecting information about the actor than a matter of undergoing close identification. In fact the more they seem to care about a personality the more they are aware of them as actors: 'Kelly Garrett is one of the Angels, she has dark hair and has won the nicest personality award for TV' (girl, 12). But if children show a laconic attitude to their favourite actors, they are unequivocal about those personalities which they dislike (cf. Chapter 1). Whereas most of their favourites have a role which is implicit in a series, the least liked are those who talk rather than act, and draw too much attention to themselves. It is those who come across with marked characteristics, or the kind that could be most easily identified with, that are most disliked. Politicians are often cited, but any who show distinctions of character are likely to be cited as 'big-headed', 'a show off' or 'he gets on my nerves'. While some younger children make a bow to the standard norms of fantasy and profess a dislike for Dracula or Frankenstein, children from the age of eight are clear about their dislikes and their reasons for them:

'He is always being stupid.' (Tommy Cooper)
'He is so stupid and wears too much.' (Garry Glitter)
'He is daft and he looks horrible.' (Ken Dodd)
'He never laughs or makes you feel happy.' (Luke Ferbech)
'He is fat.' (Frank Cannon)
'She shows off.' (Lena Zavaroni)
'He makes stupid jokes.' (Bob Monkhouse)
'He reads news.' (Gordon Honeycombe)
'He is a big head.' (Mohammed Ali)
'He is boring.' (any news reader)
'She is an old bag.' (Ena Sharples)
'He looks horrible.' (Clement Freud)
'He asks dirty questions.' (Robin Day)
'He gets on my nerves.' (Frank Spenser)

Children are able to express an instant judgement with the greater vehemence because it is inconsequential. 'It's rubbish' or 'It's great' will be a more common judgement than anything more ambiguous. The less salience a personality has, the easier it is to be enthusiastic; the more personality intrudes over the action, the easier it is to be dismissive. Hood (1980) suggests that it is only those with power who look directly out of the TV screen at the audience: others are mitigated by the interviewer. But children show themselves to be most dismissive of just these kinds of personalities that assume this power, that seem to be endowed with identifiable characteristics. Instead, children like their heroes to be more anonymous. For to them the heroes have distinct parts to play, and their popularity depends upon the programmes rather than the other way around.

6 The real and the fantastic

'I'd like to have bionics and be famous.' (girl, 12)

In their favourite programmes children perceive the close association of the leading characters with the actors that they undergo. Each series is a familiar ritual of events and reactions, with conventions that dictate that the 'hero' will always win and that after suitable trauma there will be a happy ending. During this inevitable course of events the heroes will underline their identity with a series of characteristic gestures that children recognise and appreciate. Children become aware of the consistent nature of a series, and are groomed to accept the role of such heroes, dependent on a world that is obviously fantastic. This does not suggest, as Bailyn (1959) and others have tried to maintain, that there is an automatic tendency for children to identify with such figures. The very fact that the younger children's favourite characters are nearly all fictional, with powers or strength or 'bionics', suggests that they cannot find it easy to apply such powers in their own surroundings and must recognise the fantasy for what it is. The argument that children muddle the distinction between the real and the fantastic through their preference for 'fantasy' heroes rests on the assumption that they become so closely involved with what is happening on the screen that they subsequently transfer the lessons that they have learned to their own lives.

Given the amount of television children view, and the way in which they watch it, it is difficult to sustain the argument that they are closely and assiduously involved. Nevertheless there are a number of studies that see in children's reactions to television an imaginative extension of their inner fantasy lives. Noble (1975), citing the work of Feshbach (1955 and 1961), suggested that children become nourished by what they see on television, that far from being frightened by violence they actually appreciate it by recreating on the screen what is already part of their inner fantasy lives. It is suggested that 'escapist' material is needed especially by children who are frustrated (Riley and Riley, 1961) and by delinquents (Halloran, 1970). The fact that television is used as a medium for fantasy is seen by writers not only as a virtue but as a way of suggesting that television is a powerful force, that it can mould the minds of young children, and that they have great difficulty in making the distinction between the inner and outer realities of their lives. These assumptions are not borne out by the evidence, since the level of children's attention and the way they use television already suggests a more sophisticated discrimination. The driving force behind the arguments about the power of escapism is the hypothesis of simple modelling; that children follow, understand and copy a mode of behaviour. Even Schramm et al. (1961) made this assumption: 'A certain number of young children (and a few older ones) will inevitably confuse the rules of the fantasy world with the rules of the real world and transfer violence from television to real life' (p.163). While they concede that there is a difference between fantasy on television and the real world they still imply that children take one so seriously that they apply rules they have learned or actions they have seen, to their own circumstances. Feshbach's description of television as a fantasy medium used for cathartic purposes (1961 etc.) is based on the idea that children are deeply and actively involved in what they see. Even at this level it is very difficult to separate what children take from what children bring to television. Klapper (1960) asked the question:

> Does escapist material produce particular values and patterns of behaviour among its devotees, or do its devotees become devotees because of the values and behavioural tendencies they already possess? (p.190)

Both possibilities suggest a level of involvement and patterning that is not borne out by the way in which children respond to television. Children are not 'devotees' in such a rich emotional way. It is through their more dismissive attitudes that we see how complex is the relationship between the fantastic and the real.

Klapper's presupposition that there is a direct relationship between the 'material' seen and the subsequent 'behavioural tendencies' suggests the ability to pick out certain clues from programmes that are watched, and an ability to choose certain elements to imitate. It suggests, in its own way, the difficulty in deciding which elements are to be taken as

50

real and which are pure fantasy. The theory that children imitate what they see has great difficulties in making distinctions between different levels of attention, and between one form of content and another. Nowhere is the researcher's muddle about the fantastic and the real more apparent than in attempts to transfer the artificial conditions of the laboratory to 'real' life. Milgram and Shotland (1973) criticised the many experiments done on children copying certain actions they saw on a screen (q.v. Chapter 8) on the ground that these artificial experiments set up false expectations on behalf of the children, and that people watched television at home in a completely different way. They therefore tried to transfer these experiments to 'field' conditions. Taking a popular American television series called *Medical Center* they persuaded Columbia Broadcasting Services to make three different versions of the same episode. In one of these the villain smashed up a charity collection box, and got away with it. In the second the villain, having smashed the box, was caught and punished. In the third he thought better of breaking collection boxes and decided to be good. Even before the programmes were made there were difficulties. The authors complained that they were only allowed to change a small part of the programme. But the real difficulty lay in the experimental design which tried to prove a direct correlation between observed content and subsequent actions. The authors assumed that the plot itself was influential, that an audience would remember the moral, would model its subsequent behaviour on it, and would do so after the lapse of several days, having picked out what to model from a plethora of different programmes. When the programmes were made with their different endings the real difficulties began, since they could not check the results. In the event Milgram and Shotland invited members of the viewing public to come to the studio, although this was exactly the unreal, artificial circumstances that they themselves had criticised. Once the audience had seen the programme they were allowed to leave. One week later they received an invitation to come back to the studio, ostensibly to be given financial rewards for having taken part in the previous viewing session. When they arrived they were each confronted by a notice telling them that the office was closed. This was the 'frustration'. A charity box, like the one in the film, was placed nearby, this being the 'trigger' to remember the action of the villain they had previously seen. Had they emulated the villain by breaking into the charity box to steal money, the connection would anyway have been far fetched, but no such behaviour took place. The researchers, however, were not to be put off:

> We wondered whether the high level of frustration experienced by the subjects obscured the effects of the stimulus program; we eliminated frustration in experiment II. Result:

no evidence of imitation. We thought a model, or booster placed in the assessment situation, might interact with the stimulus program and produce an effect. Result: negative. We reduced the time delay between seeing the television act and the occasion for imitating it by embedding both in the same situation. Result: negative. We broadcast the stimulus material in New York and St Louis and again sought to measure imitation but there was none. We changed the material from dramatised fiction to real-life incidents presented on the news. Result: no imitation. We adopted a new paradigm of investigation in the telephone study, by giving an opportunity to any viewer to immediately imitate the act by calling in an abusive message . . . (p.65)

This experiment itself reveals the difficulties in picking out the real from the fantastic, and by its very design shows the absurdity of suggesting that 'effect' derives from the imitation of isolated elements in the content of a programme. It shows a view of television as a conveyor of fantasy that is taken as seriously as if it were real; so seriously that it carries some kind of moral weight.

Children's reactions to television show, in fact, a complex awareness of the distinctions between the real and the fantastic. They prefer the latter, knowing what it is. They take on the elements of fantasy quite happily in their discussion of what they like. But they know that in every thriller series the killings, the car chases, the muggings and the jokes are all part of the ritual of drama,like the fact the hero is always the person who wins. Children's favourite characters are nearly all the heroes of popular series., but they are also 'stars' with characters of their own, written about in magazines. They are liked for the role they play, but are also actors known by their real names, and the centre of fan clubs which provide information about their 'real' likes and dislikes, favourite colours or favourite clothes. Ninety per cent of children from the age of seven knew the real names of Starsky and Hutch, and of Dr Who. Although only about half knew the real name of Wonder Woman a few also knew the name of the woman who actually carried out the dangerous stunts, and several drew attention to their appreciation of the stunts as the factor that make such programmes worth watching. Although her programme was less popular than Wonder Woman's, Lindsey Wagner who played Bionic Woman was, due to the publicity, much better known. Children showed an ability to cite actors' real or fictional names almost interchangeably, showing how close is their identification of the role and the actor; the 'star' consists of what he does. At the same time children were perfectly clear about the difference in watching their favourite footballers and watching their fictional heroes. When asked about what *other* characters that they liked on television most children did not merely substitute another of the same kind, but thought of comedians or footballers, showing that they were aware of different kinds of pleasure and the distinction between those who act and those who are 'personalities' in their own right. For children the most important trait, to entertain, remains the priority. How this is achieved is secondary. Some children enjoy programmes such as *A Question of Sport* or other quiz shows as a chance to perform better than their favourite stars. Recognition of particular people remains important in itself. The fact that as children get older some of them are more apt to point out their favourite is a 'good actor' indicates a greater ability in pointing out objectively what they appreciate. What they mean by the term 'good actor' is the ability to play a part like Kojak with consistency. When children say how much they like the 'Fonz' in *Happy Days* they are perfectly aware that his style is placed in the context of a particular time: 'I'd like to live in the late 1950s; he says in a very groovy voice "sit on it", "cool it" and "hey"' (girl, 11). The trademarks transcend time but are appreciated for the gimmicks they are: 'He says "hey" and I like his hair style' (girl, 11).

Children's awareness of the differences between the real and the fantastic are shown in their responses to questions about being a real policeman. Many of their favourite characters play the parts of undercover policemen; they like the fact that they have violent roles. But they accept this as a fantasy world. They would like to be a hero in a television thriller (for the fame and the money, partly) but only a tiny proportion would like to be a policeman in real life. The real job of a policeman is not romantic. Children distinguish between the realities and being a star, between *real* dangers and invented fantasies of the screen. They had many reasons for not wishing to be an actual policeman:

'You sometimes get killed.' (girl,9)
'You would have to stay up all night.' (girl, 9)
'Everybody hates them.' (boy, 12)
'You get badly hurt sometimes.' (boy, 9)
'They get stuck doing papers and files.' (girl, 10)
'I might have to see a dead body.' (girl, 11)
'You have to wear a uniform.' (girl, 11)
'You have to do traffic control and things like that.' (boy,10)
'It could be dangerous and boring.' (boy, 11)
'Only in a play or film.' (girl, 10)

It is clear that the distinction between the enjoyable fantasy of the screen and the realities of everyday life is crucial.

Children's reactions to the question of fear show an equal ability to make the distinction between what is to be taken seriously and what is not. Gerbner and Gross (1974) stated their belief that fear is a more critical concomitant of violence than aggression. Lyle and Hoffman (1976) on the other hand pointed out the pleasure some children have in 'scary monsters'. Children (q.v. Chapter 8) are not necessarily aware of the implications of violent scenes, for they see them in context. Many bodies being shot piecemeal in a Western have less emotional effect than one bloody nose in a play about modern society (Shaw and Newell, 1972). Children's taste for horror films does not lead them actually to enjoy being scared. That children are capable of being frightened is clear, but this depends both on the way in which the programme is put together and the way in which children approach it. It takes more than a ritual shoot-out in a thriller or a Western to strike the audience as serious; generally the more killings that are shown the less frightening the show becomes, because the violence, whether a shoot-out in a Western or a stranglehold in *Charlie's Angels*, is an integral part of the recognised ritual. Many programmes, notably horror movies, but including *Dr Who* and *Starsky and Hutch*, are designed to give at least a *frisson* of excitement and this the children enjoy in its own terms. They do not normally think of the implications of pain inherent in the violence. Three-quarters of the children say that they positively enjoy being scared by programmes on television; but this is at the not very emotionally compelling level at which television operates. But children are *capable* of being really scared; very few said with any bravado that they had never been scared by anything on television. A large proportion of the children could cite an occasion on which they had been afraid, as in one incident on *Starsky and Hutch* that seemed to make a personal connection: 'I saw the one where Hutch shot a girl in her eye when he was going to shoot another person but he missed and shot a girl in her eye and she was blind' (girl, 7). While children liked the general excitement in a series like *Cannon* they could also remember occasions on which, unexpectedly, a deeper emotional response was elicited. Sometimes children referred to programmes seen years earlier. But while they were able to remember a unique occasion they were still capable of enjoying the more normal levels of fear engendered by television. Many of the children who said that they did *not* like being scared cited thrillers as their favourite programmes.

Children's capacity for fear is always there. Occasionally certain moments on television break through the expectations of fantasy and demand a more complete, and remembered response. A girl of eight, for example, remembered the news 'when I watched a man getting his arm trapped off'. Sometimes children could give a date when they were scared: 'Wolf man last year'; 'Monday 23 May, a thriller' (girls, 10).

Other children, however, were equally adamant that they enjoyed the thrills of *Taste the Blood of Dracula*, saying that they liked the 'scary' moments like 'when he (Frankenstein) had his arm off' (boy, 9). Most of the recollected moments were those on horror films or thrillers, but there is a school of thought that suggests that 'real' violence has far greater salience than any fantasy (Meyer, 1971). In such a thesis the news would be seen as the real threat to children's well-being, since they are capable of taking action thrillers in their own terms and able to distinguish between the real incidents and the fantastic stories. The news is one of children's least favourite programmes but there seems little correlation between dislike and fear; most children suggested that they had never been frightened by the news (cf. Chapter 7). Those who had nevertheless said that they enjoyed being a little scared, as if they had turned the ostensibly 'real' into a kind of fantasy. Those who *had* been frightened either by the news, or by an incident in a horror movie, related the incident closely to their own circumstances. On very rare occasions therefore, children could see the connection between actions, and consequent pain, as if it could happen to them. At these moments they were genuinely scared. Otherwise what they saw on television was all one.

The fact that children see all of television in terms of entertainment does not mean that they are capable of distinguishing between what is real, or what is true, and what isn't. For them television is not of such high salience that the distinction is particularly important. We know that the audience is able to take up the fantasy of *Crossroads* as if it were real, and able to recognise the star of a series by the role he plays, just as Conan Doyle used to complain of being addressed as Sherlock Holmes. But this is a different phenomenon from actually viewing what happens as real life, and analysing it as something to be copied like stealing money from a charity box. The life of the imagination has its own power and can take the imagery of television as part of its world (see Conclusions). If television were taken seriously at face value in the way that Liebert et al. (1973) and Ward and Wackman (1973) suggest, the children would take advertisements so seriously they would not be able to control what they were actually doing.

By the age of ten children appreciate the presentation of advertisements as something quite distinct from the products advertised. Only the very young children have a tendency to believe that what an advertisement says is true. Even with them the question of 'truth' is a complex one, for truth can refer either to an objectively ascertainable fact or to the way it is described. Those who feel that children might be disappointed if advertisements present a false picture of the world (Bever et al. 1975) suggest that children closely connect what they see in the advert with the real world. Given that their favourite advertisements are often cartoons or include anthropomorphism, it is difficult to make such a translation. The Advertising Standards Authority refers to 'truth' as 'all descriptions, claims and comparisons which relate to matters of objectively ascertainable fact' (1976 4.1). While this leaves out the whole question of the meaning of phrases such as 'you can take a White Horse anywhere', or 'Pure Gold' or 'the Effect is Shattering' (cf. Chapter 14) children are aware of the fact that at one level the existence of the product in the shops makes the statement about it on an advertisement 'true'. They take the pragmatic view that advertisements are there for information, to make the audience aware of the existence of products. Those who 'believe' the advertisements in terms of having made sure the products *exist* show an awareness of the peculiarities of the Advertising Standards Authority's position. Some children said that advertisements must be true, or they would not be allowed to appear on television. But as children grew older so they learned to believe advertisements less and less; children of seven believed at least in the established norms about what is allowed on television; more than half the children of eleven no longer believed even that. Children develop a sophisticated attitude towards advertisements that includes an appreciation of their value as entertainment together with a clear realisation of the market forces that underlie advertisements. They accept them as pleasant fantasy interludes but do not really believe them:

> 'They only make people want to buy.' (girl, 7)
> 'So many washing powders try to prove they're better.' (girl, 8)
> 'I don't believe Bovril because people are paid just to say Bovril's good.' (girl, 10)
> 'I do not believe what they say, especially the advert with Daz because they could have washed their clothes with any powder.' (girl, 11)
> 'It's because, for example, an advert is about the best paper to read and then another says that another one is better.' (girl, 11)
> 'Mars is not true: A Mars a day helps your teeth rot away.' (girl, 12)
> 'Because when you buy it it isn't like they say.' (boy, 7)
> 'Because they all say they're the best but they aren't.' (boy, 8)
> 'One advert when they test whiteness, I think that when they push a thing down on the other shirt they put it on the button not the shirt.' (boy, 10)
> 'They always make it out to be better than it really is so

many people will buy it.' (boy, 10)

'They say a lot about them so you will go and buy what they are showing.' (boy, 11)

'The monkeys are just a gimmick to get folk to buy their products.' (boy, 12)

Children's realisation of the progeny of advertisements, or their 'real' nature, does not prevent them enjoying them as entertainment. But they are aware of the ways in which advertising works. Some quote cases:

'On *Nationwide* once they did an experiment on Persil Automatic and it worked for all detergents. And on *That's Life* they did one on Frolic with six dogs and several other dog foods and none of the dogs went for the Frolic.' (boy, 12)

Those who take the advertisements more literally are just as liable to be disappointed:

'My mum bought some Flora margarine because she thought it was soft but it was frozen.' (boy, 12)

'Shout, the spray that you spray on your blouse; I asked mum to look for it but it wasn't in the shops.' (girl, 12)

'Shampoo, they say it removes dandruff but does it?' (girl, 9)

'Because my cat does not like it and it said cats love it but it is not true.' (girl, 8)

Children are familiar with advertisements and there are anecdotal cases when some are influenced by advertisements enough to badger their parents into buying certain products. They also can be persuaded by advertisements to foster certain hobbies or trends. But this does not mean that they confuse the advertisement's gimmickery of presentation with truth; they have a sophisticated awareness of the reality of advertising even as they accept their entertainment value. Most of their favourite advertisements are, in fact, for products that have no particular appeal to them (Chapter 14).

The complex matter of the definitions of truths and falsehoods is well illustrated by the ways in which children cite examples of falsehood. Just as they can take truth literally to mean that if a product is advertised, and exists in the shops, that is 'true' in so far as it goes, and just as they accept the pragmatic version of truth as defined by the Advertising Standards Authority, so they can apply this level of truth to the fantasy elements of advertising and point out how absurd is the fantasy: 'Jam doesn't go "toot" ' (girl, 11); 'Monkeys can't talk' (boy, 8), or 'I do not believe that chocolate animals can growl' (girl, 8). Truth at the level of a statement like 'better' (than what?) or 'tastes good like a cigarette should' are obviously absurd in any strict sense of the truth. Thus a boy of nine points out, 'Penguins can't play football; but it's a good advert'. To children a good advertisement, like a good programme, is one that entertains. The product is of less importance than the production. They see the fantasies for what they are, without believing that every level of presentation is real. Children's attitudes towards commercials show a far greater sophistication and awareness of what they are for than earlier reports suggested (Ward and Wackman, 1973). Williamson (1980) also showed that children are conscious of selling motives and the fact that each advertisement is just one point of view. By the time children are nine and ten they have developed the habit of expressing their immediate disbelief in advertisements, with many examples and reasons. Bogart (1973) found that in the United States only 12 per cent of children thought that advertisements told the truth *most* of the time.

Children's pragmatic attitude to advertisements, their combination of pleasure and disbelief, shows an ability to distance themselves from close involvement in the fantasy worlds presented. They do not subtract elements in which to be caught up, even if there are moments when each of them becomes genuinely, and surprisingly, frightened. They do not 'read' into the multifarious images presented to them a carefully constructed emotional picture of the world. Halloran's (1963) suggestion that an audience for commercials would be made to think that all the best products were associated with leisure, thereby creating a 'false' picture of the world, supposes an unrealistic involvement with, and analysis of, the material on television. Children see through the falsehood on one level, and accept 'falsehood' as pleasure on another. Children's involvement with fantasy is a far more complex matter than either close personal identification or the inability to discriminate between different levels of the real or the false. The real world and the make believe of television are not readily confused in the act of watching. When Schramm et al. (1961) suggests that the fantasy world is transferred from one to the other, they assume that the same level of attention is paid to both. But the rules of the 'fantasy' world are clearly different, a difference children readily acknowledge. It is because of this difference that Noble (1970) suggests that children actually need the fantasy to sublimate their inner lives. But the difference between children's attitudes to heroes and *real* policeman shows that if any projection takes place it is at a level of fantasy that hardly captures their sense of the real world and their place in it.

When the Rileys (1951) discussed the film *The Lone Ranger* as an escape from the real world in which demands are unrealistically high they were surprised, on closer analysis, to find that children did *not* sublimate their anxieties in the programme. They were never so deeply involved. Children learn the 'appropriate', if equivocal, emotion that accepts television at a far less intense level. Occasionally expectations of ease are broken and a 'real' incident breaks through, whether on *Nationwide* or a thriller. Otherwise children enjoy the kind of 'scare' that television provides (Lyle and Hoffman, 1976). The Rileys were the first to suggest that escapist materials are more likely to be popular with children who are frustrated, and although their findings have since been disproved (Noble, 1975), they are still fairly influential in attempts to prove a direct connection between television and other people's delinquent children. The problem with the idea of taking fantasy seriously is that it suggests a level of involvement, of emotional commitment, almost wholly lacking in children's reactions to television. Early researchers assumed that those people who spent a large proportion of their time watching television were the lonely and the unsatisfied, but there is no evidence to support the view that 'alienated' adults spend more time with the mass media (McLeod, Ward and Tancill, 1966). Even Bailyn (1959) found that children do not use television as an emotional escape. Sargeant and Stempel (1968) also showed that 'high anomie relief people' do not use television for escape. The level of demand is emotionally not high enough for such a level of cathartic relief. 'Alienation' is a strong feeling, like despair, and the mass media do not evoke such strong feelings, apart perhaps from outrage against what is shown. Inattentive viewing is far closer to the norm. Thus children's ability to distinguish between the real and the fantastic shows both sophistication about television and a detachment from it in terms of involvement or emotion. But the question of fantasy also reappears at a different level.

7 Looking at the news

'My mum said that if there was any more fighting she thought there would be a world war.' (girl, 11)

One of the children's least favourite programmes on television is the news (q.v. Chapter 1). This is partly because the subject matter itself bores them, partly because the style of presentation is too verbal, and partly because the tone is too serious. The news does not fulfil the criteria of entertainment. Children do not generally dislike the news because it makes them frightened, nor because it makes them think too much. They find it very easy to ignore. But children are capable of taking the news seriously and occasionally do so. Those moments when the news has a direct emotional impact are nearly always the ones which children relate closely to themselves and their own circumstances. Moments of close involvement with what they see on television are so rare and so clear in children's minds that they contrast strongly with their more habitual style of viewing.

Children who have been frightened by an item of news illustrate the well known journalist's dictum (Diamond 1975) that '10,000 deaths in Nepal = 100 deaths in Wales = 10 deaths in the local town = 1 death next door'. The arithmetic in children's case would be even more strongly biased towards the significance of the local. Children do not find themselves concerned with large-scale disasters, but are affected sometimes by rumours, by any possible personal threat, whether based on a specific incident like a local murder, or a general one, like the application of a general incident to their own circumstances. Children's sense of fear reveals a greater sense of threat to their own lives than a sense of being imaginatively engaged in the horrors of the world:

'When there is a murder near because you never know if he could be in town.' (girl, 8)

'When they say that some bad police was going round.' (girl, 7)

'When I hear about people have been raped.' (girl, 10)

'When the murder in Carlisle was committed.' (girl, 10)

'About the murders and death quite near Cockermouth.' (girl, 11)

'When I was in the north last week and there were two armed robberies near by where I was staying.' (girl, 11)

'When the news about UFOs was about I thought they would invade.' (girl, 11)

'When the man fell in the river.' (boy, 8)

'It was when it was about killings. It is frightening to me because it is getting nearer Cockermouth.' (boy, 10)

'When there is robberies and things in Handsworth.' (boy, 10)

'When there was a murder in Brigham. When a man was supposed to be going round with guns that had infra red sighting.' (boy, 10)

'When there's a murderer on the loose, especially in Cumbria.' (boy, 11)

'When a little boy got tortured by two men.' (boy, 11)

'In America the sun was blotted out; I hoped that it would not happen here in case the sun was always blotted out.' (boy, 12)

The news that frightens them is that which impinges on their own lives. Reality has a strong sense of the local. Incidents that are more likely to be part of an entertaining thriller, like murders or mutilations, *can* frighten them but almost invariably do not do so.

When children are asked to cite what they remember from the news, local and domestic incidents also predominate. But their memory for particular items is very poor. Few children can give a coherent account of what they have seen on the news. But then Stern (1971) found that half the adult audience of a national news programme could not recall even one of the nineteen news stories shortly after they were broadcast. Despite the general inattention to the news it is a particular content of the mass media that is often singled out for attention on the assumption that it makes a deep impression (i.e. Adler and Cater, 1976). Based on the assumption that the audience is both fully aware and waiting to be influenced, many studies have been made on the way in which the presentation of the news can be manipulated (Altheide, 1976; Tichenor et al. 1973; Wade and Schramm, 1969). But in contrast to this level of concern, a large proportion of children could not remember any item of the news, let alone be aware that it could be interpreted. Those children that could recall the news cited domestic items; only about 20 per cent of nine- or ten-year-olds could cite international news even in a vague way, such as 'space-shuttles' or 'Russians in space'. Most of the news stories of which they were aware had only made an impression in the vaguest terms: 'strikes', 'murders', 'accidents', 'football' or 'royal baby'. The royal family were considered the most significant news items apart from their own locality. For to a majority of children local items and minor incidents that struck them as interesting were of greater salience than larger headlines. Children found it difficult to recollect anything more than the vaguest expectations of what might be on the news, or was generally on the news, such as 'strikes' or 'fighting'. These were the generic cases they associated with the news, as if they had remembered only what they had expected to appear (q.v. Chapter 10). What children extract from the news, in terms of significant events, is very vague and yet they are generally able to cite the more trivial incidents with greater precision. Boys tended to note stories such as 'Pele Retiring' or 'Manchester United out of Europe' or 'England versus Italy'. They were attuned to receive those items that interested them.

Children's citing of the news reflects the way in which television news is put together. It includes world headlines and important disasters on the one hand and items of light relief or curiosity, and football scores, on the other. Television news provides information at a number of levels. Kay's (1954) suggestion that messages on the news have cathexis (magnet-like) fields concerned with entertainment and familiarity, as well as local involvement, relates closely to the way in which children cite news items they consider the most important. Thus girls of nine and ten would cite items such as 'kids attacked: Rugby player dies; Accident at Bridgefoot', or 'TV violence; pocket money; oil slicks', 'Coach crash; people shouting at each other; bombs' or 'Duchess of Kent; skateboards; where Kermet got shot'. This last item, when a teddy bear got shot by a gunman who was aiming at a little girl, was mentioned by several girls; achieving that personal salience Kay would define as proximity. Boys of nine and ten mentioned items such as 'Pele retiring; skateboarding; and Russians in space'; or 'great white shark; car shut out of plant; fall down Everest'; 'Kevin Keegan not playing for England; Ian Evans broke leg; RAF man shoots woman'; or 'space craft; Scout boys on TV; we should have peace'. Whatever happens in the world the items of news that are noted are either those often repeated such as 'strikes' or 'murders' or those which achieve personal importance. One boy of ten said that the most important news was the fact that 'the price of pocket money is going up'.

The close relationship between the trivial and the weighty in children's attitudes to the news can be attested through many examples of children's responses. Their readiness to note what is repeated most often or what has immediate impact is clearly demonstrated. Children of seven and eight are especially concerned by local news, car crashes in particular: 'When three cars crashed on the same corner' (girl, 7) or 'On the news there was cars sinking in the snow' (boy, 7). Their sense of the importance of the local and the personal is shown repeatedly: 'There has not been any around where I live' (girl, 7) or 'I heard on the news that a boy got bashed to bits by his dad' (girl, 7). Those items that are remembered have a common personal thread:

> 'Motor bikes are important and cars because they have crashes on the road and at racing matches.' (girl, 8)
> 'When a dog at Derwentwater went through the ice and died.' (girl, 8)
> 'There was murderers going around killing lots of people and stealing money and jewellery.' (girl 8)
> 'When the children were off school.' (girl, 8)
> 'If we are going to have a strike or we are not going to get enough oil to fill cars up or take people to work in taxis or a bus.' (boy, 7)
> 'When the workmen were fixing pipes.' (boy, 8)

Children of seven and eight therefore stick to news that has some kind of local or personal centre. By the age of ten children's awareness of the news is wider, but is just as much a mixture of the general and the trivial with certain items important to them for personal reasons. There is no sense of mental order being *imposed* on the news, or its significance (or the bias in the reporting) being weighed up. Their attention and comprehension shows a curious mixture of different levels of importance:

> 'Queen and Prince Charles' trip and the money strikes.'
> 'Queen's visit and the baby that the men took away and her mummy put cigarette ash on her.'
> 'A girl's dog was savaged by dogs; the people going on strike.'
> 'When a lady got a new job then went into a graveyard and some of her friends they were boys. They took a pretend coffin into the graveyard and one of them dressed in a white cloth and when she saw the coffin open and somebody came out with a white cover on she just fell to the ground.'
> (girls, 10)
> 'Avon has arrived at a house.'

'Vietnam and China are fighting; everybody is rushing to kill people.'
'The discovery of Jupiter.'
'About two killings at Broughton; this means that killing is coming further into Cockermouth.'
'The accident of John Burke, a rugby league player for Workington Town.'
'American eclipse of the sun.' (boys, 10)

Children have great difficulty in signifying which are the important items of news; the easiest way for them is to cite the recurring strikes, or commonplace murders. But they are all put together in their memory items at a variety of different levels of significance; not only those things that strike personally but those that seem interesting, or amusing for their own sake, as if at least part of the news was a medium for entertainment:

'The civil war in Iran; Pelicans having cold feet.' (girl, 11)
'Well I have a boyfriend and my brother got out of hospital.' (girl, 11)
'Jack the Ripper; Test tube baby; fighting in Iran; Manchester United winning the FA Cup; all the snow; the lorry strike.' (boy, 11)
'My dad's factory may close down on weekends.' (boy, 11)
'I might be getting a horse.' (girl, 12)

As children get older their ability to cite the news becomes less; they are more circumspect about the fact that they do not actually like to watch the news:

'Can't remember any.' (girl, 12)
'I haven't been watching the news.' (boy, 11)
'To tell you the truth I've forgotten.' (boy, 12)

Television has always been considered an important source of information (cf. Murdoch and Phelps, 1973), although children prefer not to watch those programmes that give information. They tend to avoid the news and documentaries by choice (BBC, 1978), although they cannot avoid the fact that these programmes are part of an evening's package of programmes. But nearly all the attention given by research to the presentation of the news on television has been devoted not to the audience and its reactions but to the presenters and the way in which they control and manipulate what is presented. The assumption made is that the audience imbibe whatever is given; that it *can* be biased by a particular slant given by the producers. But there is no evidence given by the audience that such manipulation takes place, despite the analysis given by critics; the gap between the editor's 'casting' of the news and the ground on which they do so is extremely wide. The concern with political bias in news reporting depends on fascination with the workings of editorial control; just as politicians are consumed with passionate interest in what they themselves are trying to say, might have said, or have been reported as saying, so presenters of the news assume that the way they put the news across can make significant differences to the political perceptions of the audience. The first long study of the forming of news, with the implication that the audience's opinions would reflect editorial bias, was by the Langs (1953) and has remained as influential as the phrase 'making the news'. The Langs described the power of the commentator and the importance of the placing of cameras for what they revealed and what they ignored. They analysed the 'landslide effect' of giving the impression that General MacArthur's homecoming elicited unified euphoria, when it was only by careful editing and the camera's concentration on the few people that had come to greet him that such an impression could be made. Tichenor et al. (1973) showed how the editors chose what was newsworthy and defined what topics were controversial. De Sola Pool and Schulman (1964) pointed out that good news was more accurately reported than bad: 'Persons writing about good news tend to produce supportive images, while persons writing about bad news tend to produce more critical ones' (p.150). Breed (1955) found reporters strongly influenced by the policy of the institution for which they worked, whether conscious of this policy or not (cf. Sigelman, 1973). Breed (1958) also came to the conclusion that two-thirds of the items not reported are politico-economic and that this reveals a dislike of exposing institutional faults. This last point was taken up by Whale (1977) together with a recurrence of the idea that the media are effective because they reflect their audience; it has often been pointed out that the propensity in *all* news presentations is to go for the most lurid and the most violent.

A great deal of attention has been paid to the political bias of all news reporting, even if it tries to be objective, and to the power of the press in promoting the interests of particular parties. The Glasgow Media Group (1976, 1980, 1982) believe that the presentation of news is governed by fierce right-wing bias and establishment control. The BBC, on the other hand, has been continually attacked for showing left-wing bias in its presentation of alternative points of view. The problem with this research, however, is not the question of whether it is accurate or not, but whether it is relevant to the consciousness of the audience. The fact that an audience is unaware that there is bias suggests that it is the more easily manipulated. But television audiences are not just unaware of bias but unaware that there *are* points of view; they do not look at television as if what is presented were significant. Their refusal to change opinions (qv. Chapter 13) does not derive from being unaware of political bias, but from the lack of significant 'opinions' about these definitions of politics. Thus the presentation of the news, and the subtle ways in which it is done, is at one level; the attention of the audience is at another. Very rarely are the two ever connected.

Children are clearly unaware of the controversy surrounding political bias. This is not due to the fact that they have not been taught about politics, the significance of voting, or the attitudes of different political parties. Children do not look at the news with that attention which might include such a form of interpretation. The most that they deem necessary with television is a recognition of certain items of interest, and acknowledgement of a few essential facts. The sheer amount of news makes it hard for them to remember, unless there is a continuous piece of news night after night about an event like the Falklands crisis. Even then what they will see will reflect their own interests, and not the interpretation given by the presenter. While they will be able to parody overheard remarks that give an indication of political chauvinism, they do not seem to pick this up from the television news itself. Connell (1980) points out that we do not see through the news bulletin to the reality, but see the bulletins themselves. Children see the images and recollect them accordingly to the interesting way they are presented (cf. Park, 1972). Items of great importance or utmost triviality will juggle for attention in children's minds; and both, unless there is some personal connection, will be hard to remember. Sports news is of greater interest to some children and easier to respond to because they look forward to it and anticipate the expected. Interest devoted to an item that is awaited is far greater than to the relaying of new things. The one unifying factor in the presentation of the news that can be expected is the role of the presenters. These are amongst the children's least favourite characters since they talk and talk seriously. Although the news might occasionally include interesting pictures of excitement, generally it rests heavily on the earnestness of the unsmiling presenter. Even the efforts of John Craven to cajole children into interest are generally doomed to failure; children *can* look with close critical attention, but generally don't.

Nevertheless children cannot avoid looking at the news altogether even if they wish to. The news is an inevitable part of the evening's schedule; during the early part of the evening between children's programmes and later between children's favourite programmes, thrillers, comedies and horror films. While it might give them a chance, like advertisements, to 'go to the toilet', it cannot be ignored any more than other programmes. Yet children are only slightly aware, when they survey the evening's viewing, that they have seen the news. They mentioned the news as one of the programmes they would see, but generally forgot they had seen it when asked about a previous evening's viewing. It is as if there were an automatic shutting out of the news; half the children said they did *not* watch the news even if they had watched a whole evening's programmes. Children prefer almost any programme to the news. It seems to them to lack variety, imagery, and the juxtapositions of familiar colour that characterise their favourite programmes. The variety of the news lies in the content, not the presentation.

Although the news tends to concentrate on the more exaggerated incidents, on the bizarre and the abnormal, children tend to see it as a rather dull programme with inevitably dull subjects such as strikes, even if there are moments that, by their personal relevance or proximity, become interesting by chance. But most of the incidents that take place that concern children do not actually make the news:

' . . . everyone is always drunk and when they're drunk there
is always fights . . . small fights and things that don't make
the news'. (boy, 14)

The news, like advertisements, is therefore part of the inevitable texture of television. But it rarely emerges from its general texture. Bias is not of as great significance as those items of news that by chance are of some personal interest. Thus children are aware of a general violence, but only concerned with those manifestations which are local.

8 Violence

'Kennedy was hit in the shoulder but he shot the man with the tommy seven, Sam dived for the gun . . . he shot two men until a man stepped out and he got it right through the head.' (boy, 14)

When children are asked to cite the characteristic behaviour of Starsky and Hutch they give a list of actions that makes them sound like the very worst criminals. They 'smash doors and windows', 'jump on car rooves', 'bash people's noses', 'shoot and kill people', 'drive fast in cars', 'chase girls and are in gun fights'. The image that children report includes a series of violent acts, some large and some small, but all of the kind that, when written down and analysed as a percentage of content, gives a picture of complete depravity. The fact that children are perfectly aware that Starsky and Hutch are on the side of the law, that they 'fight crime', 'catch criminals' and 'solve mysteries' seems a fairly fragile gloss to those who wish to complain about levels of violence on television. *Starsky and Hutch* is a popular series that has been singled out for criticism as containing the kind of material which would inevitably deprave the young. The Annan report (1977) suggested that the show was much too violent, and this point was taken up by most newspapers as well as those agencies that have been campaigning for greater control over the number of violent incidents on television.

When there was a move to cut out the violence in series such as *Starsky and Hutch* many viewers protested, not because they relished the brutality depicted but because they saw these violent acts as part of the style of the programme. Surveys of audience reactions to various programmes (e.g. BBC, 1978) reveal that people are, in fact, unaware that what they are watching is violent. When written down or isolated as a type of content it appears that people watch a great deal of violence, but most of the incidents in a Western, as in boys' adventure stories of the nineteenth century, seem to the audience part of the inevitable texture of the programme. To children the actions that Starsky and Hutch undergo are all 'stunts'; they are part of the performance of the battle between the good and the bad, part of the excitement, like the Hollywood genre of car-chases. Seen in the gloss of ritual, the detective story seems no more than story and, however many actual deaths, seems far less violent than a single nose-bleed. It is as if the more deaths that are depicted, the less realistic is the programme. It is very difficult for children to talk about incidents isolated under the heading of violence since they will agree that something is shocking if it is explained to them as being so, but will not have noticed it as such in their normal viewing. Nothing is worse than the relish for violence, or a fascination with torture, but that lingering over the pornographic is not the state of mind in which children approach television, even if it might be the case for those who buy the most bloodthirsty videos. Children are all occasionally struck by the brutal or the frightening; whether in *Starsky and Hutch* or in a horror film. But this moment stands out uniquely against the general rough and tumble of a thriller, when the streets of America or London are ostensibly crowded with car-chases, shoot-outs, and fist-fights. For children 'stunts' include the use of guns; they do not think of the consequences of their use. The difference between description of violent incidents, when they sound callous and brutal, and the way in which they are habitually perceived is very great. Content such as that described by children as typical in *Starsky and Hutch* would, if copied by those children, turn the whole world from China to Peru into nothing but a continuous fight. But the audience does not perceive violence in this way. When Shaw and Newell (1972) interviewed families about their concerns about television they found that violence was not only an issue of little moment, but that much of what they defined as violent was not even noticed. Having shown their subjects films containing 'killings' they found that even after vigorous prompting the audience did not agree that what they saw was violent. The popularity of programmes containing violence (McIntyre and Teevan, 1971) might suggest a bloodthirsty audience whose jaded palates demand even more exaggerated sensations (cf. Read, 1969). But it could also suggest an audience unaware that the rituals of gangster movies have any real reflection on their own lives, are anything more than entertainment. Children are accustomed to high levels of violence without being aware of its significance. Content analysts list violence in terms of incidents which show anyone being hurt, by a gun or a knife, a fist or a bomb. But violence is not perceived by viewers in this way; to them violence includes emotional involvement. In terms of content analysis television contains many 'violent incidents', especially in cartoons. But the greater the number of violent incidents, the less likely it was that the audience would perceive them as violence felt personally. A Western with twelve deaths was not perceived as violent; a programme about a young man drafted into the army who had a realistically simulated fist fight was seen as far more so. One was taken as a ritual; the other as more personally applicable. The fact that children watch violent programmes does not imply that they even see the violence as such, or relate *Tom and Jerry* into real terms.

It is unfortunate that one of the donnés about the effects of television on children is that they imitate all they see, that they are mere reflections of the accumulated violence of television programmes. Distaste for the content of programmes leads to the assumption that television violence affects the whole of society (apart from commentators themselves). Bronfenbrenner (1971) gives a typical example of this assumption:

> Given the salience of violence in commercial television, including cartoons especially intended for children, there is every reason to believe that this mass medium is playing a significant role in generating and maintaining a high level of violence in American society, including the children and youth. (p.114)

But this assumption in commentators has become one of the major hypotheses amongst researchers who have tried to prove a direct causal link between television and violence. The United States Surgeon Generals Scientific Advisory Committee on Television and Social Behaviour was set up to prove the assertion of an earlier commission:

> In 1969, the President's Commission on the Causes and Prevention of Violence declared uncompromisingly: 'Violence on television encourages violent forms of behaviour and fosters moral and social values about violence in family life which are unacceptable in a civilised society.' Yet, as acknowledged elsewhere in the Commission's report, there is no evidence that television is an actual *cause* of social violence: for, as in the million-dollar Surgeon Generals' report that followed in 1972, the Commission's findings were purely correlative, equating the two main factors in what is scientifically a pretty arbitrary fashion.

As Eysenck and Eysenck (1964) indicate: 'Correlational analyses are important, but they are merely permissive, not "compelling", and they involve Thurstone's maxim that "a correlation is a confession of ignorance" '.

(Baggeley and Duck, 1976, p.ix)

Most of the research on television and violence is designed to demonstrate a clear connection between what is seen on the screen and what is enacted in real life. It rests on the hypothesis that children imitate what they see, that they model their behaviour on this aspect of television. The two most influential psychologists who have explored this question are the Americans Berkowitz and Bandura. Both have relied heavily on the Buss aggression machine (Buss, 1961, 1971) which is designed to measure a reactive behaviour following a film. The machine records the amount of electrical charge that the subject is willing to administer to a victim. The essential hypothesis is that if the subject sees a violent film, rather than a neutral one, he will be willing to pass on the immediate sense of aggression through administering high levels of pain, through the electrical charges. Most of the vibrations on this hypothesis are concerned with frustrating the subject in some way before putting him in a position of power over someone else who is supposed to answer various questions (unrelated to the film). If the 'victim' gives the wrong answers the subjects are encouraged to give a series of electric shocks; the machine records the number and the strength of the electric shocks ostensibly given. The research based on this machine is designed to measure the relationship between the stimulus, like viewing films with violent content, and the subsequent response, measured by the willingness to administer pain. The extensive use of such a device is itself a comment both on the difficulties in isolating particular variables, and on the desire to prove behavioural outcomes in experimental conditions.

The majority of Berkowitz's experiments used a film called *The Champion* made in 1949 which concerns the actions of a prize-fighter (acted by Kirk Douglas) in a boxing ring. A particular part of the film was shown to find out whether the subjects emulate the same actions, or transfer aggression to other circumstances. In a typical experiment (Berkowitz and Rawlings, 1963) a group of subjects watched the boxing match for seven minutes while a control group saw a film on the 'innocuous' subject of canal boats. Both groups were then given the opportunity to use the Buss aggression machine. Berkowitz concluded that the subjects became more aggressive after watching the violent film because they retain an example of action, which, when they were for some reason frustrated (i.e. by the victim's inability to answer simple questions), sprang to mind as an immediate example to imitate.

Berkowitz sees the connections between the experience of viewing and subsequent action being made through frustration: 'A frustration is . . . any interference with some ongoing goal-directed activity . . . Anger "drive state" . . . produces aggressive responses only in the presence of relevant clues' (1962, p.xi). Thus, given, the right conditions, subjects were supposedly ready and willing to act in a broadly imitative manner.

Like Berkowitz, Bandura concentrated on a series of variations on one main experiment in which children are shown a model engaged in an aggressive act. They are then tested to see if they imitate it (Bandura and Houston, 1961). In most of the experiments children see an actor hitting a large Bobo doll (a plastic doll weighted in such a way that it springs upright after it is knocked down). Sometimes the children watch a live action, sometimes they see the performance on film, and occasionally they see it in cartoon form. They are then led to a separate room where they are given the same materials they saw attacked by an adult. Their 'mean imitative aggressive responses' are then tested (Bandura, 1973). Bandura (1963) concluded that 'experience helped to shape the form of the child's aggressive behaviour' (p.61). Given the willingness to imitate, children are supposed to be affected in all their subsequent behaviour because their inhibitions are reduced: 'Experience tends to reduce the child's inhibitions against acting in a violent aggressive manner' (1973, p.94). Like Berkowitz, Bandura does not think that the effect of violence is limited to one specific occasion. He therefore suggests the hypothesis of 'disinhibition' which, like Berkowitz's definition of 'frustration', basically extends the willingness to imitate.

There have been numerous experimental studies designed to prove what many people instinctively feel. Some, like those of Walters (1963), were variations on the film *Rebel Without a Cause* using the Buss aggression machine. Others, like Drabman and Thomas (1974), were variations on the Bandura experiments. Most of the two hundred and fifty or so tried to discover, in a variety of ways, whether they could elicit the temporary effects of imitation or disinhibition (McLeod et al. 1972; McIntyre and Teevan, 1972; Hanratty et al. 1969; Hapkiewitz and Roben, 1971; Foulkes et al. 1972; Stein and Friedrich, 1972; Parke et al. 1977; Steuer et al. 1971 etc.) or isolate involuntary emotional reactions through the study of galvanic skin responses (Osborn and Endsley, 1971; Thomas et al. 1977; Lazarus et al. 1962 etc.). Some experiments have attempted to find out about long-term correlations between early viewing habits and later acts of aggression (Lefkowitz et al. 1977; Eron et al. 1972; Eron, 1973; Singer and Singer, 1981). But all the experiments in this tradition of the laboratory model have been heavily criticised either for their suppositions (cf. Williams, 1979) or their methodology (cf. Eysenck and Nias, 1978). Some are attacked for being theoretically simplistic, others for weaknesses in experimental design and many for relying on unwarranted assumptions (Lesser, 1962). Many of the experiments, when duplicated, reveal quite conflicting results (Howitt and Cumberhatch, 1975). It is also possible to come to different conclusions from the same findings. The problem with these experiments is the contrast between them and the normal conditions of viewing (Staats, 1968). When there is a connection between the experiment and real life it turns out that children carry out the same behaviour which is taken as evidence of aggression in circumstances which have nothing to do with films or violence (Hanratty et al. 1969; Patterson et al. 1967). The Bobo doll, for example, is designed to be hit so that it springs upright again. Lesser (1977) said that the experiments did not take into account all the actions that children anyway use in their play. Wells (1973) found he could manipulate his observers. Many experiments relied on verbal responses (Mussen and Rutherford, 1962; Atkins et al. 1972) or stated willingness to use violence (Dominick and Greenberg, 1971) or, however complicated the methods used, relied on correlations between press-cuttings and what boys or parents think of as violence (Belson, 1978). The statistical correlations between incidents of rape and the amounts of violence shown on television (Court, 1976) have also been severely criticised (Cochrane, 1978; Yaffé, 1979).

But it seems that no amount of proof that these experiments are based on false assumptions destroys the belief that there must some- how be a correlation between violence observed and violence subsequently enacted. Even Eysenck and Nias (1978), having pointed out how badly the experiments were carried out, and having criticised the assumption of a causal relation, still tried to suggest that there somehow *must* be a link, somewhere. Even when an experiment like that of Liebert and Baron (1971) is criticised for relying on children of five and six and eight and nine being asked after watching a film to press either a button which says 'Hurt a child' or another which says 'Help a child win a prize', we still find assertions of the correlation between high levels of violent content on television and high levels of aggressive behaviour (McLeod, Atkins and Chaffee, 1971). The problem with the experiments is that they rely on strong levels of emotional arousal that children do not normally associate with television. The differences between the conditions of viewing a large number of varied programmes at home, and seeing a short clip of film in a laboratory, could not be more different. Children would not notice most of the content as 'violent' if they had not been told. They need to find something to do to please the researcher. The fact is that most of the experiments have not really been about television or children's responses, but about a different subject altogether.

Experiments concerned ostensibly with violence are not in fact about the effect of television but about the nature of obedience. Both Berkowitz and Bandura have drawn attention to the importance of the justification of aggression which underlies conscious imitation. When Bandura quoted a similar experiment by Hoyt (1970) he clarified an important point in his work on behaviour modelling:

> In a related study, Hoyt found that exposure to filmed aggression in which the victorious aggressor was portrayed as avenging a past unfair beating generated more aggression in viewers than exposure to a film in which the aggressor was portrayed as defending himself against a dangerous attack, or to the same film shown without references to any justifying circumstances. (Bandura, 1973, p.133)

Hoyt was measuring obedience to a model. Other experiments by Bandura also explored subjects' following of justified violence. Berkowitz and Rawlings (1973) found that a particular set of conditions made a fundamental difference to the ways in which subjects used the ag–gression machine. If the film appeared to suggest that the violence depicted was justified, the subjects were subsequently more virulent in their anger. In an experiment based on a news film of an episode in the Vietnam war, Meyer (1971) demonstrated that a narrator justifying a particularly brutal act caused subjects to behave in a more primitive manner than those who watched the same film without hearing the commentary. In such experiments (e.g. Lovaas, 1961) the crucial factor was not the medium or the violence depicted, but the authority which suggested that the subjects should follow the example being offered. Thus, as in the classroom, it is possible to make children follow examples (see Powers and Geen, 1972). In certain circumstances 'seeing others carrying out punitive orders calmly . . . increases obedient ag-gression' (Bandura, 1973, p.177). Television can be *used* in the right circumstances as a substitute model, as an aid in justifying particular actions, like a teacher using a film to teach a particular point of view. The conditions of the laboratory, combined with the willingness of children to obey, and their desire to please, naturally leads them to be able to respond to tasks required of them. The actual presence of a teacher and the conditions of the laboratory make viewing television into an examination.

One side effect of the presence of a justifying authority is that children exaggerate aggression when they are in the presence of an adult. Siegel and Kohn (1959) monitored groups of children to discover that they were far more aggressive with adults watching, as if they were challenging authority. Hicks (1968) confirmed this finding, when he worked on the effects of aggression seen on film. Dominick and Greenberg (1972) found that the presence of parents made a significant difference to the way that children viewed television violence. But the most famous experiments which explored this aspect of obedience and imitation were carried out by Milgram (1963, 1964, 1974) using the Buss machine. Subjects were asked to take part in a series of experiments ostensibly concerned with the relationship between pain and memory. They were to present a series of questions to a victim who, if he did not answer correctly, was to be given a series of increasingly powerful electric shocks. The subject sat at the Buss machine; the victim in an electric chair. It is perhaps fortunate that the victim was only simulating pain because the subjects were willing to assist in the experiments to the extent of giving enough voltage to kill their victims. This obedience to some kind of authority knew few bounds; given justification for aggression the subjects were willing to demonstrate almost incredible feats of obedient violence. They only needed the sanction of the researcher, the teacher, the official, the man in the white coat, before they would obey instructions to be violent. Television in itself, and the conditions in which it is normally watched, creates no authority in itself, although it can be *used* as a medium through which such authority manifests itself. Given the right conditions, such as those realistic ones experimented upon by Latané and Darley (1970), people are willing to imitate extreme or absurd actions. To maintain their own self-image and relate it to other people's attitudes, they will fill various expected behaviour patterns (Orme and Scheibe, 1964; Argyle, 1967; Farina, Allen and Saul, 1968). We also know that people have a capacity for role playing in which the role can take them over completely (Zimbardo, 1973). But the conditions in which these experiments took place were all ones in which the subjects were closely, actively and emotionally involved for a short time. The contrast with television viewing is such that it is a curious transfer to apply discoveries about obedience, the following of 'justified' instructions and role-playing, to violent content on television.

Children are not emotionally caught up in what they see on television. There are, of course, occasions on which they are suddenly, despite themselves, pushed beyond their pleasure in 'scary' things. But these moments of horror spring almost invariably from a lingering image rather than from a violent incident in the conventional sense (q.v. Chapter 9). Children are not just indifferent to violent incidents defined as shootings, killings and hittings; they do not see them as such. When children *are* aroused to strong emotional reactions it is more likely to be with horror or distaste, a nightmare rather than a desire to repeat or emulate the action. Children *can* be aroused by the excitement on the screen (Greer, 1982) but this does not have to be linked to violence. The arguments about the biological basis for aggression (Lorenz, 1966; Maccoby and Jacklin, 1980) or about early learning influences versus genetic factors as the prime influences (Tiegler, 1980), all rely on the need for the 'Drive' state of high emotional arousal on which people need to act. This might be simulated on the screen, but it is not watched with the passion it depicts. When Carpenter (1976) allowed young children to make cartoons he found they made a series of violent incidents; in a parody of the cartoons that they knew, the children concentrated on the events, and ignored the connections of the plot. They realised that cartoons depend on 'violent' incidents, but such a level of violence has almost nothing to do with the real thing.

Some researchers have gone so far as to suggest that television actually reduces aggressive responses in children. Taking a typical Bandura experiment Lesser (1963) found that children who watched a violent film played less aggressively than those who had watched a neutral one. The experiments of Feshbach (1955 etc.), based on the use of Berkowitz's film *The Champion*, have led him to the conclusion that 'Vicarious aggressive activity results in a reduction in subsequent aggressive behaviour' (1961, p.381). His hypothesis rests on the idea that human beings, given the tendency to be violent (Ames, 1966. notes that children of three to five years old tell stories of great violence and aggression even if there is no outside source for such stories), need to sublimate their feelings by identifying with a type of aggression or by releasing the emotions through cathartic involvement. As an antidote to simple models of imitation of violence Feshbach's hypothesis remained influential (cf. Noble, 1975) despite the fact that it, too, came in for a great deal of criticism (Liebert, 1971; Lefkowitz et al. 1971, etc.). The advantage of Feshbach's position is that he does, at least, recognise the distinction to be made between the real and the fantastic, even if he does include the 'conventional' view of imitation:

> A child's acting out of aggressive tendencies should be lessened or unaffected to the extent that dramatic content functions as fantasy in the larger, cognitive sense, and is perceived as fantasy in the narrower, fictional sense. If the dramatic content is perceived as 'real' the possibility of facilitating aggression through such processes as imitation, instruction and disinhibition should be considerably enhanced. (1971, p.321)

Fantasy violence is supposed to reduce aggression. One ironic result of this hypothesis is the conclusion that any form of hooliganism carried out in real life, like gang fights at soccer matches, is not really violence at all, but a necessary exhibition of 'aggro'; ritual fantasy play (Marsh, 1978).

Audiences are often unaware that what they see on television is violent. Verbal acts of aggression and ridicule create more unease in children than any physical aggression, especially when they take place in circumstances that could apply to their own lives (Himmelweit et al. 1958, p.19). As Orwell (1945) first pointed out, it is more likely that seeing a real football match in which the home side is losing to foreign opposition will cause feelings of anger and frustration (especially if it is a rough match) than being entertained by a Western, however many and brutal the deaths. The lack of strong emotional reactions to television places the idea of violence in a very different context. To list a series of 'violent' incidents derived from different physical acts might read like a catalogue of brutality, but it is not perceived as such. Rubenstein's (1974) suggestion that there should be an index of violence so that television companies have to reduce the amounts shown misses the point. Besides, most indexes do not include verbal abuse or football fouls. The Independent Broadcasting Authority (1975) nevertheless presented a compromise directive that suggested that there should be 'less' violent actions shown during the early part of the evening. The problem is that the 'effect' of violence is not a measurable quantity. It is easy to look for, and be shocked by, the analysis of violent incidents in *Starsky and Hutch*. The fact that some critics are appalled is understandable, for, if such content is looked at with strong emotional arousal, then it does strike the imaginative viewer with horror. But the callous way in which violence is presented is met with indifference by the audience. Violence in thrillers or Westerns makes good entertainment because it is the means through which stories are enacted. Children's interest in fairy tales, or battles between good and evil, and their capacity for relating similarly violent ones, show a concern for constructing patterns through a repetition of structural devices and ritualised endings. They accept the 'moral' justification of the hero winning at the end because this is part of the optimistic convention of a story (Chukovsky, 1923) and because this conforms to the ritual of expectations (Appleby, 1978). Ritualised violence offered as entertainment is distinct from the genuine threats that impinge on the normal world. Children enjoy 'scary' things although they would not call most thrillers 'scary'. The use of television characters, like puppets, in children's games says more about their imaginative play (Roberts, 1982) than the source from which they derive their ideas (Singer et al. 1977). Children playing 'cops and robbers' or 'cowboys and Indians' are not assuming that they are in the 'real' world when they say 'bang bang you're dead' (Opie and Opie, 1969, q.v. Chapter 6) or when they parody the style in which thrillers are written. The transference of attitudes from television to normal circumstances is a more complex matter than simple imitation. The difference between real violence and that on television remains clear.

9 The style of television

'One can learn from the professionals.' (boy, 10)

There is such a great variety of styles on television that it seems, at first glance, almost an anomaly to suggest that television has an overall 'style' of its own. The distinctions in pace between domestic comedy and thrillers, or between cartoons and farming programmes, the juxtaposition of advertisements and the news, or *Top of the Pops* and *Tomorrow's World*, let alone the differences critics see between examples of the same genre, would all suggest that television creates such a mixture that even if it is looked at in a particular frame of mind, the contrasts would predominate. And yet television is associated by children with a distinct style of its own, with a particular tone. The very mixture of differences makes the whole seem the more unified. Children have distinct favourites amongst programmes and will always be clear about the order in which they would like to see their programmes, but they are, beyond these preferences, far more conscious of the general style of entertainment. They will try to avoid all those programmes that break the tone, that make a different set of demands. Far from being a significant event, or a special outing, television is a medium for conveying a happy mood at any time it is switched on. Its rhythm is not supposed to change, and although there is a sense in which different tones are appropriate to different times of the day (Conrad, 1982) the overall gloss is supposed to be one of humour and lightness of touch. The dislike of documentaries and children's programmes, and the preferences for thrillers, and comedies, together with a liking for personalities that smile and are jolly, create the way in which television is expected to perform. Details of style differ; the effect of the style is the same.

The very exaggerations of the changes in picture and the very richness of the images displayed on television makes it very easy to watch. And yet those images that children tend to remember most clearly stand out from the constant changes, either because of their repetition or because of the way in which they are presented. One of the best examples of the power of television images is the very popular programme *Dr Who*. The plots are quite complex and it relies on lengthy verbal explanations and yet is very popular with six- and seven-year-olds. The reason for its success lies in the way in which it tends to rely on a series of clear images embedded in familiar material. A typical episode of *Dr Who* began like this:

Shot 1. A Police Hut.

Shot 2. Looking down a tunnel that looks like the bore of a rifle.

Shot 3. Th Face of Dr Who.

Shot 4. Looking at a Kaleidoscope.

Shot 5. Title.

Shot 6. Close up of a Skull.

Shot 7. An obviously foreign doctor talks to the skull; and then to a girl.
He says 'Volcanic element, 12,000 million years old: *Too* old; impossible'.

Shot 8. Man with a rucksack on his back walking through a forest (branches, artifical smoke, the sound of whistles) at night.

Shot 9. The foreign doctor goes into a laboratory full of apparatus and TV monitors. There is the sound of bubbles. He says 'Phase one power. Phase two power'.

Shot 10. Close up of the Skull. The girl comes over to look at it. The skull *seems* to change.

After a time the skull turns into a face. By the end of the episode the plot was beginning to be clear. But young children found it very difficult to relate what happened. All they could think of was the image of the skull.

'A skeleton. It makes you scary. The skeleton's face turned orange. The lady tried to kill a soldier.' (boy, 6)
'Woman turned into an old skeleton 100 years old. She did

'this computer and her head turned an old skeleton face.'
(girl, 7)

'Hairs all over his hands. They were going to kill the girl.
Tried to kill her head.' (boy, 7)

'About a skeleton. Skull changed into a woman's head then
back to skull. Can't remember any more.' (boy, 6)

'Did that skull turn into a lady and back to a skull? I don't
know what else happened.' (boy, 6)

'A lady got killed by a skeleton. She just fell down.' (girl, 7)

All they could remember was the central image, which both fascinated
them and 'scared' them. The visual tricks made far more impact than
the outline of the plot.

The one consistent, almost static, image of any programme, however,
is the style associated with the hero (or, in the case of *Dr Who*, the
recurring Daleks). The appearance of Dr Who himself is characterised
by children as depending on curly hair, a large coat, and a long multi-
coloured scarf. There are certain underlying factors that they also
recognise as part of the paraphernalia of the programme such as the
police-box ('Tardis') in which Dr Who travels through time and space,
the mechanical dog ('K.9') and Dr Who's propensity for Jelly Babies.
Children also point out that he inevitably 'fights monsters' and 'travels
through time'. Some are aware that he is generally 'looking for the
keys of time'. Each of the cited characteristics is a mark of the recognisably familiar. The details are there to be attuned to, and children soon
learn that those items give clarity to the overall image. Each of the
popular heroes on television are recognised as carrying a particular
style. *Wonder Woman*, for example, is a programme that depends upon
the transference of the ordinary woman into a super power. The fact
that she can jump high and run fast must be built into the plot; the
sequence when she spins round to be transformed from one character
into the next becomes the most significant part of every plot because
it is the most repeated. It is as if the images presented at the beginning
of every week as part of the credit sequence were not only those most
easy to recognise but the very substance of the programme. Wonder
Woman does not, every week, hold back a tank with one hand from its
attempts to crush her, but this image is typical of what she *does* do,
week by week. It becomes hard for children to separate the repeated
credit sequences from the individual episodes, the repeated images from
the single plot. Thus when children are asked to say what happened in
the most recent episode of *Wonder Woman* they focus as much on the
central images of her prowess as on any event that was significant to
the story.

'Diana Price spun round and turned into Wonder Woman.'
(girl, 7)
'Diana changed into Wonder Woman and she started to chase
two men.' (boy, 7)
'Wonder Woman jumped very high out of a trap and ran fast.'
(boy, 8)
'She changed into Wonder Woman and threw a bomb out of
a cave.' (boy, 10)
'She jumped up and cut wires in half.' (boy, 11)
'In a cave she got away and span around and she jumped up
on to the aeroplane and when she was down she caught the
men.' (girl, 8)

Her powers are the basis for each plot. Children know what to expect.

Children's ability to recognise familiar material, together with their
clear expectations of what this material should be, helps them learn to
perceive particular images, associated with the appearance of the hero,
or with a style of presentation, or a pattern of repeated actions. Thus
the memorable points in *Starsky and Hutch* might be the way in which
one of them lifts his gun to shoot, or the way they talk to each other,
rather than the circumstances of the plot, or the denouement. Children
learn to process the information that television offers according to its
style, and according to the fact that television is not expected to force
close cerebral attention. Children have clear expectations of what the
material on television should be. They expect a succession of familiar
images, a pattern of repeated actions that in their repetition become
like images. While there are strong similarities in the structure of plots
(it has been suggested that there are very few basic plots to choose
from), the stories themselves seem to be of less salience than the structure produced by the expected images. The logic of the argument is
certainly lost in the pattern of the pictures. The 'context' of the story
is not easily distinguished from the content; so that the children learn
to tune in to their expectations and learn from that (cf. Hilgard, 1964).
Children therefore do not readily analyse or discriminate between the
material that is generally agreed to be significant and that which is considered trivial or incidental. Although they have the capacity they do
not consider it appropriate to do so. Any audience subconsciously or
consciously looks for what it expects to see (Bruner, 1974). In the case
of television the expectations are of a style in which not too much edge
is given to an argument, and the succession of images becomes the more
important. This recognition of repeated images is not a product of the
conscious desire to visualise. Children do not bring their *own* imaging
powers to bear on television as they do when closely reading a passage
of prose (Winkley, 1975). Attention can actually be distracted by
attempts to visualise (Valentine, 1962). The stereotypes of television

are perceived through the repeated recognition of the familiar, rather than the conscious attention given to the irregular, the unexpected (Berlyne, 1958) or to the novel (Berelson, 1964). This is why violence is no longer perceived as such. Children exhibit the tendency for perceptual hypotheses to fixate after receiving a minimum of confirmation (Bruner, 1974, p.81).

The succession of expected images becomes a style in itself. It is for this reason that MacLuhan (1964) made so much of the individuality of each of the media. While an audience could run the whole gamut of emotions in responding to a series of programmes, they actually rest relatively calmly in a sense of watching television; the activity of watching is more dominant than the details of content. The way in which children perceive the style of television can be best illustrated by the particular use of language. Although children do not want too much attention to be drawn to the meaning of statements, television is hardly ever only a succession of visual images, but a barrage of sounds, drawing attention to the pictures, emerging from the pictures and becoming part of the pattern of the pictures. In the language used on television there is an implicitly friendly private voice speaking personally and intimately to the single individuals of a vast anonymous public. The popularity of many television shows depends on the ability of the compère to create a friendly atmosphere. The language must be personal, and the tone chatty, in contrast to the formality of newsreaders and politicians.

Children find the personal tone of chat show compères, or the laconic 'one-liners' of their action heroes, easy to emulate, and to parody. The language of the advertisers, for example, in its off-hand assertiveness, has a distinct tone. Leech (1966) and others (Schrank, 1975; Hall and Whannel, 1964) have pointed out the syntactical tricks of this language such as the vocatives, or the displacement of the nominative, but the idiosyncrasies of the language used do not depend on the syntax as much as on the tone. The suggestion of command – 'try . . .', 'enjoy' – are in fact versions of cajoling; drawing not too much attention, but asserting something that can easily be ignored. The language of advertising depends on the speaking voice allied to a rather offhand friendliness and the knowing air that despite the assertions is not to be taken too seriously: 'Ensign by Van Heusen. As of now, still a strictly masculine satisfaction. You could, obviously, let her wear yours. But then, is nothing sacred?' As Leech points out, the advertising world assumes that even 'highly available copy means copy which it is also easy to read out and listen to' (p.62). Advertisers have a particular point to make, and wish to communicate a message, and still use the friendly tone. For it is through this style that the 'message' is most effective; like the throwaway remark or the assertions that do not draw too much attention to themselves. At the Rank Foundation's CCTV studios near Watford business men are taught that on television only the very simplest messages communicate. Whatever needs to be said on television must not only be easy to listen to but must be asserted, spoken with conviction. This is the tacit learning from television that is more pervasive than the learning of information. Some of the incidental information young children acquire (Siegel and Stevenson, 1966) depends on the tone in which it is conveyed. This is one of the reasons why children find it easier to remember advertisements. Labov et al. (1968) compared the narratives of eleven-year-olds about personal fights with their narratives about *The Man from U.N.C.L.E.* and found in the television narratives an absence of evaluation. Television programmes do not depend on evaluative responses; assertions come more readily. Instead of rational argument television presents successions of verbal clichés as well as repeated images.

Children tend to expect television to provide characters who assert their own opinions, and readily take on the tone of this dogmatism — 'Football is the top sport in England' (boy, 9), 'Liverpool is the only club' (girl, 11), 'Carlisle is rubbish' (boy, 13) — as readily as they recall the tone of advertisements: 'I like Toffos a lot because they have a lot of taste in them' (girl, 9) (cf. Chapter 14). Even in their writing children tend to exhibit the tendency to use the speaking voice: '. . . and put him in a plastic box. No! I tell a lie, it was a cardboard . . .', (girl, 12); 'Honestly, a holiday's never gone so slowly in my life, really' (boy, 11), 'O.K. lets lay it on the line and so the guy's a ——' (girl, 13) etc. Advertisers as well as politicians know the importance of keeping their statements on television clear, simple and short. Children more easily learn the tone than the message politicians and advertisers are attempting to convey. For the overall tone of television, as befits a medium perceived as functioning for entertainment, is one of personal friendliness. There is an obvious juxtaposition between the remarks of the compère directed to the audience and the 'overheard' conversations on *Coronation Street*, but they are more akin to each other than to the ratiocination of a news reader.

The differences between programmes can easily be pointed out, but these differences are rarely as significant to children, despite their preferences, as the similarities. To take one clear example, the tradition of Hollywood thrillers with their emphasis on action and the outdoors is quite different from the British tradition of thrillers based on the availability of stage actors and studios and on the development of character. Yet children do not see the distinction between programmes made in the studio and those made outside (Gomberg, 1971; Lyle and Hoffman, 1972). Noble (1975) also demonstrated that children cannot easily discriminate between 'live' programmes and those filmed on location. But the style of a programme does not depend upon whether the content is seen as 'real' or not; such discriminations seem to children beside the point. The level of children's response is such that they will see the differences in the pace and imagery of a programme more than the way in which it has been put together. 'Style' to them is not a matter of the means of production but the result; the content is not as important as the way in which it is presented (cf. Baggeley and Duck, 1976). Whether the scene is obviously fantastic, like a thriller, or obviously taking place in the studio, like *Blankety Blank*, the similarity in the audience's expectations is more important than the differences in venue.

The overall style of television cannot be judged in terms of differences in content. To know that television provides a mixture of sports, drama, variety shows, quizzes, information, news, children's programmes, advertising and personality programmes does not get us very far in understanding the effects on an audience, although the variety of content is itself part of the overall effect. Content analysis, based on the idea that an audience becomes what it sees, misses the point when it bases this assumption on the number of violent incidents, the number of weapons used or the surroundings in which they take place (Gerbner, 1972). Children's sense of the content of television works on a less cerebral level; the images that are depicted become more clearly associated with their expectations than the sense of characters as victims or perpetrators of violence (Gerbner, 1970), or the realisation that more than half the heroes depicted are aged between twenty and thirty-nine (BBC, 1972). The case that television makes a cumulative impact (Ellul, 1964) or creates new social moralities (Fiske and Hartley, 1978) must rest on a more subtle analysis of response than either the learning or stereotyped social relationships or the ability to model behaviour on perceived characteristics. The way in which children make sense of the style of television, its rituals and myths, includes what they bring to bear on it, their expectations and the sense with which they put it all together. Underlying individual responses to individual programmes, or images within programmes, is the general condition of viewing. The perfect mode for any stimulus is one which does not make demands by being either too loud or too soft, and neither too little or too much (Berlyne, 1960), so that the most attractive kind of stimulation comes from a perfect balance of elements (cf. Feilitzen, 1976). Television, through its combination of sound and picture, and its overall tone, achieves this balance, neither imposing too much on the audience, nor assuming too much involvement from them. The very fact that there is little room for free selection supports the desire for ease of effort (Furu, 1971). Thus children expect to be entertained through those elements of style most easily recognised; through the images most clearly presented and through the pervading tone.

PART III
WHAT CHILDREN LEARN
FROM TELEVISION

'And shall we just carelessly allow children to hear any casual tales which may be devised by casual persons, and to receive in their minds ideas for the most part the very opposite of those which we should wish them to have when they are grown up?'

Plato, *Republic*, Book 2

10 Recall and recognition

'I watched the most recent but I can't remember.' (girl, 12)

Children's knowledge of the programmes that appear on television is both detailed and comprehensive. They are aware not only of a wide range of titles but of the times of which these programmes are shown. This knowledge derives from their experience; they are aware of what is on because they have seen so much. Their knowledge of popular thriller programmes is particularly impressive because they are able to bring to mind the essential imagery even of a series shown some time previously. They can cite, with complete accuracy, an evening's viewing, and they know by a glance how to recognise which programme is on. This ability to remember what they have seen contrasts with their inability actually to recall details of what they have seen. The more that they watch, and the greater their capacity to recall the main images of a series, the less they can remember about the plot, or anything that happens within the programme. Of all the information that children will have seen over an evening's viewing, of all the hours of action, children remember very little. They know that they have *seen* the programmes but can say almost nothing about them.

The capacity for children to remember large quantities of information, such as new words and meanings, let alone facts, is well established (Miller, 1977). Whatever the limitations that come about over a much longer time span (cf. B.J. Underwood, 1957) the ability to process and store information is very strong (Tulving, 1972 etc.). This capacity for recall is actively encouraged in schools where intelligence is measured in many subjects by the ability to store and recall information. Even on television programmes, intelligence is almost exclusively associated with the capacity to remember. Programmes like *Mastermind* equate 'great brains' with knowledge of a subject; other programmes like *A Question of Sport* apply this capacity to remember to more specific events. The encouragement of memory is not limited to items of obvious importance or erudition; much time is spent on magazine programmes in inviting recall of pop music or sport. There are many quiz shows concerned with facts and statistics — the capacity to quote the number of goals scored against Darlington in a particular season, or the name of the drummer of a backing group. Placed in the right conditions children can bring to mind a whole array of small visual details in a film clip they have just seen. The capacity to recall part of a popular programme can be demonstrated by a boy aged seven describing *Wonder Woman*.

> In the last programme I saw there was a peace talk and there was a man who was in the bar and a boy came up to him and asked if he could take a picture of him and the man said 'yes' so the boy took a picture and then he gave the photograph to the man and he had been thinking about his wife and his thought was in the picture. The boy said his wife was wanting to talk to him so the boy took him to his house and they dropped a photo and Diana Price found it and the boy took some more people to his house and two men got Diana and put her on a conveyor belt and tied her up when she fell off the end. She turned into Wonder Woman and didn't get hurt. Then she dressed up and went to the boy's house and she talked to the boy and she told him she was an agent and she said that his uncle had lied to him. The boy didn't believe her. 'But it's true' said Diana. When the boy went down the people put their hands together and closed their eyes. Then Diana turned into Wonder Woman and tore the curtain down and the people saw that they had been working it on a machine.

Despite one or two ambiguities this account demonstrates a clear retention of a sequence of events. But this account is unique both in its length and its lucidity. The difference between children's capacity to remember and their actual performance is great (Birnbaum, 1969).

The boy remembering the plot of *Wonder Woman* revealed a grasp of the events rather than mere knowledge of the main images or actions of the protagonists. He had clearly concentrated on this programme (he was one of the few to have seen very little television) and applied his mind both at the time and afterwards. Other children did not reveal either the same application or the same powers of retention. In fact, the more programmes they had seen the less well they remembered them. The older children, with their greater abilities in remembering, were actually less good at recalling what they had seen than younger ones. The very knowledge of scheduling, or looking forward to programmes and knowing what to expect, seems to mitigate any awareness of what they have just seen. They know they have undergone the experience, but have not consciously stored any of the content. Thus a series of programmes seen over a year earlier were just as clearly in their minds as one seen the night before; for both had little hold. A 'series' tended to mean a certain kind of experience, a fulfilment of expectations, rather than a distinct story line.

What children clearly remembered about their favourite thriller programmes was not the plot but the familiar gestures and looks of the leading characters. Over 90 per cent of the children were regular viewers of *Starsky and Hutch*, and had looked at the most recent programme. And yet, whether they had watched it as recently as the night before or a week earlier, they found great difficulty in bringing any significant details to mind. Half of the children could hardly recall anything that made the programme distinctive. They liked Starsky and they liked Hutch; they would certainly watch again next week. They looked forward to the excitement, to the sight of the fast car, to the experience of the two heroes shooting at people, or throwing them against walls. But last night's programme seemed to have exactly the same hold on their minds as their expectations of what was going to happen on the programme a week later. Under prompting, or, better still, a recording of the particular programme, children would recognise that they had seen it. A quarter of the children, however, could not recall anything more than that. Another quarter could only indicate one episode that lingered in the mind — 'There was a hijack'; 'There was a car chase'; 'There was a shoot out'. A third of the children were able to pin-point the main incident — 'A man was trying to murder a group called Wolfpack'. The rest were able to recall two incidents or more. The children were not well equipped to answer questions. They had not expected to be asked and had therefore not treated viewing *Starsky and Hutch* as a comprehension test. Nor did they think that any particular programme was significant. They approached the programme as part of a particular experience in which the plot itself, apart from giving Starsky and Hutch the opportunity to play their parts, was not significant. Children's indifference combines with a certain unwillingness to remember; but there was no *refusal* to try to recall. They show a strong link between the attitudes with which they approach a programme and its subsequent salience. Children do not think it appropriate to remember the hours of information they see; they do not, therefore, approach the material in the same way as if they did think it significant.

When children do recall part of a series they do not always recall the most recent episode. It sometimes happens that one particular incident has left a deeper impression and become symbolic of the rest. Thus a moment that frightens them, or seems to them more closely associated with some experience they have had, will subsume the symbolic gestures of subsequent programmes. As Posner (1969) demonstrated, visual memory is not necessarily sequential, so that the images within a programme can be subsumed within the image of the whole programme. Children's recall of one episode is almost like a reference point, a proof that they have seen it. But the high recognition value of heroes like Starsky and Hutch works against more than a rudimentary recall of the plot. Those who try to cite a significant incident find difficulty in bringing to mind something that is unique to that programme; what springs to their minds is the knowledge of what Starsky and Hutch tend to do with a car. Thus the overall image of a series dominates to such an extent that one programme tends to merge with another, and the most recent one is merely another link. Sometimes children prefer to cite a programme they have seen some time earlier; for what they *do* retain, which is very little, remains once it has been processed in their minds. Thus children's recall of *Kojak*, which had not been screened for over a year, was not that much worse than that for *Starsky and Hutch*, which was on every week. Younger children aged five to seven in particular, having seen an episode, could bring some clear details to mind: 'He jumped into a window and saw a man with a gun and at the end he was in a garage and suddenly he saw one of his men dead and he caught the killer' (boy, 6); 'One of his men were in the car park; so was the thief. He was in a car and Kojak's men was after him and he got shot' (girl, 7). Older children did not show the same capacity to remember. Instead they showed knowledge of the *tone* of the programme, the general outline, and, most of all, the recognisable gestures and looks of the eponymous hero. Their responses showed an awareness of what the programmes tended to show rather than what appeared on a particular occasion. Thus the typical overcomes the distinctive: 'A lady had landed and came to meet Kojak and he said "I love you baby" ' (boy, 7).

The dominance of the typical gesture over any idiosyncrasies of plot is illustrated consistently in all the popular thriller series that children enjoy. The recurring situation, or the particular starting point, is easy to place, but the recent episode is not. Apart from the boy of seven who demonstrated the capacity to recall *Wonder Woman*, the children found themselves either citing the starting point or unable to recall more than the general outline: other boys of seven would recall; 'Wonder Woman saw a boy called Matthew and he took a picture of her and they took her into a house'; 'There was a boy called Matthew and he took a picture of the man and of the persons that died and the person on the picture would be the person that died'. Older children tended to be more laconic: 'A boy would take photographs of people who were dead and bribed people by the power he had' (boy, 12); 'They were photographing and hypnotising people' (girl, 11). They knew enough to be able to tabulate which episode they had seen, but were unable to expand this into a clear, lucid and detailed outline. Some could not recall the most recent episode at all, but could give a general recollection of an earlier one that had made some greater impression, like the detail that the boy was called Matthew. Children were looking for recognisable items to recall but even their willingness did not give them more than a hazy impression of anything but the central point of recognition.

Charlie's Angels is another programme with clear recognition appeal for it has the essential idea of three girls with different coloured hair working for someone they have never seen, creating a continuous sub-plot of speculation about who their employer could be. Younger children were more capable of recalling a fairly clear outline of what had taken place: 'A girl's father had been killed and the little girl wanted to help but Charlie's Angels would not let her. One of Charlie's Angels took the girl to her beach house and got kidnapped' (girl, 7). But the majority tended to cite the programme in the following terms: 'People had been hijacked in a bus and Charlie's Angels pretended to be old women'. They could not expand on this outline, although they could bring distinct images to mind: 'Someone shot at them but they missed' or 'Someone got run over'. The programme was better known than any individual episodes. This distinction between the knowledge of a series as a whole and the recollection of a particular programme is maintained in children's recall of *Bionic Woman*. They know the heroine and what she does, but when it comes to reciting what actually happened they have great difficulty. The more clear the awareness of the series as a whole the less is the attention to a distinct episode. Apart from indications of one episode − 'She tried to save a girl in a car getting demolished' − children would bring to mind illustrations of bionic powers: 'Fell off a cliff without getting hurt', 'Jumped from a helicopter', 'Ran fast after a man'.

The very popularity of these series, and the regularity with which they are watched, seems to diminish children's capacity to recall them. It is therefore interesting to compare these levels of remembering with a less popular series, *Petrocelli*, in which the hero did not have the same high recognition value. Beyond knowing that the hero is an American lawyer of foreign extraction, children cannot bring to mind any gesture, look or unusual power that is associated with him. When children were asked to say what happened in the last episode they did not show any greater capacity for recall, but were less inclined to allow the image of the programme to prevent them from trying to cite the raison d'etre of the plot. Referring to the same episode typical answers were:

'A boy was arrested for murder.' (girl, 11)
'A man was accused of stealing drugs.' (boy, 10)
'A boy killed a man but Petrocelli got him off.' (boy, 11)
'A young boy was accused of killing a man and taking drugs.' (girl, 10)
'Boy was accused and caught killing a man.' (boy, 12)
'Petrocelli proved that the mental boy was not the murderer; the boy called Petrocelli Mr Tony.' (girl, 11)

They all gave indications of how they would recognise the same programme again; but they also knew how they would recognise the style of Petrocelli, as opposed to more familiar heroes. The earliest type of recall is that which is based on recognition (Shepherd, 1967). It is not surprising that the main images of programmes are most readily recalled, but it is noteworthy that this in itself seems to create difficulties for children in recalling more than the familiar. To some extent children actually shut out material that seems to them irrelevant. As Allyn and Festinger (1961) demonstrated, there is a capacity to look for and remember only what people choose to see. In the case of dramatic thrillers actions have higher salience than the plot. Thus when the heroes follow their familiar routine and chase the villains, children recognise the expected and partake in the easiest form of learning (Gagné, 1965). The pleasure of a thriller programme lies in the ease with which it can be watched, in the fulfilment of the expected. It is from these patterns of recognition that children's recall is derived, rather than from any deliberate attempt to learn. They remember those things they want to (Fitzgerald and Ausubel, 1963) and approach the programmes with certain expectations in mind.

It could be argued that popular thriller series are a distinct phenomenon: that their very reliance on repetition results in low levels of recall. Children were therefore asked to recollect one programme they had seen the night before. Their responses made it clear that programmes which were *not* part of a series were, in general, more fully recalled, but it was also clear that their powers of recall were never very high. The more programmes they had seen the less capable they were of recalling one in any detail. Most were able to give at least one detail; enough to indicate that they *had* watched a particular programme. But even the fullest descriptions of a programme seen the evening before were fairly rudimentary, reading like a parody of the summary given before the programme so that viewers can 'slot in' to the next episode easily:

Crossroads

'Gill decided to take in husbandless women with young children. The 'Three Chimes' shall become their home and when she does Adam shall leave. Glenda has told everyone to mind their own business.' (girl, 12)

'Gill has decided to make 'Three Chimneys' a home for expectant mothers. When she does Adam will leave. Chris Humber has accepted a job. Glenda has told everybody to mind their own business. So has Mr McFee. Rosemary has decided to leave.' (girl, 12)

Charlie's Angels

'A man called Harry murdered people who he imagined as his father. Harry was a disc jockey at a disco and Charlie's Angels went for jobs there. The manager had a wife who was always nagging on and he thought she had sent Charlie's Angels.' (girl, 12)

Fawlty Towers

'This American man came with an English wife and was asking for a waldorf salad. The cook had gone out and Basil Fawlty had to pretend that the cook was in. Near the end he gave up and went outside. It was raining so he came back and asked for a room.' (boy, 11)

Sometimes children give the impression of emulating the style of those who would promote the programmes, as if they had caught the tone. They could nearly always indicate the characteristics of the programme. Those which were not part of a series elicited recall that also centred on details that make the programme unique:

Tomorrow's World

'It was about a man who had a bad heart. He took seven types of drugs a day. He stopped and ate different food and he's better now. And about a mirror that can see all of yourself from three foot away.' (boy, 10)

Blue Peter

They planted some cherry trees and shrubs. They showed a clip of film about Vivaldi. They talked about Roland Amundsen and they also went up to Simon's dad's farm to see how the lambing was getting on.' (girl, 11)

The capacity for children to recall essential details was more consistent for those programmes that were not part of a serial. But nevertheless most children would only give the essential details, the particular point that made the programme remembered:

Blue Peter
'It showed all sorts of dogs. It showed little dogs and big dogs. I like the little dogs best and Goldey entered it.' (girl,8)
'They showed you the recipes so that you could make them at home.' (boy, 7)

In many cases they could give an indication of the main point that had struck them as significant.

'The dogs walked to heel and lay down and sat.' (boy, 7, of *Blue Peter*)
'There was a murder by one girl.' (boy, 8, of *The Saint*)
'The man was ill. The lady went shopping at the shop.' (girl, 7, of *Coronation Street*)
'Terry was mad because his ball would not bounce.' (girl, 8, of *Feet First*)
'Went to the pub. Danced. Got a new dress.' (girl, 10, of *Coronation Street*)
'Miss Jones dressed up as Rigby's wife.' (girl, 11, of *Rising Damp*)
'Well, he dropped his cups and saucers.' (girl, 12, of *Sharp Intake of Breath*)
'A lady won a telly.' (boy, 10, of *Blankety Blank*)
'The team lost three-one.' (boy, 11, of *Feet First*)
'Emlyn Hughes team got beat.' (boy, 12, of *A Question of Sport*)

Children find it far easier to recall programmes if they have seen a smaller number of them. The amount they could remember was at an inverse proportion to the amount they had watched. Those children who could give a fair account had watched an average of about three programmes. Those children who could give only a rudimentary detail had watched an average of nearly six programmes. The heaviest viewers seem to pay less precise attention and do not burden themselves with attempts to recall. Children's capacity to pay close attention for the sake of learning information is not automatically applied to television when viewed in the home, especially as television is seen as a medium for entertainment rather than instruction. Their retention of the material is made the more difficult because of the juxtaposition between the ostensibly significant and the inessential. This is why children suggest that the application which goes into remembering is inappropriate to television. Their level of attention is rarely on the same level as that which is tested in laboratory conditions with explicit demands on their capacity to process content (Leifer et al. 1970; Halloran, 1969;

Gomberg, 1961). Children's attitudes to television can even include a palpable dislike of recall. But if there are any distinctly different levels of response there are also distinct levels of memory. Those items which are consciously learned are quite different from those items, less easy to categorise, which become subconsciously part of an audience's pattern of associations.

That there are different kinds of memory, as well as different kinds of response, has always been implicit in research on memory since William James (1890), but these distinctions have often been ignored. By far the most substantial bulk of work has been concerned with the prepared recall of items specially set up for testing and categorising in an attempt to assess information storage (e.g. Broadbent, 1966; Baddeley, 1970; Tulving, 1972; Kiss, 1969; Deese, 1969; Collins and Quillian, 1969, 1970 etc.). Even when the nomenclature has changed, or the theoretical models are different, the more easily testable part of memory is that of receiving, categorising and storing information semantically processed. Thus the bulk of research has concentrated on verbal recall of set items in experimental conditions. It is for this reason that the pioneering work of Bartlett (1932) is still an important corrective. The conditions he deals with are far more analoguous to the way in which children actually watch television. They do not apply their minds in such a way that all variables in the task of information processing can be isolated or limited. The problem with television is that its complexity applies not only to the content but to the attitudes and circumstances of the audience watching it. It can no more be assumed that the words of a pop-song or advertising jingle are carefully heeded than that they are written down and deliberately learned; yet this material, ostensibly ignored, can be undeliberately remembered.

The ability of the mind consciously to process only a certain number of items was first explored by Miller (1956) in his analysis of the span of absolute judgement: 'There seems to be some limitation built into us either by learning or by the design of our nervous systems, a limit that keeps our channel capacities in this general range' (p.86). The capacity to concentrate on particular events or items, like the capacity to learn what to ignore, to focus only on the relevant, is one which children learn as they get older. At first, and with television, children do not know which items are the ones supposed to be significant in the way that an experiment by Newell and Simon (1972) on a unique solution to a complicated cryptogram would suggest. When Yntema and Muesner (1960) discussed Miller's idea of a 'chunk', the capacity to take only so many items of information at one time, they were also careful to single out specific tasks, for they found that the capacity to recall was far greater if there were fewer variables. If the mind can only process a certain amount of information at a time, it continually needs to ignore much of the material being offered by television. For this reason children seem to look for recognisable clues, even if these clues are not an obvious part of the original conception of plot. In this way von Wright (1968) found that his subjects were, even in an experiment, unable to carry out a task until they had recognised a clue that was essential to them, but irrelevant to the experimenter. Posner (1969) pointed out that visual memory cannot be said to be organised in a sequential way because of the differences associated with recognition. Some of the images on television are like ones that invoke memories in a more complex manner; for images remain in the mind even when the mind has processed what it *wishes* to retain (Underwood, 1976). While the idea of a 'chunk' as a 'span of attention' refers usually only to the conscious manipulation of recall, subjects 'see' much more than they can report (Sperling, 1960). There are many items which are not consciously retained, but it does not follow that they are not retained at all (Sperling, 1963). 'Recognition' is a sign of the storage of information which has not been processed in the normal way. Cue items, recognised rather than recalled, give a different structure to memory than those items which are presented especially to be recalled.

Children not only respond to semantic stimuli but select information on the basis of physical ones (Darwin, Turvey and Crowder, 1972). Bartlett (1932) drew attention to this when he demonstrated the differences of response between the familiar and the unfamiliar; the material eliciting conscious response was not necessarily better remembered (p.19). Ausubel (1968) pointed out that familiar material is neither completely ignored nor forgotten, but accumulates in the memory. As Craik and Lockhart (1972) demonstrate, memory does not depend only on 'chunks' of semantic clues but on a combination of visual as well as verbal material. Broadbent (1958) argued that Miller and others were wrong in presuming that seven items could be recalled at one time; he suggests that only three could be stored, let alone recalled, at one time. But whatever the limitations in amount, we see that children retain, on a more subconscious level, only a small number of basic facts or images about programmes. While they can give sequential accounts of what they have seen, they find it more natural to recount one or two basic points, in terms of the programmes' central images. Miller and Broadbent's work applies to items of information presented over a short period of time rather than a complex succession of visual and auditory experiences. In the latter case it seems that the limitations of the amount that can be recalled are still there, but applied in a different way, as if the central items had been accumulated over a long time. Just as the 'chunk' can be repeated and changed, so that the capacity remains but the items change, so children learn to concentrate on those details that make a programme recognisable, the 'one in which' as if recognition rather than recall were being explicitly brought into play.

The most lucid way to describe the existence of different levels and types of memory, together with their inter-relatedness, is in terms of recognition and recall. For recognition takes place all the time, is unaffected by other states of recall or other tasks (Goodwin et al. 1969) and can, through repetition, become almost another kind of remembering in itself. Children retain an awareness of tunes and pictures, of images and associations, in which the love of the familiar is very important. Television offers a balance between new material and repeated images. Recall is voluntary; recognition is not. Children can actually remember more of the surrounding details to which they do not pay close attention. Whereas recall shows a normal curve of forgetting, recognition shows great powers of retention (Shepherd, 1967). Bartlett even goes as far as to say that the desire to recall is related to actual forgetting. Children do not study the images that they see on television, but, as in the case of faces, they quickly become familiar with them (Goldstein and Chance, 1971). Naturally the connection between recall and recognition is close. Kintsh (1970) talks of a double process by which recall involves both search and decision, whilst recognition entails only the latter. Tulving (1976) defines recall as a more complex version of recognition. Anderson and Bower (1973) relate recognition to associative memory. Thus recognition should not be taken as a purely passive response; even sensory perception is active and discriminating. Recognition includes a parody of the original, a view which responds to certain familiar clues. Unlike the semantic logic required in complete recall, recognition elicits more vague responses that include many of those clues, like tone and context, that recall in the narrower sense leaves out.

Recognition naturally depends upon familiar material. Sometimes the familiarity of recognition is so strong that it disturbs the ability to recall anything (Tulving and Pearstone, 1966). Recognition is like subconscious memory; children recall little of what they see and hear on television but they recognise a great deal. The ritual of television programmes depends upon a balance between repetition and variation, between the familiar and the unexpected. In structure and tone, as well as the central imagery, a popular series remains very much the same. Children look forward to the familiar. This is why the formula of programmes, and the actions of the hero, are so much better remembered than the plot. Constant repetition is a way of learning through recognition (Zielske, 1959; Krugman, 1955). Familiarity breeds remembering.

11 Educational television

'You learn a lot from television. My favourite programmes are *Starsky and Hutch, Six Million Dollar Man, Bionic Woman...* I like *Charlie's Angels* as well.' (girl, 9)

The power of television to communicate information has nearly always been taken for granted. Its pervasive presence, its ability to combine the moving image with sound, the lavish resources available for the preparation of material and the curiosity with which it has been approached have long made television a symbol of educational opportunity. McLuhan's vision of the 'global village' was one manifestation of the belief in television as a powerful influence on people too far flung ever to gather in schools to hear their teachers. Many countries all over the world have experimented with different types of educational service (Klees, 1973) using television as the primary mass source for communication. The founding of the Open University as well as the development of Schools broadcasting have seen this belief in television clearly manifested. Educational technology is even becoming a specialist subject in its own right. This belief in the possibility inherent in this form of communication has nearly always provided a counter weight to the fears expressed about the power of television to do harm.

In contrast to such belief in the possibilities of television as education, the actual result of the investment has been clearly disappointing. One reason is that it has been assumed that television can be a substitute teacher; that it is better to provide a magnificent lecture on the television screen than to provide any number of less erudite or less interesting presences in the classroom. Another reason is that television has been assumed to be an automatic conveyor of information to such an extent that the audience is supposed to view it as a teacher. This view depends on a model of the classroom in which children pay careful attention, and, through the application of their minds, remember all that they hear. Even if this were true of the classroom the contrast with the conditions of viewing in the home is very clear. Nevertheless, the image of television as teacher still remains; analyses of children's programmes concern the extent to which television can successfully take the place of a teacher in conveying a wide variety of facts (H. Lesser, 1977). Television has been viewed as a means of ensuring that children 'know more', through children's programmes, educational programmes, documentaries or the Open University, and as a substitute for other ways of learning, replacing books, comics and the radio as well as schools. But television has an ambiguous role in education. As teachers have seen television as a substitute teacher so they have tended to expect it to do all the work by itself, from presenting facts in an interesting manner to stimulating discussion. In this they have obviously been disappointed. . . . More disappointing still is the fact that even such carefully presented information does not seem to make the expected impact. Even those who accept the model of television as a conveyor of facts to an audience panting with eager anticipation learn that there is something about the medium which does not lend itself to such treatment. This is something that McLuhan intuitively felt when he realised that the very universality of its provision somehow dimmed the pedagogic value of television.

Educational television has been used sometimes as a replacement of the teacher and sometimes as an extension of the teacher. Theories underlying the creation of programmes for children have depended largely on Piaget's view of children's cognitive development (Lesser, 1977; Noble, 1975), whether the television programmes are used as aid to teacher's presence or whether they have been delivered as an entity separate from the classroom environment. The common starting point remains the same:

> The implied (but rarely stated) psychological basis for teaching by television is the hypothesis that learning occurs in response to an appropriate stimulus or stimulating situation and that a highly skilled and well-informed teacher may provide a more effective stimulus by way of 21 inch screen than is provided by a mediocre teacher who is physically present in the classroom. (Woodring, 1964, p.290)

It is significant, however, that television has been found invariably more effective as a means of education when it has been used as an addition to a teacher rather than a replacement. For effective learning the teacher needs to draw attention to, and reinforce, the content conveyed on the screen (Schramm, 1977). Hoban (1960) found that a teacher's participation in a programme designed to stand by itself was essential to its success. He also found that devices such as arrows, as if these were a justifying presence pointing out significant details (q.v. Chapter 8), made a crucial difference to the amount which children were subsequently able to recall. This necessary outside presence was needed whether embedded in the programmes or not (Vernon, 1962). Educational television programmes without such support have always been found to be less effective (Schramm, 1960).

The power of television to convey information in a more general way has been found to be very limited without such external aids. One early example of the discovery of this fact is the experiment carried out by Star and Hughes (1950) in the first flush of enthusiasm about the ability of television to teach its audience useful and significant facts. All the media in Cincinnati were flooded with information about the United Nations; the newspapers conveyed statistics, the radio presented copious descriptions and all the television schedules were dominated by exciting details and sermons about the significance of the United Nations Organisation. After an extensive period, during which time the vast bulk of the population must have come across a wealth of information, Star and Hughes and their colleagues discovered that the vast majority remained ignorant about the United Nations Organisation; the vast majority were in fact ignorant about its very existence, despite all they must have seen, heard and read. The only people who learned anything about the United Nations were those already interested and knowledgeable; those already committed to learning. But even when new facts are learned at a particular time, they can be as quickly forgotten as the context in which they were presented. When people in the United States were asked about their reaction to the assassination of President Kennedy in 1963 they were asked to name the three other American presidents who had also been assassinated (Wade and Schramm, 1969). As a result of the publicity at the time a certain number were able to cite the names, but after a short time additional items of information such as this were completely forgotten. The authors also pointed out that the audience tended to remember general events rather than specific facts.

As audience retains a general 'feel' of the information presented on television rather than anything more specific. Ever since the experiments on the film *The Battle of Britain* (Hovland, Lumsdaine and Sheffield, 1949, 1953), many have corroborated the findings that information is less clearly remembered than emotional attitudes. When Wade and Schramm (1969) tested the results of the learning of science through educational television they found that the '. . . chief information that rubbed off was concerned with science politics rather than science itself, and with a general picture of the environment rather than a deep understanding of it' (p.208). This discovery is confirmed by the Open University which has found that its most successful programmes are general ones on foundation courses; what they call 'change points' rather than specific items. But then very few Open University students actually watch any of the programmes. Even if the television is consciously attended to, there is far less subsequent recall than most teachers would expect. Belson (1967) found that even when people listened assiduously they were able to recall less than one-third of the information presented. 'Even major or central points were no better understood than were minor points and small details' (p.145). On the other hand when Belson tested audience reactions to a programme about learning to speak French he found that:

> 'The results indicated that the programme had produced a slight increase in viewers' knowledge of the words and phrases, and of the facts presented, but that this was accompanied by an increase in viewers' apprehensions about language difficulties, and in general about visiting France.
>
> (p.193)

The distinction between emotional responses and recall of information is again apparent, even in an educational programme as popular as French, popular, as Schramm (1960) points out, because it is viewed with a distinct sense of purpose and approached for a measurable result by an audience that knows exactly what it *wants* to learn. The audience for educational television is very small: '. . . those persons who are most devoted to the idea of becoming educated or informed will watch television only if they can see exactly what they want' (Schramm, 1960, p.67).

One of the best examples of high expectations and subsequent disappointment is the case of *Sesame Street*. The programme was imbued with all the techniques associated with television entertainment; it was seen as a combination of slick presentation and noble educational purpose. It was accepted that because it was competing against the attractiveness of other programmes, it needed to be produced in a rather different and more imaginative way in order to be effective. When G. Lesser (1972) discussed the principles on which the programme was based he stressed the importance of gaining the child's full attention. He concluded that the three principles underlying *Sesame Street* were that learning would occur through children's desire to learn, through direct teaching and through modelling. H. Lesser (1977) also pointed out the additional requirement of an adult's participation to make such attentions effective. It became clear to all those who were researching the programme that despite its publicity and despite the pleasure that parents were deriving from it, and despite the considerable panache of the producers, it was not making much impact on the children. The style of presentation was of greater interest to many than the children's responses (Halloran, 1978) as if complex visual sequences would automatically create learning (cf. the criticisms of H. Lesser, 1977). But not only did attention to *Sesame Street* not increase with age (Salomon et al. 1972) but there was little improvement in recall. *Sesame Street* was designed to bridge the gap between educational and popular television and for that reason was a subject of great curiosity. But despite the energy that went into its making, it became apparent that the gap between its design and effectiveness as an educational programme was wide (H. Lesser, 1977). Even those who had at first been thought to have benefited were found to have been specially selected and imbued with the 'Hawthorne' effect of fulfilling the researchers' expectations (Cook et al. 1975). Otherwise its success depended entirely upon the role of mothers; on their additional enthusiasm.

The complexity of the process of learning is apparent even when applied to something comparatively easy to analyse in laboratory conditions as language (Lock, 1978). Even in terms of the classroom, observable phenomena such as teachers' styles, ideals and organisation (Bennet, 1976; Sharp and Green, 1975; Galton et al. 1982 etc.) do not reveal the complex responses of individual children and the extent to which their idiosyncratic differences and expectations influence the way they approach the information offered them. It is clear that the assumption that learning is a simple process and that television is merely another means of helping this process is one which has not been borne out even in those experiments based on testing distinct items for recall. The presence of a justifying authority and the careful control of conditions can make a difference to learning, but even there the process of learning is clearly not always at one level. The conditions in which children for the most part watch television are so different from those of the classroom it is as if we were discussing two different media. But even under the most rigid of pedagogic treatments such as Programmed Instruction (Cronbach and Snow, 1977) it is difficult to isolate the particular elements that make one thing understood and remembered and another forgotten. Heidt (1978) also reminds us of the importance of understanding the variables of individual personality as well as of the medium. In most classroom applications of television, however, such complexity was not taken into account; hence the subsequent disappointments.

Even in the conditions of the classroom television is not closely attended. Those items which are ostensibly learned, whether French or science, seem to be more a matter of attitude or general politics than detail. It is as if what James (1890) called the primary memory were not being applied. James considered information in primary memory to be that matter which is in current consciousness. Information within 'secondary memory' was seen as that which had been absent from consciousness at some time. The secondary memory, even if less 'conscious', was more permanent. James therefore understood the limitation of studying only conscious responses: 'Another variety of the psychologists' fallacy is the assumption that the mental state studied must be conscious of itself as a psychologist is conscious of it' (p.197). He invoked, as Waugh and Norman (1967) did later, this crucial distinction between capacity and performance. That children *can* learn, even to the extent of being manipulated by the justifying authority to imitate the peculiar gestures of a model, is clear. But such capacity is more often applied to other educational experiences, perceived as such, than to television (Kausler, 1974).

The difficulties in promoting clear cases of learning through television arise because of the distinctions between recall and recognition and because of the different levels of memory. Whether the terms used to describe the difference between primary and secondary memory are those used by Waugh and Norman (1965) or Atkinson and Shiffrin (1968 and 1971), or whether the processes of forgetting are seen as decay or displacement in short-term memory, or interference in long-term memory (Craik, 1970 etc.), it is clear that what children are remembering from television are not those points to which they are necessarily paying conscious attention. The assumption that nothing is permanently remembered unless carefully rehearsed might apply to the classroom; but it is rarely applied to television where the most rehearsed items are those which are incidental or secondary. As Bruner (1974) points out there is, even within the consciousness of the material being invoked, a defence against remembering. This 'defence' can be directed to the conscious, psychological presence, as it can be to the explanations given on a documentary, to the semantics. This leaves intact what Tulving (1972) defines as 'episodic' memory, 'about temporally dated episodes or events, and temporal-spatial relations about these events . . .' (pp.385–6). Television, even in its earnest educational form, is complex in its relationship to memory. It has direct relationship to what Bruner (1969) calls 'memory without record'. Thus Bartlett's (1932) still useful distinction between reactions '*by means of organised psychological material*' and '*reactions to*' (p.196) organised material is also relevant. The danger of too narrow versions of information theory is that they put too much emphasis on verbal responses, as if the 'content' or input on programmes could be defined, and were learned in verbal terms. It is possible, as with jingles, or the words of pop-music, to bypass the semantic store when remembering even verbal items (cf. Craik and Lockhart, 1972, p.674). Thus the assumption that educational television is, like a teacher, a means of conveying semantically coded and testable material subsequently organised into a permanent memory store is not borne out by the evidence of those programmes watched in classroom conditions, let alone those programmes seen at home.

Children are not generally very fond of educational television programmes. They might prefer to watch television at school than undergo a more traditional lesson, but programmes that set out to teach them things are not their favourites. Their dislike of politicians is one symptom of their dislike of anything that seems to have designs on them. Nevertheless, just as the argument that television causes harm through children imitating what they see continues, so does the similar argument that if the content of television were changed, so would the subsequent behaviour. This argument is seen in the opinions expressed by parents about their children (Woodrick et al. 1977) and in those experiments to test whether children can be made more willing to help through seeing examples of good moral behaviour (Stein and Friedrich, 1972; Sprafkin, Liebert and Paulos, 1975; Shirley, 1974; Friedrich and Stein, 1975). But even in this distinct use of educational television, in conditions in which children knew they were supposed to be learning something, it was clear that the influence of the adult, or a secondary source of justification to the actions seen on the screen, was important. Thus the labelling of actions by an adult increased children's knowledge of what was taking place (Coates and Hartup, 1969). Children *could* learn from models if they were previously reinforced to imitate (Gruser and Brinker, 1972). But otherwise even 'pro-social' television had little influence on subsequent behaviour. But then educational television draws attention to a distinct level of information processing. Normal viewing conditions are somewhat different.

12 Television as a conveyor of information

'I like to be able to answer the questions better than the personalities.' (boy, 8)

In 1959 Wilbur Schramm conducted a large scale survey that came to the conclusion that there were no instances of real success in educational television. In 1980, after a series of experiments on programmes including *Sesame Street*, Palmer and Dorr pointed out that Scramm's conclusion could be repeated in every detail apart from a change of programme titles. The lack of effectiveness in educational television, however, does not mean that television does not convey any information at all. Many teachers are frightened by what they see as the capacity of television not only to convey unnecessary facts but misguided opinions (Murdoch and Phelps, 1973). Postman (1979) argues that commercial television is itself the primary curriculum as far as young children are concerned, and that formal schooling is comparatively a secondary matter. Some children do feel that watching different kinds of television programmes for pleasure is justified by the fact that they are gaining something from it educationally, just as adults sometimes feel that watching television is given a kind of earnestness by attending to the news. This idea that 'you can learn from watching television' is not one that is sustained by children for very long, because they do not continue to approach television even with that excuse. As Piepe et al. (1975) pointed out, the 'educational' appeal of programmes such as quiz programmes was greatest for those with limited education.

Children do not associate television with learning as such, despite their ability to parody their parents with educational justifications. They more readily associate television with play when, although they might learn something, they do not think that it is incubent on them to do so, for the distinction between work and play is strong. Even when children look for information television 'tended to make no impact where the child could turn for information to his immediate environment, parents and friends' (Himmelweit et al. 1958, p.18). While children have the *capacity* to use television as a source of information and, by dint of the teacher's cajoling, can learn what they are meant to learn, they do not actually think of television as a container or purveyor of facts. The ways in which recordable information is normally conveyed, as a definition or a clear statement, is itself rather different from the overall atmosphere of television, not only as a source of pleasure but one which makes few purely cerebral demands. The qualities of television, in terms of techniques as well as content, are those of perceptual ease. The level of attention given to television is not the same as those given to books; nor are the expectations.

All the attempts to make educational programmes more like programmes designed for entertainment might have made a difference to the amounts that children were prepared to watch, even if they made little difference to their ability to learn. Zillman (1980), for example, found that the use of humour in educational programmes greatly increased exposure. Children are quite agreeable to watching anything which entertains them. But their expectations are such that they view programmes with a suspension of belief which is undisturbed until they (occasionally) look back and apply a different standard of analysis. Although it is possible to analyse the content of *The Professionals* in such a way that it appears depressingly brutal and cynical, this is rarely done, since children do not bring this level of moral analysis to bear. They do not suggest that some of the characters in *Coronation Street* are less than salubrious, nor do they look at a Western questioning matters of authenticity. Subsequently children can apply the level of analysis that breaks through the suspension of belief, just as they can apply their minds if they intend to. To take one example, a girl of nine describing *Dr Who* said about the previous episode:

> 'K.9, Dr Who's dog, nearly got melted in a furnace. But Dr Who saved him by going through a secret door into the furnace and getting him out. I am not sure why Dr Who did not burn to death.'

This last point is the kind of question that if commonly applied would bring to an end pleasure in a majority of programmes from *Dallas* to

Grange Hill. All programmes beg questions about the application of real judgements to fantasy events; even those that did not would lend themselves to a satirical view. First the viewer would ask why Dr Who never got killed, then how he goes through time, and would end up questioning the idea of 'finding the keys of time'. Subsequently the viewer would need to ask why he was watching the programme. Thus the application of judgement leads not to modelling but disbelief. Few children ever choose to follow this line of questioning, or, if they do, settle for the thought that the reason for watching is that it does not require such cerebral analysis. Children have a natural interest in those programmes that are easy to watch because of their fast pace and because of the immediacy of the feedback (Wakschlag et al. 1981). Lorch, Anderson and Levin (1979) found that there was no immediate correlation between visual attention and recall, despite the fact that educational programmes are designed around this assumption. Calvert et al. (1979) discovered that when the central point of the programme was presented mainly through verbal dialogue children recalled it less well than when it was presented with a lot of special effects, music and action. It is as if children are geared to picking up those essential clues they need, like the main recognisable features of their favourite programmes, through peripheral detail. Nugent et al. (1980) found that the presentation of material at a high level of abstraction, with attention drawn to its significance beforehand, could increase the audience's comprehension but that it also put them off, having negative affective consequences, and ultimately less success. Thus the previous warning that they were to learn certain things, usually a pre-requisite for close attention, had negative as well as positive effects. Children can usually react against material to which their attention has been drawn, as if Underwood's (1957) rules on pro-active interference had been deliberately invoked.

In moments of fear, or heavy demand, children react *against* a programme. The salient features of programmes for children are those that do not call attention to themselves but are part of the recognisable tone. The style of entertainment, fast tempo and background music prevented children taking educational programmes in an educational way, and significantly impaired their acquisition of central information (Wakschlag, 1982), even though they were better attuned to the programmes.

The type of information which is generally used in test conditions, as in exams, contrasts with that which children easily take in from television. The conflicts in the findings are explained by this. As Salomon (1979) points out, most research on children's responses to the media has focused on children's ability to comprehend plots, with the aim of seeing whether a particular type of information is stored and recalled. As we now see, the style of children's perception of information is quite a different matter; the ability to learn by recognition makes a profound difference to what they take in. All the attempts to show that children learn a consistent attitude of mind towards the world, or a clearly stereotyped view of race, rank or religion, have come to nothing because they have been carried out at an inappropriate level. Children's traditional ability of comprehension and recall are generally left untouched by television. They do not analyse the structure of a television programme in the way suggested by Collins (1979) as if they were reading a book. This is revealed even in those experiments that treat television like a book. Collins found that young children had great difficulty in comprehension analysed in his terms, and that older children were worse at recalling extra material, since they had learned to concentrate for him on the salient features as a means of shutting out all extra material. It is far easier to analyse and recall an obviously distinguishing feature than a subtle amalgamation of image and event. Thus a programme about a specific occurrence like Cruft's Dog Show might not have much appeal but be easier to recall 'because it is a change from the usual TV programmes' (girl, 12). But after a time the parts of television which go on conveying information of the kind that children are sure to retain are those which are expected and recognised; those markers that denote a particular pattern of entertainment.

Gagné (1965) has pointed out that recognition is the easiest form of learning. Children grasp those points which are the more repeated, and learn the familiar rather than new information. The kind of information they acquire is of a particular type; it consists of those points of recognition which are automatically recalled when the same context is presented a second time (Goodwin et al. 1969). Thus features of style and features of gestures, characteristics of humour or facial expression or the pattern of the opening sequence or the familiar tune all become part of the information that television conveys, a level of information which is not given to semantic analysis and is not complete enough to provide models upon which to base subsequent actions. Children do not analyse a particular picture of the world, apply it to their own lives and then become disappointed because they do not possess those riches that are presented to them in glossy fantasies of luxurious wickedness such as *Dallas* or *Dynasty*. Nor do they associate themselves with the equally fantastic (if more humble) quarrels of *Crossroads*. Much of the material which children see is 'non-essential' if essential material means significant meanings that can be recalled clearly. Hale et al. (1968) found children more able to disregard non-essential features as they grew older. Children choose what kind of information to take in, and what to regard as essential; to many children the inessential means anything that is not entertaining.

The ability to concentrate on significant clues or a particular source of information is a necessary basis for perception. Both ears and eyes focus on certain elements out of range of auditory and visual clues. Thus when people are distracted by extraneous sounds they can adjust to the interruption by listening to the main message even more carefully (Festinger and Maccoby, 1964). Indeed the presence of outside distractions can even lead to a marginal improvement in the recall of a message upon which people are concentrating (Hockey and Hamilton, 1970). But the most interesting fact is that while distractions can be overcome for the sake of concentrating on a chosen source, distractions have the least effect in the first place on 'irrelevant' information, as items which would not require close attention to start with. Children tested by Maccoby and Hagen (1965) on their ability to undertake two tasks at the same time were able to remember those details irrelevant to the main task far better than the 'significant' facts after they had been auditorily distracted. Concentration *can* shut out all but the relevant facts but in conditions of distraction, with more than one thing taking place at the same time, 'irrelevant' details remain powerful. The conditions of distraction can either be *within* the complex variables of television or the circumstances in which television is viewed. Children go on taking in details at a subconscious level; forewarning them to attend to specific items would not enable them to shut out what Allyn and Festinger (1961) called 'unanticipated' material. The perception of those unattended messages is not a matter of 'late selection' in the sense of choosing later to recall an item (Underwood, 1976). Children adapt to the minimal clues that provide them with recognition, and as they learn to ignore what seems to them 'irrelevant' material, such as explanations or reasons, they also learn to watch repeated images, like the hero's gestures, with a familiarity which is not thought out but subconsciously attuned. Thus the lack of close attention for items of distinct information is allied to a recognition of repeated images that make up the background material. The formula of television programmes is thus recalled, rather than the plot.

The distinction between a response which depends on low arousal and one which makes greater demands is an important one which also applies to recognition. Only those items which do not demand active response are successful in their repetition. Continual repetition of items of high salience can have a 'boomerang' effect once the audience is aroused (Cox, 1964). Children do not like characters that 'get on their nerves'. Thus the items that are easily recognised are those which are not of central importance in themselves but become familiar through repetition. These can be a tone of voice, a gesture (like sucking a lollipop or putting on a hat), or more significantly the style of lighting, the editing and the colour which make the presentation of a Western or a cartoon. As well as pro-active interference (Underwood and Schultz,

1960), we find children's previous knowledge sets up definite patterns of expectations; children show a *desire* to recognise anticipated material. There is a tendency to assume that certain items are familiar even if they merely remind the audience of a previous experience (Anisfeld and Knapp, 1968), for new material is moulded into their previous patterns of expectation. Ausubel (1968) suggests that:

> The fact that forgotten materials can be *re-learned* more effectively and in less time than that required for original learning is ample proof of the existence of sub-threshold dissociability strength; because of its presence, less new learning is required to reach any given threshold level. (p.97)

The distinction between recall and recognition is maintained in children's attitudes towards information. Even in experimental conditions children's ability to recall is related to subsequent forgetting. Kleinsmith and Kaplan (1964) discovered that words recalled the more easily at first were afterwards rapidly forgotten. Slow initial response to emotional stimuli is closely connected to the ability to recall the same stimuli (cf. Bruner and Postman, 1947). The emotional tone of television can be said to make its impact through a barrier of conscious recollection. Recognition is a part of state-dependent learning. When the same context is presented for a second time, items learned previously are more easily, even automatically, recalled (Goodwin, et al. 1969). Thus children look forward to their favourite programmes knowing what to expect; they do not subsequently suggest that the experience is recalled as exceptional. The 'state dependence' lies in the enjoyment of anticipation and recognition. Anything that disturbs the pattern is remembered less well (Berelson, 1964).

Pleasure in the familiar includes emotional atmosphere as well as details. Some of the detailed items are indeed 'transferred' in the mind to a far longer term emotional state (Helmreich, 1972). Those items which were immediately recalled with greater clarity were afterwards far more vaguely remembered; those that had not made such a clear cognitive impact remained more definitely lodged, especially if they were associated with a pleasant emotional state. This is why so much material that is remembered is so vague, and why so many seemingly trivial details are recalled. Recognition is a type of reflex; the repetition of items on television ensures that the kind of information that children learn is more a matter of tone, gestures and attitude, than hard facts or stereotypes of the world.

13 Television as propaganda

'Do you know the biggest joke on television? Margaret Thatcher.' (girl, 7)

Those who discover that they have an opinion on a subject find it very hard to change their opinion, once they have formed it. The question of the effects of television on children is itself a good example of this fact about human nature. The mention of the subject is enough to unleash a series of statements which are supposed to sum up the whole of learning: 'People copy the violence,' or 'It's all a question of stereo-types'. Television is used, as Williams (1979) concludes, as a subject on which simple assertions or anecdotes are supposed to be evidence, since everyone knows that they are right. Even many who have lavished years researching the influence of television have spent virtually all their time testing and trying to prove their opinions (or hypothesis) in such a way that in all the literature there is no real indication of any change of mind, or even the forming of conclusions as a result of the evidence. For once an opinion is formed no amount of evidence to the contrary seems to be enough to unfreeze it. Even in the face of the greatest evidence opinions remain the same.

Given this tendency in people it is both surprising and unsurprising how many have feared the power of the mass media to form and change opinions. This tradition of fear is itself one hypothesis about the nature of society in which television is a powerful tool in the hands of a minority of controlling groups: 'Radio and Television do not exist as media outside their existing regulatory system' (Smith, 1973, p.57). Given that it is seen as a powerful social weapon (cf. Halloran, 1963; McQuail, 1969) it automatically becomes a means by which its powerful rulers insidiously manipulate the audience and re-possess and re-package any thing that comes their way (Usherwood, 1979). Sometimes television is seen as manipulating the audience in a more subtle way : 'Insistence on "correct" speech has been one of the most insidious ways in which the educational system has hitherto accomplished its repressive task of social segregation' (Groombridge, 1972, p.24). Thus while television, through its power to convey information and opinions, is seen as a powerful force, it is seen as one that can be turned to good in one's own hands, or to harm in other people's. Control of the 'media' for the sake of the domination of opinion has been seen by many people to be the most important consequence of their development. But such power rests on the assumption that the audience will listen and will be persuaded, that one opinion will prevail against others.

Both the belief in the power of television and the fear of its power was founded on the development of propaganda in the 1930s, especially by Goebbels. The ability to manipulate the mass rallies through loudspeakers, the use of radio and the showing of films like Leini Riefenstahl's *Triumph des Willens* (1933), seem to lie at the heart of Fascism. It was soon seen as lying at the heart of all modern politics. The development of such media for communication gave rise to the concept of a 'mass' rather than a collection of individuals, and delineated leaders swaying their listeners through their knowledge of how to use the media effectively (cf. McLuhan, 1967). Goebbels was certainly the first to articulate the belief in the power to use modern techniques to service a demagogue: 'Whoever says the first word to the world is always right'. One of the main traditions in the study of television's influence on the audience's belief and attitudes is the literature on propaganda developed during the Second World War, out of the suspicion that Goebbels might have been right when he developed Hitler's famous dictum that 'The great masses of the people . . . will more easily fall victims to a great lie than a small one' *(Mein Kampf, Chapter 10)*. The tradition of research in this field was continued especially in the United States in trying to find means of countering first Fascism and then Communism. But on the same assumption of effectiveness a parallel tradition has arisen in which television is seen as a means of controlling what the audience sees as information (cf. Glasgow University Media Group, 1976, 1980, 1982), and as a means of subtly persuading them to buy certain products (Packard, 1957). In this version of television as a source of subliminal persuasion the controlling power of the state is taken over by large corporations or big business interests (Mills, 1959).

The ability of the audience to take in new information from television is not very great. but then the audience does not generally turn to television with learning in mind. The extraction of certain items of knowledge from television only takes place in limited conditions. But this leaves the possibility that the audience can have its attitudes and opinions changed or moulded by television without recourse to facts. It is possible to assimilate facts when they are useful in supporting an already held opinion. The literature consistently reveals that just as an audience does not imbibe new knowledge, so it is not given to changing opinions. Audiences are not necessarily impressed by, or converted by, listening to rational argument. Children actually resent presentation of the ratiocinative. Although it is reasonable to assume that an audience could be persuaded by what it sees on television there is no evidence for this assumption (Greenward, 1968). The audience for television, given a suspicion of argument in the first place, does not readily wish to distinguish between different points of view. Instead it uses the information it receives in an idiosyncratic way, fitting it into pre-set expectations.

Far from being subtly turned into holding more left-wing, or more right-wing, opinions by a television company that biases every item of news reporting to the right or to the left, the audience sees, individually, what it wishes to see. All these politicians or the Glasgow group who demonstrate how one-sided television reporting is (cf. Chapter 7), always biased against the left, or always slandering the right, are, in fact, behaving like the rest of the audience to the extent that they see in it what they wish to see; they seek evidence to bolster their own opinions. But in another respect they differ from the rest of the audience in being far more deeply engaged in analysing the proofs for their position. For the most part the audience lets the subtleties of bias pass them by.

The one consistent finding to emerge from research on opinions, however, is that television works far less well as an agent for change than as a means of reinforcing opinions already held. This is either because of the emotional refusal to give salience to facts that conflict with a view already held, or because any statement is seen with so little attention that it does not possess the credibility to be rationally considered. The ability to shut out opinions is as strong as the ability to ignore or retain information. Klapper (1960) could not find any measurable changes of opinion in an audience as a result of television, even in conditions in which they were made to pay close attention: 'Persuasive mass communication functions far more frequently as an agent of reinforcement than as an agent of change' (p.15). Allyn and Festinger (1961) demonstrated that the bias against new opinions could be strengthened especially if subjects were forewarned about a particular communication. Hovland, Lumsdaine and Sheffield (1955), after their experiments on the propaganda film *The Battle of Britain* made for Americans to persuade them to enter into the conflict against Hitler

(1949, 1953), discovered that an audience would be more highly biased against an opinion if they were aware that someone had designs on them and wished to persuade them. When Hovland and his colleagues summarised the evidence that had accumulated out of the interest in propaganda during and after the Second World War, they stressed how audiences refused to give any credence to views conflicting with their own.

This unwillingness to change an opinion is also manifested during political elections. Great play has been made of the role of the mass media in forming mass opinions, and attention paid to the attractions of individual politicians as performers. Television is assumed to be so important that there is a tendency to gear political rallies or the choice of candidate around the ability to act or to be attractive to the medium. But no evidence has emerged to give support to this assumption, at least in any immediate form. Marshall McLuhan (1967) suggested that during the series of television debates between Nixon and Kennedy in the American Presidential election, the former argued too much for such a 'cool' medium and that Kennedy's more woolly thinking was significantly more attractive. Given the level at which an audience responds to television, and given the audience's general distaste for the ratiocinative, such an argument sounds plausible. But all those who tested the audience's reactions found that there was not the slightest evidence of any change of opinion during or after these debates (see Diamond, 1975). Those who supported one or other of the candidates felt equally sure that their own man had won the argument each time. Star and Hughes (1966) showed how little information was conveyed to an audience despite the best endeavours. Trenaman and McQuail (1961) demonstrated how little television influenced voting. They also found that the medium reinforced pre-existing beliefs and attitudes. In what has been called the 'congruence' theory (Bauer, 1964), subjects were found to be better at remembering information if it already agreed with their point of view. Fitzgerald and Ausubel (1963) found that subjects remembered passages about the American Civil War only if they already agreed with the controversial slant with which they were presented. This kind of selective retention had already been established by Levine and Murphy (1943). It takes place not only because an audience chooses to watch those programmes which accord with their views (Klapper, 1960) but because they are suspicious of any content which conflicts with their expectations (Janis, 1963). When students were asked to write out material that conflicted with their own self-concept they wrote it badly and slowly (Greenberg and Tannenbaum, 1972) this was also true of those who were asked to write statements contrary to their own beliefs (Bettinghaus and Preston, 1964). This desire for congruence is also reflected in the need to concentrate on one thing at a time: the consciousness of the need to comply with rules of correct spelling and grammar itself inhibits the ability to write persuasive arguments (Glynn et al. 1982).

The love of the familiar and the desire to fit whatever is new into the familiar means that alternative points of view are readily ignored, even if they are noticed. Hovland (1957) found that once an opinion had been expressed people will stick to it in the face of all evidence to the contrary. Schramm (1955) had also shown that if a message seems to conflict with the recipient's personality, he re-interprets it into a form which he finds more acceptable, subconsciously removing those parts of it which conflict. Thus the evidence sees what it wishes to see and is not persuaded by clear, ratiocinative argument or supporting evidence. Television therefore does not act as an agent for change. The opinions of the audience are more affected by information which does not draw attention to itself or which fits into prior beliefs. While changes of attitude *can* take place, in a number of subtle and complex ways, such as through overheard remarks, the statement of a clear message designed to influence the audience makes little measurable change to the audience's opinions or knowledge (McGuire, 1964; Roberts and Maccoby, 1973).

It is only when more trivial, less challenging ideas are conveyed that there are any changes to the audience's opinions or ideas (Klapper, 1948). The more vague or emotional the appeal, the more chance it has of making an impact (Hovland et al. 1953). An audience will accept a different point of view if the issue is trivial enough (McQuail, 1969; Piepe et al. 1975). For this reason advertisers have long been the most sophisticated researchers in this field, even if some of the research is an attempt to establish the fact that particular advertising campaigns are succeeding, rather than finding out how the audience is reacting. Lazarsfeld and Merton in 1948 pointed out that advertising is directed towards the canalising of pre-existing behaviour patterns or attitudes. Thus the findings of propaganda research have been both extended and practised by those interested in the buying habits and associative recognition of the audience (Cox, 1961).

Too much attention drawn to the argument, either for a product or a point of view, can cause the audience to react against the argument. Just as Lang and Lang (1959) suggested that political argument may result in the audience's suspicion of *any* point of view so advertisers have generally sought for campaigns to be entertaining rather than informative. The great fear has been that the audience might react against a product because of their dislike of argument; that the audience would react with 'defensive avoidance' (Cox, 1961, p.363), because they realised that their attention was not only being drawn but their minds challenged. The power of repetition to persuade depends on low arousal, on not being strident enough to irritate (Klapper, 1960). Those items connected with anxiety are difficult to recall (Nunnally and Babren, 1959). Thus the familiar is more easily absorbed since it does not challenge the pre-existing beliefs of the audience. This is why much of the material that children remember is either vague or trivial. Great issues are emotionally and subconsciously rejected; the small ones are absorbed.

Reaction against strong demands has often been demonstrated (Bruner, 1974; Hovland et al. 1953). Children can actually choose to pay even less attention if intense feelings of anxiety are aroused (Hovland et al. p.78). Children's dislikes of particular programmes such as the news or documentaries centre on their reaction against the demands being made on them as well as on the love of the familiar. Children's expectations of television are such that they resent a type of performance they would accept in different circumstances. When, for example, McMenamin (1964) organised the same lecture to be seen live and on television, the reactions to either were quite dissimilar. Those who saw the lecture live enjoyed it and found the lecturer 'poised'. Those who saw it on the screen resented it and found the lecturer too 'emphatic'. The style was felt inappropriate to television, like a stage version of *Othello* with all the gestures appropriate to the theatre confined into the more personal intimate constrictions of a film. Children react against certain types of exaggeration and cite as 'boring' not those programmes that they have already seen but those that they do not wish to see because they suspect they are likely to make demands on them. The tendency for an audience to cling to an opinion in the face of all evidence is reflected by children's desire to avoid the unexpected in their putative entertainment. They refuse to entertain any possible threat to their beliefs (Roberts and Maccoby, 1973), as if they wished to immunise themselves against those things that might challenge (McGuire, 1964).

Television is associated in children's minds with an absence of challenge. It is, therefore, not surprising that it is on the level of low arousal that the most influence can take place. Ever since Hovland's work it has been repeatedly demonstrated that television audiences are more easily persuaded to take on a new opinion if the subject presented to them is obviously trivial, as in the case of an advertisement (Krugman, 1970). The more lightly held the belief (the preference for one brand over another is an example) the more likely it is that an audience will accept a different point of view (McQuail, 1969). The more trivial the subject matter the greater interest the audience shows (Klapper, 1960). Most of the experiments on propaganda have been in conditions more conducive to rational change of opinion; a justifying authority and the atmosphere of the laboratory. It is the more telling that at the level of rationality little change takes place beyond a stronger determination to stick to an opinion already held. And yet people do hold opinions. The first explorations of the psychology of rumour (Allport and Postman, 1947), the discovery of the importance of the overheard remark (cf. Katz and Lazarsfeld, 1955) and the realisation that vague statements have more potency than rational argument, all give a consistent finding that over-insistence is the least successful form of persuasion, a finding confirmed by children's attitudes towards programmes and by the details that they can recall. Children accept the conventions of television in which interesting statements are either part of the plot, or a recognisable repeated remark, or a joke casually told. Many statements are asserted on television; the vast majority are to do with matters of little general importance. Thus when children assert their own opinions they do so the most vehemently when it is just as rational to hold a different point of view. The ability to demonstrate enthusiasm or taste by liking a particular thing becomes a parody of the information they glean from television, when knowing facts for quiz programmes gives information its most substantial raison d'etre. When children talk of their opinions they show a tendency to exaggerate, without a sense of earnestness about favourites, whether in popular music or football:

'The best pop group are *Abba*. I know all their names.' (girl, 10)
'I think *Manchester United* are the best team in the world.' (boy, 9)

The opinion is stated in a take-it-or-leave-it way as if this level of opinion mattered more than further explanation or justification.

'I am interested in one pop star and that is *Rod Stewart*.' (girl, 13)
'My favourite pop stars is Elton John and Rod Stewart. My favourite team is Liverpool.' (girl, 13)

There are few shades of grey in the assertion of personal tastes:

'I used to go to the Carlisle matches and cheer the home team but now I don't bother because I think they're a load of rubbish and they'll stay in the Second Division and maybe drop to the Third Division. My favourite team is *Manchester United* and I have got a united top because they are the greatest team. Their top crowd is 55,000. O.K.' (boy, 13)

Children learn from television that assertion can be without threat. Instead of being made to learn something to please the teacher, to repeat an exercise, they see a means of entertainment that has no such demands. The picture is always moving; someone is always talking; statements are continually being made. But little attention is sought by most of the programmes. Those that attempt to manipulate a point of view are more resented. Most of the successful assertions are those that are amusing and repeated, such as advertisements. If anything succeeds it seems to be the trivial; the emotional attitude can be better manipulated than a specific argument. Children react against persuasion (Festinger, 1957, 1964) and greatly prefer the undisturbing (Krugman, 1966). The realisation that television does not cause immediate changes of opinion any more than it causes close identification or imitation might be comforting in the wake of Goebbels' propaganda. But such a realisation, given people's refusal to change their opinions even in the face of clear evidence, would not have stopped Goebbels continuing to try, had he had the chance.

14 Advertising

'What washing powder does Kojak use? Bald.' (girl, 11)

Persuasion is a difficult art, for the greater the obvious desire to persuade, the less the success. An overheard remark is more likely to change someone's mind than a carefully constructed presentation. For every audience reacts against the message that has designs on them; and dislikes the ratiocinative rhetoric of politicians. Only the item that does not draw attention to itself, that does not seem to matter, succeeds in communicating. Advertising is the best example of this phenomenon, and illustrates how techniques have been adapted to convey the trivial in an entertaining way. Just as children dislike those personalities that draw too much attention to themselves, so they show the least liking for advertisements that insist directly on the message, or on a comparison with other similar brands. Washing powder advertisements are often criticised by children for their high-pressure sales talk, and absence of humour. They were the ones most often cited as being disbelieved. The more strident the claims for a type of product the more suspicious children were. Children are more likely to dispute a claim that is stated starkly than an advertisement that does not suggest the possibility of such a response: 'It says that Persil makes things whiter than others, but it doesn't' (girl, 8), 'I hate the way they talk on Daz' (boy, 7).

The danger of advertisements drawing too much attention to themselves in terms of a rational message had long been recognised. One carefully mounted campaign in the United States sought to convince the audience of the importance of eating prunes because of their obvious benefits to health, but the audience merely associated the prunes with the constipation they were being promoted to relieve (Packard, 1975). Cox (1961) in his summary of findings concerned with advertising confirmed that the stronger the appeal to rationality the less possibility there was of persuasion because of what he called 'defensive avoidance' (p.364). In all the market research concerned with advertising objectives, despite the fact that the end product is evaluated in terms of sales, and despite the temptation of advertisers to write for each other and their clients rather than the audience, there are a certain number of ground rules that develop this notion of avoiding any sense of urgency or threat.

Even logically presented explanations make more of an impression on an audience's general awareness than on its knowledge of the information conveyed (Ehrenburg, 1974). Changes of attitude and habits of purchase are the results of manipulation of already existing motivations rather than changing opinions or the generation of new ones (Abelson, 1972). For this reason only a small proportion of advertisements on television give information about the product that is being sold (Winick et al. 1973). Too much information might make the audience react against what is being presented. Halloran (1964) noted that the unawareness of being 'got at' was directly related to the approval of the content presented. Lazarsfeld and Merton (1948) demonstrated that advertising is directed towards the canalising of pre-existing behaviour patterns and attitudes, just as influential advertisers like Hepner and Dichter were instinctively exploiting this finding.

The fact that advertising on television is based on such established ground rules is reflected in its popularity. Nearly all children were consistent and positive in expressing their liking for advertisements. Even amongst those who did not express such strong pleasure, the ability to explain, discuss or recite from them was undiminished. There was a tendency amongst some of the younger boys to suggest with false bravado that 'they were a load of rubbish', but the vast majority, while never citing advertisements as their favourite programmes, nevertheless clearly appreciated them as part of the entertainment offered by television. Those children who said that they did not particularly like advertisements said that it was because they interrupted their favourite programmes. Most children, however, did not feel that the pattern of entertainment was affected since they found advertisements entertaining in their own way. They were seen as short programmes in their own right, the better for being repeated. Children's reasons for liking advertisements underlined the pragmatism with which they were seeking to be entertained. A very high proportion of the children saw in an advertisement something that was funny, or contained interesting characters or involved a curious incident. Thus their favourite advertisements were liked because, for example,

'It is a little cartoon.' (girl, 7)
'The snowman melts.' (girl, 9)
'They sing and have funny caps.' (girl, 11)
'I like the way they use a skateboard gang which are always falling off the skateboard.' (girl, 11)
'I like the music.' (boy, 8)
'She . . . strips off and takes a bath.' (boy, 10)
'It is funny.' (boy, 11)
'Morecombe and Wise are on it.' (boy, 12)

In nearly all children's favourite advertisements the product advertised is not as important as the style of the presentation. Singer and Singer (1981) in confirming the popularity of commercials single out the attention paid to particular characters. Children's favourite advertisements are often recognised through the use of a particularly identifiable 'character', especially in cartoon form. Thus the 'Honey Monster' that appears on advertisements for Sugar Puffs was itself a favourite, partly because of its association with the phrase 'Don't forget to tell them about the honey, mummy'. But many other cartoon characters, like Yogi Bear, the Tiger on 'Frosties' or the Space men on 'Smash' were appreciated for their entertainment value. These cartoon characters were far more popular than the real personalities associated with the product they were paid to sell, like Pam Ayres with Bacon, or Benny Hill with Slumberland. Some boys, however, did like to see a footballer like Steve Coppell appearing for Gillette, but that was for the sake of football rather than the product.

Children's liking for advertisements for their own sake bears a very ambiguous relationship to children's knowledge of which products are being advertised. Children are *aware* of which products are being advertised and appreciate the connection between the entertainment and the product. Reasons for liking advertisements include the product:

'Because it is a biscuit.' (girl, 7)
'They have nuts in.' (girl, 11)
'Because if you run out of milk it's always there.' (girl, 10)
'They are nicer than Topic.' (girl, 11)
'It makes me have an apple.' (boy, 7)
'I like shoes.' (boy, 8)
'They are delicious.' (boy, 10)
'I like playing with mine.' (boy, 11)
'They are nice and weigh very little.' (boy, 11)

These are examples of children who fulfil the expectations of the advertiser, who appear to be convinced by the advertisement to the point of trying the product and endorsing it. Ehrenburg (1974) gives the marketing point of view that awarenesss of a product must lead to a trial, and that buying comes about through this. Corkindale and Kennedy (1975) also suggest that clear advertising objectives create an audience awareness that inevitably leads to a shift in buying habits. In fact the proportion of children citing the product as a reason for liking the advertisement was very small, and showed a rapid decline as the children grow older, with very few citing the product at all from the age of twelve (cf. Meringoff and Lesser, 1980). The four main reasons children give for liking certain advertisements are the personalities, the gimmicks, the humour and the songs. While some cited commercials for pragmatic reasons such as liking the end product, most enjoyed the visual techniques, the cartoon characters and the sense of watching a short, interesting, familiar and repeated programme, that it would not be fatal to miss. Commercials with highly salient features maintain children's interest whatever the product (Greer et al. 1982). The pragmatic children who associated the advertisement and the product (the proportion varied from about one-quarter at the age of eight to less than 10 per cent at the age of twelve) described some quality that they felt was important;

> 'They are warm.' (girl, 7)
> 'Because it looks warming.' (girl, 10)
> 'I like eating them.' (boy, 11)

or else they showed an objective sense of what advertisements are for, treating them as a genuine presentation of products from which to choose:

> 'It shows a lot of nice shoes; I like the colour.' (girl, 8)
> 'To see what clothes they have to offer, and shoes too.' (girl, 11)
> 'At Christmas time you can decide what toys you want.' (boy, 10)
> 'We use it sometimes at home and I think it's nice. They tell you a lot about them.' (girl, 12)

But most children take an even more pragmatic view about the commercials and state their pleasure not with the product but with the presentation. They liked the personalities, whether these were cartoons or real animals:

'I like watching cats.' (girl, 7)

'I like the cat on it; the way the cats know what to do.' (girl, 8)

'I like the little green men on Butlins.' (girl, 10)

'I just like the characters involved.' (girl, 12)

'I like the men on it.' (boy, 10)

'The monkeys and what they dress up as and what they . . . but they don't really say it.' (boy, 11)

'It is good how they train the animals.' (boy, 12)

These are popular because of the actions that are seen; the events that mark out the characteristics of the 'personalities' rather than the concern with the creatures in themselves. Thus the most often cited reason for liking advertisements is the repeated incident that children find amusing:

'Because the boy falls off the tree.' (girl, 7)

'When the boy splashes in the mud.' (girl, 10)

'They show different sports and I like sports.' (girl, 11)

'I like what they do.' (boy, 8)

'They have got action.' (boy, 11)

'At the end of so so soup the man shoots off and the slippers go whizzing round.' (boy, 11)

Of all the techniques of advertising that elicit the approval of children, it is humour that is most appreciated. Advertisements that rely on fear, or a serious message, like the possible decay of teeth unless a toothpaste is used regularly, create reactions *against* the message (Cox, 1961; Janis and Feshbach, 1953, p.92). Humour is a way of not pushing an appeal too far, so as to avoid the 'boomerang' effect that results if a message is stressed too continuously (as happens in the case of washing powder).

It is often assumed, especially by surveyors of marketing, that children are most influenced by advertisements for those products that appeal to them. Advertisements for sweets, especially numerous during television scheduled for children, are assumed to have an immediate effect on buying habits and recall (Barcus and Wolkin, 1977). Advertising agencies would certainly like to think that children respond to the objectives of product presentation. But children in fact show that their liking of advertisements is more objective still: their favourite advertisements are more often than not for products that are neither designed specifically to appeal to them, nor of any particular interest to them. Children aged seven and eight cite and explain their liking for advertisements for coal fires, electric cookers, savings banks, for carpets, telephones, washing-up liquids, food stores, soups and nasal sprays. The proportion of products designed essentially to appeal to them — primarily sweets and toys — is comparatively small. Torin Douglas (1982), quoting from the Lintas agency, also confirms that the favourite advertisements are for general household goods like Andrex. The interest in the advertisement does not therefore depend upon the product. While it could be argued that children have an intense interest in different systems of banking as well as different brands of tea, the way in which they describe what they like about advertisements makes it clear that they recall the gimmick (monkeys at a tea party) far more readily than the brand name with which it is associated. Although it is conjectured that children are used to influence the parents (Ward, 1976), it is clear that children make a clear distinction between advertisements as a form of entertainment and buying habits. Obviously children show an interest in toys, and, in the case of girls, in clothes. Obviously the emphasis amongst advertisers in the early part of the evening is on sweets to appeal directly to children. But children are more sophisticated than to react to automatic 'triggers' or brand names. They see the distinction between the product itself and the way in which it is presented. Many of their preferred advertisements are directed towards adults, and outside the scope of any possible action. In all, 69 per cent of children referring to their favourite advertisements cited those specifically aimed at adults; for banks and for alcohol, for cars and central heating. If children liked advertisements for Cream Eggs or Chewits it was because of the way in which they were presented. One of the favourite advertisements at the time was for 'Pintsize', a dried milk substitute. Nevertheless, although children liked commercials for their own sake, they were almost certain to know the brand name. Except in the case of washing powders, which children found similar to each other, and disliked without always suggesting a brand name, and with the other exception of 'Buzby', the mascot of Telecom, children cited brand names, normally with precise accuracy; 'Vicks nasal spray, Trustee Savings Bank, Butlins Holiday Camps, Midland Bank, Citroen GSA' etc. Children are therefore aware of what is being advertised even if they are just as aware of the entertainment value of the presentation.

Children's growing awareness of the entertainment value of advertisements implies that they learn to become sophisticated about the designs that these advertisments have on them (cf. Chapter 6). From the marketing point of view there is a clear intention to cause a change of habit. That the presentation of a product on television causes a marked rise in sales is established, although the explanations for this, apart from the knowledge that such a product exists, are not very clear. But children have been assumed to be fragile in this connection; they have been seen to be vulnerable to commercials because of their inability to see the difference between the true and the false. Rossiter (1980) talks of the false modes of advertising being misleading and unfair, as if children took it at face value. Children are seen as exploited so that they can persuade their parents to spend money (Winick, 1973). Thus children are supposed to take the 'world' of the advertisements so seriously that they are disappointed when they find a gap between the claim and the subsequent pleasure (Bever et al. 1975). The Federal Trades Commission in the United States (1978) directed much attention to this aspect of children's vulnerability to persuasion. But children's responses are in fact more complex; while they are more apt to connect the product with its presentation when young, and more apt to assume that the 'truth' of an advertisement lies in its existence, they nevertheless are soon cushioned by the very fact that the repetition of the commercial makes it entertaining.

Children's knowledge of brand names is extensive, just as their preference for specific advertisements is clear. This seems to contradict the oft-cited concern that younger children will not know what an advertisement is for since they are incapable of evaluating individual messages (Bever et al. 1975). The application of general Piagetian views to children's development (cf. Winick, 1973) has implied that children under the age of ten are misguided into paying exactly the same earnest attention to advertisements for sweets or soap powders that they do to *Playschool*. Melody (1973), discussing 'routining', the juxtaposition between the advertisement and the programme within which it is placed, suggests that there are deliberate attempts to obscure the differences between the commercials and the programme by integrating the type of picture (i.e. cartoon) or the mood (i.e. humour). And yet while children value the advertisements as entertainment, they are quite clear, at least in Great Britain, where 'routining' is obviously of far less possible potency, of advertisements *as* advertisements. Given that children vary their attention within programmes, and given that they want to respond in a similar way to all of them, they nevertheless are clear about the progeny and purpose of commercials. Children are similarly clear about the placing of advertisements within and between programmes. The question of whether they would not notice the difference between an advertisement and its surrounding programme was meaningless to them. Often it was the advertisement to which they looked forward; always it was the advertisement they most easily recognised.

The awareness of advertising as a genre reveals a growing ability amongst children to accept the terms in which the commercials work. They might be influenced to buy certain products, but they know that they are being cajoled to do so. In the Advertising Standards Authority's definition of 'truth' (cf. Chapter 6) the salient point is the actual existence of the product, and its availability in the shops. The definitions of truth do not include obvious fantasy, vague suggestions or sexual innuendoes. Thus the linking of a brand of cigar with attractiveness to women, at one level of semiotics, or the suggestion that a particular lager has the ability to transform a whole variety of objects, at another, are not mistaken as being anything other than entertaining, humorous, fantastic. The linguistic borderland of vague claims (cf. Schrank, 1975) like 'helps' or 'better than' or 'natural' might each be definitions of different ways of lying, but are perceived as fantasy, accepted as meaningless in one sense, while having a distinct purpose in another. Thus children that seemed to be muddled by that relationship between truth and fantasy that so disturbs Henry (1972) or Ellul (1964) were actually giving different definitions of truth in their answers. The younger children defined the 'real' as the actual existence of the product. The implied claim, that eating a bar of chocolate was a successful way of obtaining a girl friend, or that a horde of nubile women would chase after the smell of pipe tobacco, was not important to them. As children grew older so they grew more interested in the style of the advertisement and more able therefore to see and express the dissociation between the product and its presentation. Children under the age of seven showed a greater tendency to believe their favourite advertisement, although rather fewer believed what their favourite advertisement *said*. By the age of twelve less than half the children believed even their favourite advertisement; only about 10 per cent believed what their favourite advertisement *said*. Their responses therefore showed a complex reaction; a disbelief in the commercial appeal, a pleasure in the advertisement as fantasy entertainment, and the acceptance that all the advertiser is trying to say, usually humorously, is that the product is available in the shops. To young children truth is linked to availability. Thus a girl can say 'I don't believe in Pintsize because there is a man which tells the advertisements' while liking the advertisement for its entertainment. Another girl says 'I don't believe the Mars one. I don't like the singing "A Mars a day helps you work, rest and play". I don't believe the sales either'. Sometimes the lack of belief comes through experience when a boy, citing it as his favourite advertisement, says 'No, because three of my Action men have only got one arm and half a leg'. For the most part the idea of 'truth' is absurd. 'No, fancy him coming out of the packet and going into a pint' (boy, 11). When the children were asked to cite actual advertisements that they did *not* believe, 90 per cent *immediately* gave examples. Many of these were for washing powders because of the 'hard sell' that drew attention to what they were trying to do. But children also pointed out that the products were presented as part of a curious fantasy world, in which chocolates growl, monkeys talk and jam goes 'toot'.

The fact that advertisements are not absorbed with naïve credulity does not mean that they are not remembered. One of the most important features of advertisements is that they are often repeated. Children cannot actually look forward to them, as they can to their favourite programmes, since they do not know when they are scheduled, but they recognise them when they see them. This continuous exposure has often been underlined as the most important single factor in making products remembered (Zielske, 1959). Children are able to cite a great many of the advertisements they have seen, by brand name. Their ability to grow accustomed to what they expected to see was very great, and their ability to recall what they had seen grew as they got older (Ward et al. 1977). As Krugman (1965) suggested, the balance between low levels of attention and repetition meant that the advertisements were well remembered; some children were able to cite large numbers of the advertisements they had seen, just as they were able to characterise large numbers of their favourite programmes. But in contrast to the other programmes, advertisements were clearly recalled as well as cited. Children knew, by brand name, rather than a generalised response like 'washing powder' or 'sweets', exactly what they had seen. Through the recognition of repeated actions more than 80 per cent of the children were able to give a clear account of the main events; not merely the essential point but in enough detail to show how much they had understood of the presentation:

> 'In a bar a man stands and the Milky Bar kid comes in and they get out their guns but the Milky Bar kid shouts "The milky bars are on me" so he gives everyone one.' (girl, 8)
>
> 'Yogi bear gets up. Bobo gives him the soup. He says this isn't enough for me and throws in on the floor and goes. Some people near the camp fire; he does a wolf howl and all the people at the camp fly off and Yogi bear goes back and starts eating. Bobo said "It's too big for me so Yogi has it".' (girl, 10)

Advertisements not directed at children are just as clearly remembered:

> 'A man keeps on talking and there is a French Onion man comes along. The man thinks he is French and says "Don't say you grow your own".' (boy, 8)
>
> 'A lady says "What says for the coffee". And the other lady says "Pardon". Then the other lady says your coffee is a bit bitter. "Have you tried Mellow Birds?". Then the lady says "I don't think this will teach me a lesson". "Ah yes I think it might teach me a lesson". There is a lady sitting down drinking coffee. Then she throws it away in a flower pot. The other lady turns around.' (girl, 11)

There might be a certain amount of muddle, but the main points (and the brand name) are clear. The crucial points of recognition remain, whatever the slight variations between the programme and another. The appeal of the advertisement lies in the humour and the action;

> 'There are earthlings: "See how some use Smash instant potato while others carry big heavy loads of potatoes. But how can we tell the difference between them? The ones who carry potatoes have longer arms. HA-HA-HA".'
> (boy, 10)
> 'It shows a sequence from a Manchester United football match where Steve Coppell crosses it and Gordon Hill heads the ball in the back of the net and then Tommy Docherty says "It gives me the closest shave I have had".'
> (boy, 11)

Children's ability to recall is far higher when applied to advertisements than other programmes. Given the relationship between recall and recognition this is not surprising. Whether it is because of the repetition of the ordinary (Krugman, 1965) or the repetition with minor variations (Bartlett, 1940), the most popular advertisements are clearly remembered and enjoyed. The Honey Monster of *Sugar Puffs* becomes a familiar favourite; the monkeys of *PG Tips* immediately recognised. What is more, children remember advertisements *better* as they get older, and are clearly aware of what the advertisements are for. Less than 1 per cent cited advertisements without mentioning the brand name. (The brand name is like a title of a programme.) But children's familiarity with 'commercials is mitigated by one main factor. They are sometimes more conscious of the 'punch lines' than the actions. To some extent this depends upon the style. 'Yogi bear' is a fairly complex visual display with one main selling point — 'big soup'. The Honey Monsters' actions are, however, subservient to the repeated punch line — 'Tell 'em about the honey, mummy'. The more dominant the main phrase in the advertisement the more difficulty there is in distinguishing between what is heard and what is seen. Thus, like the brand name, the main catch phrase becomes the central point of the advertisement; 90 per cent of children are able to recall the main punch line of their own favourite advertisement and, in addition, can cite many others at will:

> 'I'm the Milky Bar kid. The Milky Bars are on me.'
> 'I'm a gnu how do you do . . .'
> 'You forgot to tell 'em about the honey, mummy.'
> 'Bigger than the average soup.'

'You've passed your MOT; make 'orrible tea.'
'A last request. Can I just finish this here Texan Bar, bite through the chocolate and chew real slow.'
'As you walk through the door your pound's worth more.'
'Made to make your mouth water.'

The repeated catch phrase, like 'Beanz Meanz Heinz', stays in children's minds and becomes the symbol of the whole advertisement. The actions of the commercials are tied to the main phrase, and children are only inclined to describe what they have seen if the advertisement does not depend on a verbal message.

The predominance of the catch phrase is a result of the desire to promote repetition without the 'boomerang' effect. Just as Leech (1966) suggested in his analysis of advertising copy, the main 'one-liners' are easy to listen to and repeat. Children derive pleasure from the jingles that they hear on television commercials and find it far easier to bring them to mind when asked to recite poetry than any poetry they have read or learned at school (Cullingford, 1979). One of the reasons that children like commercials is the songs that they are able to recall with great panache. Words tied to music are not just brought to mind when the music acts as a 'trigger' but recalled with great ease by more than two-thirds of children:

'Nuts, Nuts, Whole Hazelnuts; Cadbury's take them and cover them in chocolate.'
'I am a Jamaican ginger grower and I'm very proud to say I grow the finest ginger in the world today. I know it. I grows it.'
'A finger of fudge is just enough to give your kids a treat. It's full of Cadbury's goodness but very small and neat.'
'Your profit sharing Co-op, your caring sharing Co-op; it's yours, all yours, all yours.'
'That's the wonder of good old Woolies.'
'It's all at the Co-op now.'
'Keep going well, keep going Shell; you can be sure of Shell.'

Both songs and catch phrases are a type of incantation. Most children are able to cite what they see as typical of advertising:

'And all because the lady loves Milk Tray.'
'Danish for a good meal.'
'Smarties people are happy people.'
'A hazelnut in every bite.'
'Grow your own.'

When children are pressed to suggest typical phrases that are often heard in connection with advertisements, they show themselves to be aware of the general tone:

'It's full of goodness.'
'New flavour.'
'They're great.'
'Value for money.'
'Come and buy one.'

Children seem to be aware of the style of language associated with advertisements as well as imbibing particularly familiar phrases. They are conversant with what to expect as well as remembering what they have seen.

The clarity with which children remember advertisements, and especially the accuracy with which they recall brand names, suggests that they might well be influenced in their buying habits, as well as in their styles of attention. Unlike adults, children are more likely to *say* that they have been influenced by advertisements. They are aware of the designs that are made on them, and aware of advertisements as information. Thus half the children aged nine say that they *have* been influenced, although as children get older they tend, increasingly, to deny any such suggestions. Those children who pointed out that they had been influenced for the most part cited toys, especially shown near Christmas. They said that they looked to advertisements so as to know 'what to look out for and ask for'. Other children, citing the usefulness of the information, pointed out that the advertising preview influenced them to watch films on television. Still more cited records. A very few suggested a more direct impact 'Lemon Barley Water; it makes one go and drink it' (girl, 10). There is no reason to suppose that even if children do not believe the commercials they are not influenced, since awareness of the brand is the sine qua non of buying habits. Children both understand how advertisements work and enjoy them for their own sake; at the same time, through what Hartley (1961) called 'unanchored' learning, children pick up the associations of the product and its repeated phrase. Sometimes children's pragmatism towards the information that is presented lies in the use they feel they can make of such information: 'I like the one about being drunk and need help because I think it could be true to my dad if he got drunk and could not stop' (girl, 12).

Children's favourite advertisements are not only admired for their style, but associated closely with the product. But the favourites are a few amongst a large number of advertisements that come and go, and are repeated. A high proportion of children will have seen advertisements (and therefore watched commercial television) on each evening; they can also cite accurately which ones they have seen and give explicit proof of their familiarity. But children see advertisements as part of the entertainment, more complete than other programmes and as easy to watch. Advertisements are also useful breaks within a programme: 'They are sometimes funny and when it's a film I can go to the toilet'. Never are they seen as being anything but distinct: 'Some are funny and because when a programme is end of part one, you can watch the adverts until the programme comes on.' Children's views on advertising show both realisation of what commercials are for − 'To make people buy things' − and an awareness of 'slotting', seeing quite distinctly the difference between the programme and the break (Rosnow, 1968). There are no indications that children are subsumed in the fantasy elements of commercials as if they were real (Hall and Whannel, 1964). Children's taste for advertisements showed an appreciation of the fantasy element; the cartoons and gimmicks of style. Thus children appreciate what advertisers set out to offer in what Williams (1980) calls a magic system of inducements. In many ways advertisements offer a microcosm of what children like about television; given the slight public bow towards the value of information, they actually present repetition, songs, humour, recognisability and stunts. The fact that it is far easier to persuade an audience to bolster their opinions than to change them gives advertisements the chance, recognisably and without threat, to give a sense of the familiar. Thus the leading advertisers always tried to suggest that they are providing some form of public service:

> The best modern advertising does not try to sell. It aims to help people but intelligently . . . One of the main jobs of the advertiser in this conflict between pleasure and guilt is not so much to sell the product as to give moral permission to have fun without guilt. (Dichter, 1957, p.57)
> The value of illusion to the consumer is exemplified by this advertisement. The housewife who furnishes her house in the 'spirit' of this advertisement is likely to be a happier woman than one who buys furniture that is factually described only. The pleasant emotions and feelings engendered by entrancing advertising make a worthy contribution to human welfare. (Hepner, 1941, p.11)

The picture of advertising is one which suggests that there is no point in the hard sell, but in providing entertainment as in any other television broadcast. The selling line of Bursk (1958) and others is to talk about 'increasing wants or, even better, creating new wants' (p.119).

Research on advertising reveals several important findings about the audience's response to television. It shows the importance of repetition (Hovland, 1957) and it reveals that advertisements are more effective when they do not arouse strong responses (Krugman and Hartley, 1960; Krugman, 1965, 1966). Advertising does not arouse deep involvement in children (Ward, Levison and Wackman, 1971), is not a topic of great salience (Bauer and Greyser, 1968) and does not arouse in children any deep concern for 'selling motives' (Ward and Wackman, 1973). Advertisements do sell their products but do so without great arousal (Rosnow, 1968). They tend to reinforce accepted modes of behaviour (Langholtz-Legmore, 1975) but certainly never challenge them. Thus the level at which advertisements make their effect is more subtle than that of close attention. Children, when they put their minds to it are perfectly aware of how commercials work. But they do not wish to be reminded of this; those advertisements which are obvious are those most disliked. Commercials are to children a natural part of television, not to be sought out but to be accepted. Unlike some other parts of television they are clearly remembered.

PART IV
WHAT CHILDREN TAKE
FROM TELEVISION

' . . . in sleep, in a fever, in madness or in any very violent emotions of soul, our ideas may approach to our impressions; as, on the other hand, it sometimes happens that our impressions are so faint and low that we cannot distinguish them from our ideas.'

Hume: An Enquiry Concerning Human Understanding, 1748.

15 Parents and peer groups

'. . . I like watching films and *Starsky and Hutch*, and we like watching *Celebrity Squares* and having a baby and my mummy likes watching Silver Jubilee. . .' (girl, 7)

Television is a source of a great deal of information and opinions; its potential to create images seems infinite. But television is rarely used in such a direct way. Just as children ignore it for much of the time it is on, so they ignore it mentally even when placed before it. Far from seeing television as a medium that has a direct influence, they see it as a forgettable means of entertainment. All this suggests that the position of television in the home is rather a strange one, more of a background than an obvious influence. There might be a deliberate effort by advertisers and others, as McLuhan suggests, to 'get inside the collective public mind' (1964, v.), but the audience neither perceives this, nor pays the kind of attention by which such deliberate control could be easily achieved. The conditions of viewing are such that any readiness to change opinions or attitudes would be undermined; and as we have seen, it is very difficult to persuade any audience from its set position. The ways in which influence takes place is far more subtle, and does not depend on the television by itself. The need of educational television to rely on outside sources, and the need for justifying authority for any slight change in behaviour, makes it apparent how much depends on the conditions in which television is viewed.

When children talk about television it is clear that the programmes they watch become part of the texture of their lives. Television is not viewed as a special event, nor does it replace all other activities. The time that it takes might be a dominant percentage, but it seems to fit in easily with other activities children carry out with their friends and their parents. When asked to cite what interests them, all but a handful of children mentioned particular programmes on television as one item amongst many others:

> ' . . . I watch *Starsky and Hutch* and I play in the back street, and *Star Trek*: then I went into the park to play two balls with my brother.' (boy, 7)

> ' . . . when I go in I watch *Blue Peter* and then my dad has *Nationwide* on and David play fighting. Then I get into my night clothes and I watch Janice. At dinner time I watch Rainbow and Noddy. . .' (girl, 6)

> ' . . . on television I watch *Kojak* and *Starsky and Hutch* and *Scorpio*, it's great, and when I have watched TV, and then I play cricket and after that we play football on the green.' (boy, 9)

> ' . . . I like to watch TV on Saturday nights and mornings. I watch TV on Friday nights when the *Sweeney's* on and I like *Charlie's Angels* as well. I like going to the pictures to see *The Lady and the Tramp* and watch *Dennis the Menace*. I like to go swimming, I like to climb trees. . . I like to watch *Starsky and Hutch*. . . And the bionic man and bionic woman. . . I like to go swimming; I like the *New Avengers*. I like those wonderful *TV Times*. When I play, but I like to play Freeze. I would like to go on a pack holiday. . .' (girl, 9)

> ' . . . the bionic man and woman interests me and I have got lots of posters on my walls. People say my walls will not need wall-papering. I watch both Lindsay Wagner and Lee Majors on TV and at the moment the bionic woman is on Granada at 6.40pm.' (girl, 13)

> ' . . . and I watch *Scooby Doo* always and he is on tonight and I like playing soldiers and I watch my sister wash up and I like playing with my toys and guns as well, too, and I watch *Blue Peter* every week.' (boy, 6)

> ' . . . when I come home from school I watch the *Cedar Tree* then go for a bike ride and sometimes I go to the shop. When I come back I watch the telly. . . Saturday nights I watch *Starsky and Hutch*. My favourite programmes are. . .' (girl, 10)

When children talk about their interests, without any soliciting about television, it is firstly clear that television is a most important part of their lives. It is, by far, the most mentioned commodity. But it is nearly always part of a larger pattern of play, of domestic details, of the texture of family life. Other activities are not excluded, or replaced. There might be minor quarrels about which programme to watch but nearly all the children take for granted that it is a family activity; that their parents and their friends all spend considerable time watching. As Himmelweit and her colleagues discovered (1958), children's *other* habits, like reading comics or Enid Blyton or listening to the radio, all continue, as if the same type of pleasure were derived from a variety of sources.

Watching television is an activity that does not make heavy demands; the sheer amount of time it takes up suggests otherwise. It is for this reason that the attitude of mind associated with watching television is associated with passivity (Krugman, 1970). All the members of the household can be half-absorbed in watching television, but whether they are or not they have the excuse not to talk to each other. Television is an excuse for silence. This is why, for example, a group of men on a Sunday afternoon will be able to sit in front of the television absorbed in sleep, but the moment the television is switched off will wake up and protest. It is not that they are watching but that they need an excuse to sleep; they would not share such a private experience if there were not a sense in which a dialogue was taking place between them and the television. Watching a programme is a public activity; sleeping is private. Like other more popular activities watching television is easily shared, but it is rarely discussed. Very few children talk to their parents about what they see; very few hear parents making any remarks about television. Thus the function of television is not to make a coherent centre in the family, but to be a collective as well as private source of amusement and distraction. Much has been made of the idea that television destroys traditional family life, as if there were a consistent picture of the good old days in which all would gather round the father for a discussion, for games, for stories; for entertainment at a different level. It is clear that television does *not* cause discussion or even any arguments apart from which which channel to watch. The whole family seems to spend not only an equal amount of time watching television but watching it in similar ways, sharing the same tastes.

Parents could have a great influence on the ways in which their children watch television; not only by controlling what is seen, but by influencing the ways in which children watch. We have already noted (Chapter 2) how little parents actually control the hours that children watch, or the programmes that they imbibe. Naturally there are exceptions; the most vociferous are those who point out that they have strong reasons for control. But generally parents share with their children the style of watching television; this itself is an influence on children's attitudes. Newcomb's (1953) well-known and influential (cf. Bernstein, 1961) 'ABX' theory suggests four possible roles of parents in their influence on children's viewing habits. The first is a laissez faire attitude where there are no conflicting ideas about television, and no lively interest in public affairs. The second is a protective attitude which prohibits children from speaking up, so that children watch television as an escape from these threats. The third is the pluralistic approach when children are encouraged to explore new ideas and the last is the 'consensual', wherein children are encouraged to think, but expected to agree with their parents. Many of these differences are subsumed within a more casual attitude to the medium, for even if parents are occasionally controlling, children will still look to television not as a source of stimulation to be shared, but as a casual interest that is less strong than any desire to 'escape' from the control. The 'laissez faire' attitude is the most accurate description of what actually takes place, for children are unaware of what their parents think about what is on television. To explore this further children were asked whether they ever heard their parents talk about the news on television (on other programmes there were no opinions at all). Less than 15 per cent could recall any occasion in which some form of comment had been made. Television's shared experience was a private, an individual one, as well as one of little salience. Television is not used as an instrument for discussion; some children dislike any association between the two. Thus, although Newcombe implies the active involvement of parents in forming opinions, it seems clear that any remarks made about television are casual and display general attitudes rather than reactions to specific items. Those children who could recall some occasion on which their parents had given some comment were inclined to report a general complaint, often about strikes. Their parents gave comments on 'strikes and things'. Occasionally a formative attitude would emerge:

> 'They talked about the shame of the ambulance strikes and all the poor people who will suffer.' (girl, 12)
> 'Talking about the state of the country.' (girl, 12)
> 'Talking about Leeds getting beat 2—0 against West Bromwich Albion.' (boy, 11)
> 'Wars that are going on.' (girl, 10)
> 'A girl getting burned.' (girl, 9)

As in children's own reactions to the news, local events are important. But apart from some matters of sudden importance, like a football match, the general sense is of a vague opinion, a general attitude, far more potent for a potential dislike of trades unionism or political leaders than any bias in presentation. It is clear that children's awareness of parents' attitudes towards news stories depends on overhearing remarks rather than on any discussion. Rather than shared commentary the remarks that are made seem to be directed at no one in particular. This *can* mean that they have more force in the minds of children, since overheard remarks have more influence than any ratiocinative challenge.

Both the conditions of viewing and the generalised nature of remarks mean that attitudes are more clearly conveyed than opinions as such, apart from opinions about preferences. Children can take on the views of their parents without being aware of it. In fact many children seem to parody their parents in their attitudes towards television; saying, like most parents, that they are strict in their control of what others watch even if, like parents, they do not act on what they say. The same parents who complain in theory about what is shown on television do not necessarily notice the same content about which they complain (Shaw and Newell, 1972). Nevertheless it remains common to complain of violence, and to be censorious of others. In this, as in general attitudes, children seem very close to their parents. There is little evidence of any conflict between adults' and children's experience of television (Winick and Winick, 1979). The parents who complain about the kind of programmes being shown on television are often the ones that leave their television on all evening; this ambivalence between attitude and performance is also seen in children.

One of the most potent influences on attitude is that of overheard remarks, whether by parents or peers, since they come across with all the objectivity of a fact, and seem to have no designs on their (hidden) listener. Katz and Lazarsfeld (1955) demonstrated that television itself was not enough to cause changes in opinions but that, through a second layer of opinion (the 'gatekeeper') who would pass on a message, could make an influence through the dissemination of the idea it presented, through certain respected leaders in the community. They found that opinions taken from the mass media were only effective when subsequently repeated. In their 'Decatur' study they explored the important link between the mass media as conveyors of general opinion and the ways in which these opinions were confirmed through gossip. They went so far as to suggest that . . . 'Ostensibly individual opinions and attitudes . . . (are) primarily social (in) character' (p.63). It is not always apparent from where these opinions are derived but it is apparent that the overheard remarks about the news made by parents, and the success of television in creating general opinions, are connected. Opinion change does not depend on argument; indeed when people are aware of someone arguing against them they will be less willing to concur than when they cannot see the person with whom they are talking (Short et al. 1976). The less awareness the audience has of a source, and the less they feel challenged by it, the more likely it is that they will make it their own.

Katz and Lazarsfeld's 'two-step flow' theory (1957) rightly suggests the importance of the individual's opinions rather than the authority of television, but over-stresses the distinction between the two. The connection between the general influence of the medium and the supporting social influences is very close. General attitudes, and distinctions of preferences, are shared by both. Thus the family in watching television becomes a silent peer group in itself, involved individually in a collective emotional expectation. The pervasive emotional tone used by parents affects subsequent development more than the particular techniques of child-rearing or even the cohesiveness of the marital unit (Berelson and Steiner, 1964 etc.). The parents create an emotional tone in relation to television, and tend to reflect, as well as expect, that of television. In Newcomb's terms the 'laissez faire' tone predominates; into this lack of critical attention the 'soft-sell' approach is the one that is most easily accepted (Maccoby et al. 1954). Thus children's attitudes towards the news can be influenced by the reactions they see around them; their interest in the opinions of the news are not derived as much from the medium itself as from the remarks about it (Lazarsfeld et al. 1968).

If children's attitudes towards themes of great significance on the news are rather vague, their opinions about their favourite programmes, or pop stars, comedians or football teams are very crisp. Their assertions of taste seem at first to contrast with the prevailing emotional tenor of television, but in fact the assertions are stringent because they obviously do not, in themselves, matter. The facts presented by television can be used in a variety of ways, but these depend on the nature of the peer group and on the way they use these facts rather than on the ways in which they are presented. Children use the imagery of television in a variety of ways; that their games might include Daleks is not an influence in itself but a utilisation of readily presented images (Opie and Opie, 1964). Children will readily take on the persona of cricketers (cf. the old anecdotes of young boys pretending to be Victor Trumper) or generals (cf. the even more ancient personas of Wellington or Napoleon) as well as the characters of cowboys, and the heroes of thrillers. This might be termed the transfer of fantasy into real life but it is in fact a use of imagery as a normal part of play; not a direct effect on a pattern of modelling. Children can use the images (like that of Batman flying) in an autistic, destructive way just as they can use any example provided for them. But this rare state of psychology contrasts with the more casual use of images that children indulge in during their play. The fact that some lawyers blame television for the crimes of their juvenile clients can be likened to someone fifty years ago blaming radio as the source of criminal invention, or one hundred years ago citing a tract as the begetter of wickedness.

Although children share the same images, and allow their play to be interrupted by the scheduling of their favourite television shows, they gave no indication that they talk about television to their peers. Watching television might be a shared activity but it is a private pleasure. They will enthuse over their favourite programmes — 'It's great' — or their least favourite — 'It's rubbish' — but they do not talk about them, any more than they watch with critical attention. Just as the television seems to be a subtle presence, often ignored in the home, so the subject of television is a background to children's conversations with each other. To be in the 'know' about certain things is important to children as well as adolescents (Dembo and McCron, 1978), but television itself, while sometimes the subject of peer group attitude formation, is rarely the cause of it. Thus television plays a very subtle, as well as important, part in the relationship between children, each other and their parents. It does not dominate. It is not the cause of excitement or dialogues. It *can* be the cause of a quarrel if the participants so wish, but then anything can. For the most part television makes its effect by remaining in the background. Children *can* be taught to look critically at television by parents; their attitudes can be changed by the attention that parents pay them (Schneller, 1982), although direct efforts in training parents to control and limit children's television viewing may not be as effective as giving the parents more active things to *do* with the children (Singer and Singer, 1981). But generally very few parents bother, for they have the same lax interest in what television offers as their children.

16 The idea of the mass and the individual response

'We require instruction how to resist not merely that powerful combination, Big business plus copywriter, but also the more sinister allies of Big Business — the newspaper, the magazine, the film, the best-seller, even more subtle enemies of national decency and spiritual fineness than the advertiser . . .'   Q.D. Leavis *Scrutiny* 1932 (p.72)

Each individual is, in his own eyes, the one exception to the rule that most people are all the same; products of class, upbringing, schools or political systems which mould them into products like cars. The most long standing tradition in the discussion of the mass media is that they are all symbols of the decay of society; examples and producers of new generations of an anonymous populace. The definition of 'mass' man, manipulated and controlled, is closely linked with the study of the media as symbols of that 'mass'. The underlying assumption seems to be that children are readily corrupted by what they see on television, and that those who control television deliberately exploit this power to corrupt. The problem with many of these assumptions is that they do not actually address themselves to the way in which these 'effects' actually take place. This is not only because of the difficulty in exploring the nature of individual response, but because such general attitudes to the mass media are based on a circular argument that is rarely questioned by their protagonists. On the one hand is the rather unreflective assertion that the viewers (the critic himself apart) become what they see, that they reflect the standards presented to them. On the other hand is the proposal that the media merely reflect the vulgar tastes and expectations of the audience. With this circular argument the easiest way to enter is to find out whether there is a small group (like capitalists or politicians) deliberately exploiting the circumstances. In this chapter we will briefly explore the nature of such arguments and show how little they actually impinge on the nature of children's response, and then show how different is the common response to television from response to more literary media. The idea of 'mass' might be a useful concept, but it needs to be linked to the individual as well as to social forces.

The rise of technology and the change from an agrarian economy to one in which people's habits, and means of communication, have changed rapidly has frightened many. To some (T.S. Eliot, 1948; F.R. Leavis, 1933) it has meant the loss of the relationship between the individual and his 'tradition', between the creative talent and the culture from which it springs: 'That the power age destroyed the agricultual basis of life and thereby the best soil for a satisfactory civilisation should be a generalisation trite enough' (Thompson, 1933, p.2). To such a view the content as well as the amount of the new media, let alone television, is a sign of a decay in taste because of the audience's unwillingness to be imaginatively and intelligently engaged. The new technologies are themselves blamed for changes in values (Mumford, 1923; Whitehead, 1925; Chase, 1929), even if the loss felt is not that of 'high' culture restricted to an elite (Hoggart, 1957). The suspicion of new technologies when extended to television suggests that it is at once the cause and the symbol of the decline of quality. Lohisse (1968) argues that all the mass media are concerned with the ephemeral so that all experience to do with them is reduced to the same level of vulgarity. He draws what has become a common distinction between the artist, creating a work from his own inner needs for its own sake, and the communicator who has designs on the responses of the audience.

Many of these critics (Henry, 1972) see the products of television as axiomatic of an audience's tastes and habits of thought. The programming is felt to be itself a breakdown in cultural standards (Merton, 1957); content is seen in itself as a response of the audience. One problem with this analysis is that it leaves out the capacity of the audience to respond at different levels. We have seen how *capable* children can be of the most intelligent application. Another problem is the assumption that an audience is somehow moulded by what it sees, that even at a level of indifference, certain cultural stereotypes are imbibed. The very fact that programmes are approached with an eye only for entertainment is implied to be a kind of corruption, presumably as corrupting as the detective stories that W.B. Yeats read every night must have been for him. The real problem with the argument about culture is that it transfers the sense of the mass medium to the mass audience as if one were subsumed in the other. The term 'mass' has therefore been applied both to the type of technology (R. Williams, 1974) and to those groups that the technology impinges upon (Lohisse, 1973; Tarde, 1969). The audience is seen as an undifferentiated common average in contrast to the 'great cultures (which) have always been elite cultures' (Lohisse, 1973, p.34). The 'mass' is then taken to lack clear organisation (Blumler, 1966) and at the same time to have no belief in authority (Shils, 1959). Given such a view of the audience it is easy to see the media as reflecting their tastes: 'cultural products manufactured solely for a mass market' (Wilensky, 1966, p.295). It is also easy to see why a link is made with the analysis of the shift from the idea of 'gemeinschaft' to 'gesellschaft' (Weber, 1920) in which the rise of the population and larger groups automatically means greater anonymity and alienation from traditional culture. Ortega y Gasset's (1969) definition of the 'ideal mass man' being without individuality or personal integrity is then easily linked to the power of television over the masses, since the media are manipulators as well as expressers of general attitudes. Thus Marcuse (1964) talks of 'one-dimensional man' as a victim of both manipulation and repressive tolerance, clearly at the mercy of what Marcuse calls 'an omni-present system which swallows up or repulses all alternatives' (p.14).

This rather gloomy view of society suggests that people are almost infinitely malleable (cf. Brecht, 1970, p.369). Belief in the existence of 'mass man' then leads naturally to an interest in the institutions that control the media. Mannheim (1940) defines the mass in terms of institutions, as a replacement of communities by bureaucracy. The anonymous individual is seen as helpless or afraid to respond, as a small pawn in a theory of society. But somewhere in this picture of the mass there is the suggestion that a few exceptions, within institutions, are somehow in control. While society is 'formed' by the technologies of the media, and while society is reflected in the products of the media, the explanation of how this comes about requires some analysis of the relationship between social institutions and the means of communication they control. For this reason the sociological approach to the study of television has retreated from a study of the individual response to a study either of the stereotypes of content, or the analysis of institutions such as the BBC or IBA. Lewis (1978) in his summary of traditional sociological approaches points out the ease with which content analyses are carried out and how doubtful the hypothesis on which they rest. Halloran (1963) suggests that the 'sickness' of society expresses itself in the media, and that this is the fault of the socio-economic system which determines what the media will produce. The

144

belief in the power of television and other media, which is a common starting point for an attack upon the institutions that run them, is to some extent founded on a fear of propaganda:

> The experience of the propagandists of the First World War coupled with the ensuing reaction against the black art they perfected were among the profoundest influences on the men who came to lay the foundations of broadcasting . . .
>
> (Smith, 1973, p.692)

Thereafter, the uses made of the new technologies before and during the Second World War led to a greater fear of anyone who had control over them. The discussion therefore turned from that of 'effect' to the study of the structure of society in which people behave in terms of the 'generalised other', the image of what other people approve (Mendelsohn, 1964). Whether there is an image of a 'ruling class', or the dominance of multi-national companies, there is a sense in which television forms part of a system of communication that has potential to influence as well as entertain and in which the designs on the audience vary enormously. Cohen and Young (1973) describe both the mass manipulative model where the public weakly receives a message from a powerful source, and the commercial laissez faire model where the public is given what it wants. When Golding (1974) suggests that the influence of television is not through political manipulation as such, he goes on to say that ideological communication is still the most pervasive spread of influence through television. Thus the very fact that television does not change attitudes is seen as proof that television maintains and legitimises the class inequalities of society, or 'meaning systems' (Parkin, 1971). This assumption almost always leads back to the analysis of mass media 'as an industry and as social organisations' (Golding, 1974, p.8). Curran et al. (1977) recorded this shift in emphasis towards an analysis of mass institutions in terms of their class structure. Thus the concentration is on 'who' says what, and not on the consequences. In the analysis of large institutions we are constantly reminded of the general assumption about the importance of television's role in the fermentation of attitudes and beliefs. The hypothesis that content equals effect remains intact:

> '. . . an understanding of the way in which television structures and presents its picture of reality can go a long way towards helping us understand the way in which our society works' (Fiske and Hartley, 1978, p.17)

This might be true, but does not help us understand how children respond to television, what they expect from it and what they learn. The problem with all the analyses of society as seen through the content of television is that they assume that the complex nature of response can be ignored. The 'mass' are no longer individuals, or even a crowd, but an abstraction that reflects the picture of the world, no more than the smallest atom in a large structure.

The concept of 'mass' is useful in so far as it describes different levels of response. Lying within the concepts of cultural change and expectations we inevitably find questions of value and standard, different definitions of elitist or ethnocentric culture, but always the assumption that there *are* different kinds of response, emotional or intellectual, profound or superficial. Television is seen as the archetypal 'mass' medium, not only because of the amount of time spent in viewing or the size of the audience but because it shows a type of entertainment most associated with the 'masses'. This latter 'mass' is defined either in terms of class, groups or culture or in terms of the unthinking, manipulated helpless creatures losing their identity in the face of exploitation. But it would be more helpful to define 'mass' from the expectations and attitudes of the audience. 'Mass' can be defined by what an audience expects from a given source. The audience turns the medium into a 'mass' form of entertainment by its expectations. Just as there is a clear distinction to be made between an artefact which is designed to contain a collection of ideas, and one which is designed to cause certain reactions in the audience, so can an individual, by his response to an artefact, apply his ideas or merely seek a less demanding gratification. A response to any work can either be a definition of the work or a comment like 'it makes me feel good'. It is possible to pay close and intelligent attention to all kinds of programmes, to *Coronation Street* as well as to *Macbeth*. Just because the latter is shown on television does not turn into mass entertainment; nor does the general popularity of the former label each onlooker as merely one of the 'masses'. 'Mass' can be defined by what an audience expects from a given source. Thus it is possible for each individual to view television on a number of different levels. The content is important; but so is the response. Just as it is possible to have designs on an audience through immediate reactions, as in pornography, so it is possible for an audience to seek out such gratifications.

One of the interesting aspects of children's approach to television is that they do not have high expectations of what it offers. They do not associate it with the kinds of pleasure that come from reading, or with the levels of demand made by school. They show an indifference to the content as defined in terms of cultural stereotype, and instead seek gratification of an easier kind. It is quite clear that children bring to television, as to comics, a readiness to be pleased which contrasts strongly with their capacity to learn. The absence of expectations and the poverty of recall suggests a different level of mental activity that some critics find hard to accept. Thus children do not approach comics as a study of sociological forces or as an analysis of class systems, or even seeking examples of violence. The content as such never stands out; they do not notice all those signs of racism or class that critics tend to explore. Thus the level of reaction to television is one which does not bring cerebral capacities to bear.

It is easier to test a reader's response to a written text than a reaction to television, just as it is easier to carry out experiments in laboratories than to discover individual processes in the complexities of every day life. Virtually all the work that has been carried out trying to clarify the nature of response has been confined to what is sometimes termed the 'perfect reader'; alert, concentrated and unharmed by prior expectations or prejudices. This is itself perhaps a result of a view of humanity that makes a sharp division between the inarticulate reactions of the 'masses' and the abilities of the elite. In fact all responses are far more complex and of a different type than that displayed by the literary critics, able to extract meaning through a detailed repeated reading of the text. Since the work of I.A. Richards (1924) and taken more widely through the influences of Levi-Strauss (1963) and Barthes (1969) there has been an awareness of how arbitrary and ill-thought out are the approaches even of an educated reader. Gradually there is an awareness that apart from the critical study of the text there are a whole series of questions to be asked about the reader's response. Harless (1972) explored what he calls three cathexic types in adventure fiction, suggesting that readers seek to be provided with either entertainment, self identification or problem-solving. While he found that exposure to selected novels did not show any attitudinal changes, he did suggest the importance of identification with leading characters, an assumption often applied to television. His study suggested that different styles provide a range of different pleasures. Chatman (1971) had already suggested that different styles of writing would influence the reader in different ways, depending on the type of pleasure required or needed. Both suggested that books provided distinct gratifications at a level which contrasts to most television. Holland (1975) described four principles of style and the reader's involvement in which the reader had to balance inner drives and outer reality: ' . . . The fantasy is not "in" the work but in the reader, or still more accurately, in the creative relation between reader and work' (p.117). Thus the reader 'makes sense' of the text by transforming it according to his own character. Holland (1968) also suggested that unconscious fantasy is transformed into conscious meaning, taking the psycho-analytical point that art is a type of relief through the balance of disturbance with comfort. S.Lesser (1962) also relates the scrutiny of a text to psychological needs even if the appeal to the super-ego, the ego and the id are disguised or mixed up. Iser (1976) came to the conclusion that the 'asymmetry between text and reader stimulates a constitutive activity on the part of the reader' (p.169). In all these analyses of the individual's reaction it is assumed that the reader brings with him not only an 'imperfect' host of other associations but also a definite need for a level of psychological gratification.

Many analysts of reading have tended to concentrate on either the text or the reader. While the latter's reactions tend to be described in psychoanalytical terms, the former tends to be analysed in terms of different orders of signification, after Barthes (1969), creating generalised associations and cultural meanings (cf. Williams, 1980; Dyer, 1982). This leads attention back to an analysis of content in a culturally organised picture of reality, and away from personal involvement. While it is suggested that a closeness to the style of a text in terms of personal taste influences its persuasive effect (Sandell, 1977) it remains apparent that the two go so closely together that it is almost impossible to define one without the other. The problem in each case is that single items of content are taken for analysis; either one book or a series of signs of a certain type. If magazines contrast with books in their more varied form of presentation and expectation, television in its variety and amount contrasts even more strongly (cf. R. Williams, 1974). There are signs in reading theory of an awareness of the complex interaction between the text and the reader, a relationship between the style both of the medium and the onlooker (cf. Derrida, 1977) that both illuminates and contrasts with the different style involved in watching television (Baggeley and Duck, 1976). The problem is that there is a tendency to look at the text as a construct, partly because this, being static, is easier, and partly because it is assumed that the reader's close identification can be construed in the text he reads.

The complex nature of individual response should not be taken to imply that, like a critical reader, the television viewer will be paying a high level of attention. Even more than adults, and certainly without that ability to conform to set patterns of response, children bring with them different styles of attention, and quickly learn habits of expectation. Like adults they are able to approach texts with criticism, self-consciousness and preferences (Winkley, 1975), but they also tend to watch television with such a different range of reactions that their sense of criticism and interest is full of the power of associations as well as imaging. Thus they recognise what they expect, not in the need for psychological gratification but in a kind of fulfilment of abstract desires. The sense they make of the world through what they see on television is not the same as that presented to them. Many of the designs that producers have on them pass them by. In so far as children

148

reveal the same tastes as adults they are learning quickly to be part of the mass audience. The attitudes they learn about television are as important as what they see in the content itself. Their attitudes do not vary greatly from one programme to another. Children do not exhibit (as, perhaps towards a text) moments of studiousness, moments of compassion, of horror, of tenderness, followed by terror, or relief, as implied by the architectonic juxtapositions of the whole of an evening's entertainment. Such sustained objective attention is impossible in any circumstances (Spengemann, 1980), and television, unlike a book, is not in the control of the onlooker in terms of pace. Children therefore do not enter closely into the varying moods. If they were able to respond to the height of their sensitivity, entering or identifying with the world of comedy, the tragic passion of thrillers, sympathising with the problems of the news, involving themselves with the news readers, understanding and analysing the structures of tension and irony implicit even in children's programmes, then the idea of the importance of every stylistic detail of content and the changing presentation of the world would be as important as those items singled out for attention by the hermeneutic literary critic. The irony is that children's very inattention, their lack of application, whilst it makes them more typical of what is defined as 'mass man', makes them at the same time less likely to be the victims of simple 'effects'.

17 Images and associations

'He's bald, he sucks a lollipop and wears sunglasses and shoots people . . . he wears a hat . . . and says "Who loves ya baby." ' (boy, 8)

Some philosophers argue that it is impossible to describe any thoughts that are not expressed in words; others that no such thoughts exist. And yet it is clear that the mind is not always functioning at a level which gives rise to thoughts: it is equally clear that the mind does not react in terms of 'thoughts' to all the events around it. One of the reasons that children recall so little of what they have seen on television is that they are not applying that part of their minds that they would use to describe or analyse what they have seen. That they are capable of doing so if they wish is clear; but to make use of this capacity they need to approach programmes with a particular intention. For most of the time children view television with not only an indifference to the meanings or possible meanings being offered, but a palpable resentment that there should be even a hint that they should need to derive significant meanings. As in those tracts of boredom associated with daydreams, some forms of repetitive play, reading comics or watching television, children let their minds wander in ways that are hard to describe and harder to test. It is as if their minds were functioning on a different level, below a trapdoor of language, which, when language attempts to describe it, transforms the nature of what is being described. And yet it is clear, not only in the exploration of alpha waves, or other modes of consciousness, or even in the hints that there are different styles of learning (Pask, 1975; Hudson, 1968), that a great deal of cerebral activity takes place all the time, and that there are different levels of response.

Unless a different kind of reaction is deliberately aroused, television evokes responses at a level other than that of conscious, verbal attention. The problem is that it is easier to realise the existence of such response (Baggeley and Duck, 1976) than to reveal it, although in some of the work on the complexities of the human mind there are enough hints to show something of what is going on in the act of watching television, an act both typical of those states of mind when the brain is ostensibly 'resting' and dependent on the recognition of what has been already seen. For reasons both obvious and obscure there has been comparatively little research interest shown in the ways in which children learn, whether from television, books or teachers. It is as if the most crucial facts about development were ignored because they were too difficult to test, or did not fit into readily available hypotheses. Yet much more of a child's experience is taken up with time spent not in concentration but in a more vague reflection, in day dreams or in the conjuring up of images. Television, in its presentation of a moving image, a controlled picture of the world, as well as in its tone, provides the material for such a state of response; not material for a subsequent state, but the state itself.

One of the crucial differences between the act of reading and the response to television is that one demands some form of control, or perpetual concentration; and the other can be watched without any real application of the mind. Once the patterning of the television screen can be focused upon, and the types of images understood, the screen provides, in curiously attenuated form, a parody of the real world, at least one version of what is otherwise easily recognised. The fact that a child recognises images sooner than reads words implies that one act is more 'primitive' than the other, but this earlier ability remains intact even when children learn the cognitive perspectives of interpreting significant clues while ignoring all those that obscure the central messages. Thus a child learns how to focus on an image or a voice, rather than hearing or seeing all the background sounds or images. But the background remains, and it is this that television continues to provide. What Bartlett (1932, p. 225) called 'image forming' is not just a preliminary stage towards fully conscious thinking, but an alternative or substitute, a continuing activity within which verbal reasoning is contained. Familiar images and the associations they evoke create the kind of mood that subsumes all the differences between programmes on the television screen. It is as if content and context were so closely intertwined that children find them almost impossible to distinguish. This is why there is such consistency in their tastes, their expectations and their recall.

Children's response to television should be understood not in terms of verbal processing, as in an experiment, but in terms of imaging and associating. The style of television, with its mixture of auditory and visual clues, with familiar verbal gimmicks juxtaposed to familiar images, creates a complex stimulation. While it is tempting to think that it can be likened to static pictures (Swartz, 1978: McCombs, 1966) or to a verbal message in traditional information processing terms (Tulving, 1962), the actual combination makes the effect more complex since it is difficult to ascertain which elements are important and which are incidental. Through the process of recognition children become familiar with images that are perceived as static, like the face of the hero, or which become a ritual series of actions, like a car chase, a slow-motion replay or a 'bionic' jump. The context in which these actions or images takes place, whether a panel game, thriller or situation comedy, is as important as the actions themselves; their interpretation depends upon the routine of the general conditions (cf. Hilgard, 1964). It is the 'incidental' information that is as important as anything else. Children look for expected clues, even if these are different from the designs that producers or critics would have on them. Children therefore do not readily discriminate between the trivial and the serious. In so far as they have a set pattern of expectation they prefer the information not to have serious intent, but in fact their readiness to see certain images means that all the different programmes presented to them offer some details that will attract their attention and many details that are of no particular interest. Like the Africans who surprised the producers by seeing as most significant a detail that had escaped the maker's attention, so children often picked up the unexpected clue, finding it fitting with the other associations in their mind. This is why there seems to be little outer logic to some of the statements that they make. Television is therefore both a distraction and a provider of material for distraction.

Some of the clues to the different levels of response to television can be found in the literature on imaging. Horowitz (1978) has pointed out the many types of imaging that can take place, from those categorised by context to those categorised by interactions with perceptions. Since Paivio's experiments (1970), the ability to image has been linked with the ability to recall, although it seems that the type of recall evoked by either is different. As children become more aware of the images, their ability to bring them to mind depends upon recognition. Tversky (1969) showed that subjects' ability to record stimuli in pictorial terms depended upon their awareness of what they were expected to do with the information. Just as children know that they are expected to verbalise for a comprehension test, so they realise that the images on television are there to provide a familiar context for the next appearance of the same programme rather than an event beyond the confines of the television experience. Most of the images are not consciously used. Horowitz (1978) wrote that 'Unbidden images are, first and foremost, a failure in repression. Usually dominant inhibitory influences over image formation give way to suddenly stronger facilitory influences . . .' (p.192). This level of imaging is one that *can* be controlled by verbal demands, but nevertheless has a close connection to the idiosyncratic associations of the individual child. The television pictures themselves are like unbidden images. This state of response is generally most associated with childhood − 'Children . . . think in simpler, more concrete, and more iconic forms . . . (Horowitz, 1978, p.34) − but this might just as well be so because adults learn how to disguise their imaging, and become adept not at suppressing the images but in explaining in such terms as if they were always thinking through verbal reasoning. The ability to communicate sometimes consumes all the matters that are communicated. From Bartlett's (1932) discussion of 'image forming' to Bruner's (1974) exploration of 'iconic' thinking, imaging has been taken as a preliminary stage towards fully 'conscious' thinking. It seems more likely, however, that this is said because children disguise it less well. Television shows, in its reliance not on verbal reasoning or analysis but on the power of familiar imaging, that response at an iconic level can continue. Horowitz (1978) has demonstrated that the tendency to see in images develops through different phases and is never ousted by dependence on lexical signification (p.78).

Imaging is part of a level of response less demanding than ratiocination. Children find it easier to retain the complex visual stimuli with all the perceptual details than remember simple verbal descriptions (Horowitz, Lampel and Takanishi, 1969). To explain such retention is more difficult. Paivio (1971) demonstrated that even words evoke images, and suggested that the two go so closely together that it is impossible to divide long-term memory into visual and linguistic systems. For visual material is not only recognised but also more easily retained, like the look of a face (Sperling, 1963). Even when attention is not being particularly applied, physical clues can be retained when semantic ones are not (Darwin, Turvey and Crowder, 1972). Thus children retain many of the images they see on television while much of the information is mentally ignored; they recognise patterns of familiar imagery. As children become older they learn to ignore part of their perceptual experience for the sake of focusing on what they expect (Gregory, 1966). This is another reason that children's answers about what they have seen on television are so laconic. It is not just the amount from which they have to choose what to recall, but the fact that it is the most salient images (the looks or behaviour of the hero; the style of the newsreader) that stay most readily in the mind.

Children's ability to recognise the essential imagery of television is not the same as their ability to image by themselves. The associations of what they see on television do not necessarily connect with other unrelated circumstances; each image tends to be associated with another. Just as when a new word shares any features with a word previously presented, people assume that they have heard that word before (Anisfeld and Knapp, 1968) so children learn the salient features of a programme through a familiarity that links a series of related features. Tversky and Kahneman (1973) found that any possible associations, whether conceptual or phonetic (let alone imaged) made information better remembered than before. In this sense the catch-phrase of Kojak becomes a type of 'imagery'. It is as if the familiar associations in a series were a part of state-dependent memory (see Kleinsmith and Kaplan, 1963). Children perceive more of the essential details when they are 'attuned' to the circumstances (Goodwin et al. 1969). The ability to associate with a series of expected images is an important part of children's experience of television. The personal associations — what Schramm (1963) defined as 'connotive' meanings as opposed to 'denotive' meanings — create an accumulation of expectations in the audience. These are not associations unique to each individual but a series of images that become an expected ritual of style and tone. The 'stereotypes' of television are not perceived as definitions of sex or race or money, but as people who will fulfil a role, who will perform in an expected way. The recognition factors of popular series lie in their performances rather than the sex of the eponymous heroes. The distinction between analysis and associations are clear, even in the act of reading, let alone watching television: 'The associative reader is, however, particularly liable to distort by amplification, to interpret too impulsively — a habit which inevitably leads away from accurate reading' (Winkley, 1975, p.289). In the case of television the associations are often bound up purely in the nature of the programmes; they do not necessarily enter into the private individual worlds of children. When children make use of the images that they see on television they are invoking a level of fantasy that has little to do with that of watching television.

Wright and Huston (1981) suggest that children's understanding of television depends on their growing independence from its sensory demands, and a growing familiarity with the features of production, but they are referring to the testable understanding, the ability to analyse. As they also recognise, children's attention is influenced by associations with content. What is clear in all the literature on children's early learning patterns is the importance of the way they learn to narrow their perceptions to the task in hand, to concentrate in the formal sense. It is equally clear that television does not evoke such a response. When looked at from the perspective of formal demands, analysis of production features or the testability of salient information, it is easy to suppose that children only gradually learn to apply their minds to television. In fact children learn to adapt to the perceived demands of television. They continue to allow a level of attention to associations and familiar images that contrasts sharply with the 'rules' of cognitive mental development. It is for this reason that it is surprising how often Piaget's theories of child development are invoked to support the producers of children's programmes (Lesser, 1977), since his theories are so strongly cognitive (Rotman, 1977), as if children were really moving from one mental level to another. Piaget himself acknowledged the existence of subconscious as well as conscious thoughts (1923), although he assumed that such 'autistic' levels of mind were soon left aside when children had the capacity to go further. Television however does not evoke nor demand that kind of response of which children are capable.

What children perceive is in part determined by their needs, attitudes and individual habit systems (Bruner and Postman, 1947). Their attitudes are not based on a structure of organised ideas but on a number of personal associations (Fitzgerald and Ausubel, 1963), and on different levels of involvement that include, but are not exclusively based on, conscious personal references. Krugman (1966, p.584) defines involvement as the connection between the content of the stimulus and the content of personal life; this is defined in contrast to the lack of personal involvement provided by television. Far from creating a series of models to imitate, television, despite its power to create images and to allow associations, does not create a powerful mark through connections of a personal kind. It is, indeed, because the television images have ostensibly so little to do with personal associations that they become part of the pattern of children's experience. If television images did connect to more private matters the levels of response would be far greater. It is as if television creates its own world of images, as if it were a purer picture of itself rather than a mirror of the world. Naturally the facts that are being portrayed are sometimes more important than the medium through which they are presented, as in the case of a public event like a football match, but for most of the time it is the image of the medium itself that prevails. It is significant that the most passion is aroused by an event like a football match, in contrast to popular drama series. The more obviously designed for television, the less the arousal. Far from being caught up in a crisis of identification with the heroes, children see them as images of the programme.

The blending of word and image is far easier for the audience than a concentration on either one or the other, just as the richer the colour the more arousal of pleasure (Klapper, 1960). Experiments on synaesthesis (Vernon, 1962 etc.) have shown how the ease of response that derives from the blends of stimuli causes less sharp attention. Although children take some time to 'tune in' to the action and colour of cartoons, (Zieler and Kelly, 1969) the mixture of fast movement, repetition of imagery and juxtapositions of colour constitute the simplest, most basic pleasures of the medium (cf. Winick, 1973; Gregory, 1966, 1970). Thus the specific stimuli become more important than the concepts they are supposed to convey. Ausubel (1968) makes a distinction between 'correlative' and 'derivative' learning; the former defining the transference of a rule or concept from one situation to another, and the latter bound up in specific details. On television the types of structures that children see, in the images of *Dr Who* or the *Bionic Woman*, are not concepts but familiar repeated stimuli. What is learned is not 'processed' through the conscious and deliberate transformation of information. Thus chance associations set up a pattern of expectations from the medium itself. James (1890) made the distinction between voluntary and involuntary attention; one resulting in the deliberate storing of ideas, remembered over long intervals, and the other holding on to information until attention is directed towards it (cf. Underwood, 1976). In terms of television the distinction is crucial.

18 The subliminal world of television

'When I grow up I want to be a coach driver and a commando'. (boy, 8)

The subliminal is always with us. While conscious of particular events, although choosing to pay attention to distinct ideas, we are nevertheless always affected by and responding to a range of stimuli of which we are not aware. Nowhere is this subconscious response, beneath the level of close attention and conscious recall, more apparent than in the images of television. The type of gratification which is sought itself suggests an open-ness to the subliminal that makes such influences 'normal' rather than unusual. Nevertheless the subliminal has normally been associated with the fear of deliberate, underhand, manipulation. Arising from the realisation that the masses could be manipulated and from a growing knowledge of the powers of mass hysteria, together with an awareness of this peculiarly visual and exciting manifestation of television, the fear of subliminal effects on film and television was at one time the subject of the greatest attention. Later, despite the realisation that advertising depends for its success on subconscious responses, this concern was replaced by the more simple assumption that viewers would imitate violence, and little recent work has been done on the question of the subliminal. But a concern with the subliminal was dropped not only through a change in fashion but because it was too closely tied to the case of deliberate manipulation, with the intentions of the film-maker rather than with the reactions of the audience. The traditional example of the subliminal was that of the single frame shot of an arid desert followed by a single frame shot of delicious, cool, Coca Cola, too short in exposure to be consciously perceived, embedded in the 'B' movie, before the break, so that the audience would dutifully queue to buy some of the suggested drink. But that kind of subconscious suggestion was also easy to control and legislate against. The point having been established that the audience did respond to subliminal images, the point was also lost sight of, since the banning of such techniques was itself supposed to be enough of an answer.

Nevertheless such subliminal responses continue, even when there are no such simplistic uses of the device as that of creating a desire for Coca Cola. The fact that no-one is deliberately setting out to make an audience react in a certain way does not imply that the audience does not respond at that level. Besides, the case of advertising, with its stereotyped associations and the 'trigger' images, remains an equivocal reminder of unbidden images. Advertisers do not seek to make their audiences react in a cognitive way; the types of learning they evoke are of a far different kind (Krugman, 1965, etc,). The associations that are manifested in advertisements — either a product linked with sexual success, or a brand name tied to an explicit need — are also less self-consciously evoked in other programmes which make use of recognisable patterns.   Material is learned in conditions of involuntary as well as voluntary attention (Festinger and Maccoby, 1964; Maccoby and Hagen, 1965, etc,). Children demonstrate that secondary attention is most appropriate to the conditions of television. This might imply that they are the more vulnerable to the influence of the programme, but these influences are themselves complex and contradictory as well as only being structured in the minds of the onlookers. Given the terms in which television presents itself, the associations made are necessarily idiosyncratic. It is not that we do not' know what kind of subliminal effects take place but that each range of personal images on which children might base attitudes are too individual to delineate. Nevertheless, there are clear indications that children accept certain patterns of television entertainment, and that they react at levels of response which are, for the most part, nearer the idea of the subliminal than anything else.

Even in the Pavlovian tradition there is an awareness (Sokolov, 1963) of the importance of, as well as difficulty in, understanding where the threshold between conscious and subconscious sensitivity lies. The question of subliminal stimuli heightens this difficulty in establishing abnormal, obviously propagandist or clearly threatening in subconscious influences. Even repetition is itself a way of invoking secondary responses, whether defined as sub- or supra-liminal. There is no doubt about the effectiveness of subliminal messages. Zuckerman (1960) showed a picture from which he wanted subjects to write a story he also imposed a subliminal message — 'Don't write' or 'Write more', and subjects did as they were told. Berelson and Steiner (1964) showed that hypnotic trances could be induced by mechanical stimuli alone, like the repetitive fascination of a piece of machinery or the gentle monotony of television images. The power of emotional reactions over cognitive ones was demonstrated by McGinnies (1949) using galvanic skin responses. But the most important fact about subliminal techniques is that they rely on visual rather than verbal elements. Reactive processes associated with verbal information processing can contrast at the same moment with unprocessed responses to visual techniques. This does not mean that all verbal material is processed consciously; the repetition of a slogan or catchphrase can be imbibed without being constantly reinterpreted.

Visual messages, or any repeated messages, whether presented subliminally or not, can be taken subliminally. Subliminal response depends not on the fact that a stimulus cannot be seen but on the fact that a subject is unaware of it. The subliminal really refers to effects that cannot be verbally defined and recorded. When Lazarus and McCreary (1951) through their use of Galvanic Skin Response explored sub-conscious non-verbal discrimination they discovered how many responses were half-consciously made, a response they called 'subception'. Krugman and Hartley (1970) through their experiments on responses to advertisements demonstrated the close connection between subliminal perception and passively learned material. Festinger and Maccoby (1964) showed how easily subjects could be manipulated if their attention was sufficiently distracted, not manipulated to change their minds but to want more of those things of which they already approved. Hovland et al. (1953, 1955) found that those who were distracted were far less willing to change their minds from a particular prejudice, as if their basic 'set' meant that they were deeply inoculated against any change of mind. Thus subliminal effects do not change minds even if there is an intention to do so; the suggestion to buy a brand of drinks or to respond to an advertisement must connect to an already established knowledge or opinion. Vernon sums up this phenomenon: 'A response made to a subliminal stimulus must be based upon some old and well-established association; it would not occur if the associations were weak and temporary' (p.186). Thus even subliminal influences tend to bolster the established prejudices about television; much of the hidden message of television is an advertisement for itself.

Television's establishment in the minds of children as an easy form of entertainment without demands is bolstered by all the obvious self-advertisements but also by more hidden asssumptions in the presentation of programmes. Programmes designed to be easily forgotten are part of a daily routine and are viewed in a state that Robinson (1969) calls secondary viewing. For this reason some commentators have con-cluded that one of the main effects of television is passivity (Freedman, 1961). This arises as an extension of Himmelweit's (1958) discussion about children's jaded palates. Yet 'passivity' is so much the natural style of viewing, given the amount that is seen, that the surfeit of entertainment and boredom are not a result but an integral part of the nature of television viewing. Passivity is not just a subsequent state, due to having been too engorged by the rich feasts of programmes. Children do not become jaded as a result of too much stimulation; but through too little. They watch television indifferent to the fact that television offers little stimulation. They pick out the selected images from which they can make sense of what they see, in what Hale calls 'incidental learning'. Children remember idiosyncratic points; and accept certain factors of recognition. Even under test conditions, with fore-warning, the 'major' points of a programme are not better under-stood than the peripheral (Belson, 1967). James (1890) again made the crucial point long before the advent for television: 'There is no such thing as voluntary attention sustained for more than a few seconds at a time' (p.416). This is why many of the main points are not taken in, and why, the images passing so fast, there is not a great chance to return to them to re-organise the information. This is one reason why television is not a particularly successful medium of instruction. Ease of viewing, as in ease of reading, depends on the number of items that are redundant, that can be ignored. Children soon become accustomed to picking up minimal clues, disliking programmes which reveal an imbalance of material due to the crowding of too many salient points. Children become receptive to the style of television (cf. Posner, 1969) and dislike any dissonance. Festinger's (1957) theory of cognitive dissonance is applied to conscious adaptations; the dislike of material that does not fit into a set norm. But it applies even more strongly to involuntary subconscious attention. It is at a subliminal level that children wish to make all the gestures of television fit one pattern.

The 'passivity' of the viewing experience is one sign of the mind not readily troubled; it contrasts with the passivity which is supposed to be aroused by poverty. The passivity of television is not that defined by Henry (1972), Bailyn (1959) or Schramm et al. (1961), or that denied by Klapper (1960) or Himmelweit et al. (1958), for they all talk of high emotional arousals. Instead the passivity of television is part of the viewing process, rather than a separate subsequent state (Furu, 1971). Fisher and Bruss (1976) found that viewing actually promotes perceptual passivity. Attitudes are therefore closely linked to the state of viewing, since children learn to take in only some of the details, and are as likely to ignore the central messages as the dis-tractions. For as Broadbent (1958) demonstrated: 'An increase in the amount of information presented will not produce a corresponding increase in the amount of information assimilated' (p.78). On the contrary; the habit of ignoring information spreads. The more that children watch the less they recall; they learn to watch without attention, and as they become older are the more able to pass by the details in the overall experience. Children learn through television to limit themselves to the incidental as well as the expected. Sonnenschein (1982) found that more material than strictly necessary (a normal state for popular programmes) had a debilitating effect on younger children. Anderson (1980) found that pre-school children did not absorb material to which they were supposed to pay attention any better than all the distractions.

The images and clichés of television convey certain assumptions, but these are not consciously exploited by those on television; influence is accidental and arbitrary. Those who fear that the control of television lies in the hands of the far right or far left might suggest that the very conservatism or self-absorption of television is itself a political effect. But we know that propaganda which draws attention to itself is reacted against; we also know that the only way to convey an opinion is to allow it to be received in the way of an overheard remark. Yet there is no way of knowing which piece of television will be absorbed in this way. More important than the confirmation of prejudices or opinions is the style with which such things are expressed. Hovland and Weiss (1951) first analysed the 'sleeper' effect, the idea remembered long after the source is forgotten. More important in terms of television is the tone with which the more arbitrary opinions about taste, given lightly and disingenuously, are more easily accepted than the harder edged opinions of politicians or documentaries. Television conveys within its main frame a suggestion that all ideas are matters of personal prejudice, not to be taken too seriously. Contained within the clear framework is the picture of individuals suggesting either that what they say is important to other people, or important to themselves. It is the latter, the more personal matters of taste that are listened to as if they were overheard remarks that do not have designs on the audience. It is because they are trivial, and because they are picked up in a casual way, that they are the more effective. Thus the conservative campaign of 1983 provided what the television companies called 'funnies' — shots of Mrs Thatcher doing things rather than talking — a deliberate use of the familiarisation of television, that makes the audience and the compère into an 'in' group. The importance of the overheard remark, however trivial its substance, is clear when it is connected to the authority conveyed by being in a particular group. The 'two-step' flow of opinion depends on the power of group status where an opinion, for example about the ephemeral tastes of pop music, becomes powerful as a sharing of subconscious assumptions (Dembo and McCron, 1978). Thus even groups share undefined attitudes operating at a level that is not aware of itself. Attitudes are received as subconsciously as the words of pop music are learned; pre-adolescents and adolescents who know the music well, and who can mouth the words, have little or no idea of what the words mean (Robinson and Hirsch, 1969).

The connection between the subliminal and the influence of shared attitudes on groups is an important one as it reminds us that the subliminal is not a completely separate world, but one which is part of a normal series of responses that people make to different events. Much more takes place even within relationships at a level which is not the subject of close attention than those conscious judgements which can both distance the object of attention, and make the response self-conscious. The relationship of the individual to television is not unlike that of his relationship to other people; informed by tone as much as by opinion. Thus there is no complete contrast between the world of television and the world elsewhere; television is not an escape from the 'real' world. The fact that it does not challenge, and is generally received in an undemanding way, does not mean that it is sought as a cathartic refuge, that children are looking for fantasy as a kind of relief. Although there was an assumption for many years that escapist materials are more likely to be popular with children who are frustrated (Riley and Riley, 1951), these findings have been disproved (Noble, 1975). Such a level of catharsis suggests involvement and emotional commitment almost wholly lacking in children's reactions to television. While early researchers assumed that those people who spent a large proportion of their time watching television were the lonely and unsatisfied, there is no evidence to support the suggestion that the 'alienated' seek relief in television. This is because such levels of alienation are linked closely to other factors such as poverty. Thus the level at which television enters the subconscious is not as an alternative highly charged emotional or intellectual world. Its influence lies directly in the absences; the absence of challenge, or emotional commitment.

The subliminal is therefore part of the everyday response to television; unbidden images create their own idiosyncratic messages, many of which reiterate the state of pleasure that suggests that watching television is its own record. The temporary nature of the dominance of 'drive', deliberate motivation, over 'habit' (Hebb, 1955 etc.) underlies the importance of long-term attitudes that arise from a series of personal associations; not only personal constructs but a way of approaching new stimuli according to the levels of demand they are supposed to be making. Differences between intentional and incidental learning depend, after all, on the way in which the stimulus is

162

approached rather than the stimulus itself (Elias and Perfetti, 1973). But the relationship between the two is very close; West (1975) quotes from a scriptwriter of soap operas who points out the need to start any item through the trivial since he recognises that serious issues can only be dealt with as an outcome of gossip. When children read their own sub-conscious maps of television they are becoming attuned to a series of expectations between the audience and the programmes. They can break out of this reading if they wish but just as concepts free the individual from control by specific stimuli (Gagne, 1965) so the concept that children bring can be one which allows the various underlying images to have free play; the gesture or the action becoming more important than their analysis of it, hence the lack of recall. When Vernon (1962) describes subliminal response as dependent on well-established associations these associations become so through repetition. Subliminal responses, therefore, are not so much a threat, a deliberate manipulation, but an everyday occurrence. Just as, when watching a programme on television, such as a game of football, the background, such as the advertising boards are the more clearly reflected in the nearby window than on the screen, so the subliminal images of television are only seen by chance, reflected elsewhere.

19 The development of children's responses

' The thing that most interests me (being frank) is cigarettes, money, drink and lads. They are the only pleasures in life to me.' (girl, 14)

The similarity of children's responses to television is more surprising and more significant than the differences. Across a wide range of backgrounds and cultures, facing a great variety of types of programmes and in conditions that contrast with each other, children show consistent attitudes towards television. That they also show individuality and that they are each capable of idiosyncratic judgements is quite clear. Underlying their differences is a general, shared attitude that marks out, and informs, all their television viewing. Whether they are of different classes or race, or different countries, of different religions or different ethnic cultures, this seems less significant than the similarities that join them in their approaches to television. It is always tempting to explore differences between types of child in relation to various stimuli since it is easier than exploring that uncharted territory of ways in which children learn. It is also tempting, because easier, to try to analyse differences of age or sex than the underlying attitudes that human beings hide as well as express. But the nature of response itself, across a wide variety of circumstances, is the ground rule on which differences must be based. Much of the literature on children and television is spoiled by its underlying assumption that children are, unlike adults, unsophisticated in their response to television and capable of understanding what goes on. The work of Piaget is often used as a prop to hold up theories of differences in which the young children are held up to the limitations of autism, unthinking and naive, and the adults, like the theorist himself, had the sophistication to understand everything that is going on. But much conscious cerebration ignores the complex nature of learning, both in children and adults. It is clear that the capacity of children to learn is as great as the adult's capacity to avoid using this capacity. When it comes to television the distinctions between children's and adults' responses are not that great, and therefore the more instructive.

Children learn to adapt to television in an 'adult' way surprisingly young. Their sophisticated absence from intense response and their clear expectations of entertainment parody their elders in taste as well as in their moral strictures about what they would not let their younger siblings see. They also show, nevertheless, that there are changes through which they go in their adaptation to television. While the charge that very young children respond to television in an imitative manner (Bever, 1975; Helitzer and Heyel, 1970) are not borne out, younger children do appear to have a more earnest attitude to television, a greater capacity to take seriously what they see. Older children are able to disregard non-essential features more easily than younger ones (Hale et al. 1968) but what they regard as 'non-essential' can mean serious messages rather than interesting imagery. Younger children certainly recall more, paying closer attention. Until the age of eight they do not exhibit so markedly that clearly expressed taste for entertainment that afterwards pervades their responses. Younger children from the age of six to nine recall much more clearly than older children. This correlates with the fact that they watch rather less. The more that is watched, the less closely it appears to be watched, whether the growing inability to recollect what has been seen is due to the amount that is watched, or (a closely connected fact) due to the way in which large amounts of television are watched. Even from the age of eight to thirteen there are parallel changes in the inability to recall (despite the growing capacity to do so) and the greater insouciance with which increasing numbers of programmes are watched.

There are some differences in taste between younger and older children. Only after the age of eight is a preference for adult thrillers over children's programmes confirmed. Younger children have a particular liking for cartoons, perhaps because of the high levels of frenetic action (Zeiler and Kelly, 1969) as if the essential ingredients of television were reduced to their simplest form. As children become older this preference is replaced by an interest in other forms of comedy with less obvious visual impact. Cartoons are obviously fantastic; situation comedies less so. When children learn to appreciate the latter they are more aware of the element of fantasy in all programmes and the more inclined to turn to television for these elements, since they are what make the medium so rich in entertainment. Younger children are also more inclined to enjoy the 'realistic' children's programmes such as *Blue Peter*, and to take seriously what is offered them. This seriousness of approach also manifests itself in the way in which younger children (up to the age of eight) approach films about war or horror. They are the only ones who think that horror programmes are anything to object to, and tend to be suspicious of them as they are of the news and documentaries. Older children continue to dislike documentaries but take horror films less seriously. This fascination with what is horrible includes, as it might with adults, an element of bravado, of deliberately mutilating sensitive reactions, but even if such taste is itself a curious symptom, it is not a sign of imitation, or the sense that the real world is being mirrored. By the age of eight most children have extensive experience of late night viewing; very few have not seen at least two horror movies. But the connection between late night viewing from 9.30p.m. (viewing until 9.30 is too regular to be called late in this context) and children's taste in gore is less and less important since the rise of the video means that children can at any time watch horror films that are too violent to be broadcast. But this is a new phenomenon, not yet explored.

The capacity of children to remember more, and recall more clearly, as they get older is established; but this capacity is less and less exploited. The fact that younger children up to seven and eight pay closer attention, at least for shorter periods, is substantiated by the fact that their ability to recall more than a rudimentary item or label is far greater. Partly a reflection of their capacity to bring single images to mind, and a sign of a more complex response, younger children show that they bear in mind at least the main outline of imagery. The very youngest of five and six remember images even if they have not understood the arguments or the plot. They receive and recall a few important impressions while older children learn to accept images as part of a more general whole. Younger children remember especially those static images exploited in *Dr Who;* older ones the images that are the recognition factors that appear from programme to programme, whether as a prop, a gesture or even an item of clothing. When they attempt to recall what they have seen the previous night younger children do much better; as the capacity increases so does the diminution in what is recalled. Older children are not so impressed by what they have seen. Only when they are prepared beforehand to talk about what they have seen, especially with friends, will their performance match their capacity.

The crucial shift in attitude towards television to a more detached, sophisticated indifference to content appears to take place around the age of eight. In younger children both the images and the ideas appear more important, although they also like the knockabout actions of cartoons. As the ability to image declines (Richardson, 1969) and children rely on more analytical responses at school and learn to link themselves to what is expected of them, so television enters a domain that is otherwise less consciously applied. It becomes part of the subconscious background to other events. Younger children reveal the power of images and associations more clearly; the fact that older children cover it up with a greater indifference does not mean that such techniques of learning do not continue to take place. Younger children are better at 'reconstructing' the material they have seen. As they become older the ability to anticipate images, to know what is expected, to be less surprised, shows a gradual adaptation to a medium in which few startling events will appear, in which little will disturb the expectations. Younger children therefore recall certain moments like a shot girl or a shot teddy-bear; and older children those signs of recognisability that are popular television's equivalent of associations.

Part of the clear expectations of programmes lies in the 'stars' and the gestures that distinguish them. To older children these stars are a part of the pattern; younger children see them more readily as separable from the programmes in which they appear. Thus younger children appreciate their favourite personalities for being 'nice' and 'kind'. But as older children understand more clearly the part that their favourites are paid to perform, so they understand the distinction between the part and the man. They are more likely to appreciate the 'acting ability' of stars, or the 'good looks'. But at the same time that children learn to see the actors as such so they appear to take them less rather than more seriously. The tendency to dislike characters as 'real' as politicians is reflected in the fact that older children become more and more dismissive of various personalities; 'idiot' is a favourite phrase, even when used with some measure of ironic affection. But just as children dislike those personalities that make demands on them so they have a growing tendency to like those who are amusing, or 'funny'. Older children learn to acquire a taste for 'stand-up' comedians rather than cartoons. 'Nice' characteristics are replaced by those which are amusing. When younger children cite their favourite characters they include a description of their looks, together with the fact that they are caught up in actions, either good or adventurous. Older children have a more cynical air. They admire the ability to do 'fights' or 'stunts'. Younger children therefore appreciate more the 'looks' or the 'kindness'; older children appreciate the entertainment that the characters can offer them, showing a shift of emphasis from closeness of attention to content, to the pleasure in its effect.

The greater involvement that younger children show is also manifested in their approach to favourite single programmes when they are more likely to mention something specific, rather than a series. Their recognition of the significant image can include those that are not repeated. This is one reason why *Blue Peter* is still quite liked by younger children; a programme about animals, or a hobby or a charity can still make a singular impression. As they get to the age of eight children's tastes switch to more adult programmes, when they learn to appreciate the expected and the familiar. It is hard to have a 'pragmatic' reason for liking thrillers. Despite their general taste, however, it is possible for older children to be surprised into taking one-off items seriously; such as a story on *Nationwide*. But generally children are well-wadded with a layer of indifference, and far from panting with the emotional excitement that would be demanded if they took what they saw seriously, they learn to look with a more jaundiced eye. Although younger children are more likely to be scared by a programme they soon learn to adapt to the fact that the violence they see is for the most part only a series of pictures in which the most life-like are merely the most carefully and cleverly rehearsed. Being 'scared' therefore becomes a kind of thrill; although older children show a clear awareness of times when they have been scared, they also show a greater taste to have such a threat repeated.

Perhaps the clearest example of children's increasing sophistication towards television is their growing disbelief in advertisements, coupled with their growing pleasure in them. Younger children say more readily that they believe their favourite advertisements, since, like the Advertising Standards Authority, they assume that what is stated must be true, 'truth' being the mere existence of the product and its availability, and not the semiotic implications of the language or imagery. Younger children make more of the link between the product and the advertisement (like the link between the hero and the programme) and often cite the product as a reason for liking the advertisement. Younger children not only suggest that the advertisement is to promote the existence of a product rather than its quality but like advertisements which deal with a version of the real world rather than ones which deal with make-believe. As children become older the distance between the 'message' and the entertainment becomes greater until they look on an advertisement as a programme to be enjoyed under similar conditions as the rest of television: songs, humour, gimmicks and stunts, and all that is easily recognisable. By the time children are twelve only 15 per cent show any interest in the product depicted, whatever their buying habits, even while they enjoy the presentation. This liking is not, however, characterised by great enthusiasm. As children learn to appreciate what television offers so they link it increasingly to being bored and feeling tired. For they learn that the entertainment offered is not gener-

168

ally that which makes demands. Younger children still have some of the excitement of expectation and the closeness of attention which goes with it. But by the time children's viewing habits are more established and their experience of a range of programmes becomes far wider, they seem to accept the fact that television is rather boring, and it leaves them feeling tired. Younger children do not link television and boredom; older ones do.

The clear similarities that underlie all the individual differences, therefore, are acquired by about the age of eight. This does not mean that children stop developing but that they have already learned a mode of response to television which is significant and formative. One can make broad distinctions in some ways between children under and over the age of eight. When it comes to differences of sex there are a few cases where in terms of taste there are clear distinctions to be made, although in most of the evidence boys and girls react in very similar ways, and as in the case of class or country, the similarity of characteristics are far more significant than the differences. In some rather obvious ways boys' tastes differ from girls, ways which appear set before the onset of television viewing. When asked what they most like girls from the age of five almost invariably mention horses; boys never. Instead, boys mention some form of transport, usually cars or trucks. When asked about their favourite programmes on television it is only boys who make a play for some form of sport, especially football but also boxing. Girls instead show a greater tendency to like comedies, or even *Coronation Street*. Boys' liking for football comes across again in their taste in advertisements, for whatever the product, a glimpse of football seems to them a significant thing. Boys also like seeing advertisements for toys rather more than girls do. Boys also cite sportsmen as their favourite characters in a way that girls do not.

The heroes of television being mostly men, both boys and girls, without any sense of personal identification, cite as their favourites the leading men, although a proportion of girls (nearly 25 per cent) also cite female characters, rather greater than the 5 per cent of boys who do so. But girls also mention good looks when boys never do, and furthermore show a greater tendency to describe characters as 'nice' and 'kind'. At the same time girls are conscious of these valuable characteristics in their preferred heroes rather than in 'real' personalities such as sportsmen. While boys have a greater tendency to cite 'real' characters as favourites they also show a far greater tendency to cite 'stunts' as the most important characteristics of their favourites. But then boys also show a preference for comedians and for comedy such as *The Goodies* or *Monty Python's Flying Circus*, while girls prefer situation comedies. Girls show a greater tendency to be frightened by the news. Otherwise the attitudes, the recall, the expectations and the taste in boys and girls are very similar.

20 Models of effect

'I think that is all that interests me. It really isn't much.' (girl, 9)

The notion of 'effect' or 'response' is very complex. Far from being a simple matter of stimulus and reaction, the variables implicit within each circumstance in which effect takes place are almost countless. To isolate one stimulus is almost impossible; add the mood, character, the recent experiences and the situation and the difficulties in trying to understand what goes on inside the mind, and it is clear why the whole notion of effect is so complex. But the problem with many of the studies of television is that they have been based both on attempts to isolate a particular variable out of many and on very simple notions of effect. The temptation to draw up a simple 'model' is very great, but to fall into temptation is not very illuminating unless such a model carries with it both a complexity that shows it is not merely the application of an unproven hypothesis, and the simplicity of insight that arises from fresh evidence. The most famous formula about effect suggests a very simple and mechanistic view of what takes place. The problem with Lasswell's (1948) formula — 'who says what, to whom and with what effect' — is not only that it does not define itself or that it gives a behaviouristic sequence but that it has remained implicitly influential. Many of the experiments have been carried out in unnatural conditions to test the simple hypothesis that 'who' effects 'whom'. However complicated the variations on the same theme, the assumptions have not changed:

What are the manifest (and latent) functions (and dys-
functions) of mass-communicated surveillance (news)
correlation (editorial activity) cultural transmission and
entertainment for society, sub-groups, individuals and
cultural systems?   (Wright, 1964, p.93)

Very rarely is the idea of 'effect' defined. Instead it tends to be left as
a clear result of a process or 'function', the end of a one-way flow. This
explains the concentration on different aspects of television; on the
producers, on the content, or on the behavioural outcomes. However
complex many of the models of effect, and there are many, they tend
to repeat the basic Lasswell pattern:

External Constraints → Internal Constraints → Media
Constraints → Media Uses → Effects (from Faber et al.
1979, p.240).

Effects are an appendage; an outcome even in a model in which many
complex variables are noted.

The 1950s, in the wake of Lasswell's influence, produced the first
spate of models of effect as the study of communications first began to
be taken seriously in the United States. The various models showed a
realisation of the problem of defining human behaviour, but came to
few solutions, partly because, perhaps, there was little connection
between the work of psychologists on behaviour (mostly animal
behaviour) and the work of social scientists. Thus many of the subsequent assumptions about the nature of television and its audience
are based on the work of the theorists of the 1950s (Gerbner, 1956;
Westley and Maclean, 1957; Schramm, 1954; Riley and Riley, 1959,
etc.). But even those models that tried to bring the work of cognitive
psychologists to bear, with the different models of short- and long-
term memory storage or information processing, still relied on an
underlying structure of stimulus on the one hand, a series of complex
variables in between, and a clear result on the other.

There are many interesting models which attempt to illuminate
the nature of communication, well and succinctly summed up by
McQuail (1982). But few are based directly on evidence and even fewer
concern themselves essentially with the response of children. Those
that are concerned with television rather than all forms of media
communication tend to centre on the behaviourist approach. As Tracey
(1977) points out:

The bulk of this effects research has involved a short-term,
stimulus-response, direct effects approach, and even

though innumerable studies and the expenditure of large amounts of research funds have produced little in the way of conclusive evidence on the alleged impact of the broadcast media on the lives of the population, the work on 'effects' still predominates in mass-communication research. (p. 10)

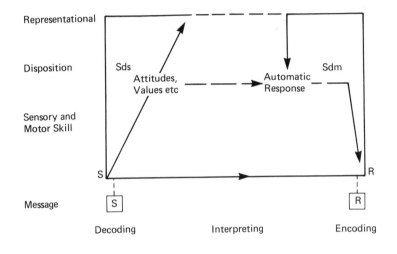

(Source: Schramm, 1955, p. 11)

One of the difficulties with theories of the way in which television affects children is that most people's consciousness is dominated by the question of violence. The interest in measurable change and in behavioural outcomes derives from this. Thus when De Fleur and Ball-Rokeach summarise theoretical positions in studying effects they refer essentially to the behavioural problem of violence. The first

172

approach they summarise is the catharsis theory which suggests that children use the mass media to sublimate their own problems. The second is the theory of stimulating effects which states that exposure to models of violence leads to higher levels of physiological and emotional arousal, and then to anti-social behaviour. The third is the observational learning theory which suggests that children learn to emulate the models put before them. The last is reinforcement theory, which concludes that popular culture merely reinforces established behaviour patterns, as if there were no effect at all, or as if all content were so uniform that it reflects the tastes and mores of the individual. Each of these approaches explores the nature of response from a fixed position; each assumes that violence is caused by television. The most popular and the most simple of these theories is that of observational learning. It derives from the idea that children learn by modelling their behaviour on what they see and what they choose to imitate. Bandura's experiments with Bobo dolls are based on his broader psychological work on children's identifications. His suggestion is that the fundamental basis of learning is the patterning of thoughts, feelings and actions on a model of which the child approves (Bandura, 1969). The child first orients himself to the model's behaviour, relates this to his own needs and then rehearses them himself. This behaviour is reinforced if rewarding. Clearly the ability to imitate rests on the high salience given to the original model; thus when a teacher hits a Bobo doll it is more likely to be imitated than if the same action is part of a cartoon. As Bandura himself points out, identification depends on linguistic explanations of the model's behaviour, as in obedience. Thus the condition of television watching is seen as the sharp focusing on a particular element, the sense that what is isolated from the many images is satisfying to copy, and then repeated (Grusec and Brinker, 1972).

Bandura himself has suggested that an adequate theory of imitative behaviour is lacking (Bandura, Ross and Ross, 1961), but his laboratory-based theory of simple learning has nevertheless been applied to the different conditions of television. Berkowitz's explanation of effect also depends on high emotional arousal. His concept of aggressive drive is that it is heightened by frustration and an eliciting clue in the environment (Berkowitz, 1963). The original idea that frustration was an important part of violence (a conflict of 'drive' and 'habit') was first suggested by Davik (1952) and Hamer and Brown (1955). Since then there have been many attempts to prove this hypothesis experimentally. Anger 'drive state' is supposed to lead to aggressive actions, given the relevant clues. It is never clear whether television provides the clue since Berkowitz's experiments use violent material as a starting point before a frustration is introduced.

Each model of effect that is based on a concern with violence implies the imitation of some kind of action, a conscious series of stages in learning; understanding the context, isolating an incident, approving the model and acting upon it. Thus television violence is supposed to overcome the inhibitions which rest on fear of punishment (Belson, 1978), or it is suggested that conditioned reflexes are overcome by repeated viewing (Eysenck, 1961, 1974, 1978). Because these approaches ignore different types of presentation and different conditions of viewing they are under constant attack, even by those who put them forward in the first place. They suggest on the one hand a very simplified view of learning and then on the other that children do not learn to counter this particular message of violence by all the other experiences of learning they undergo. It is as if countless tests of the hypothesis (as in the case of the US Surgeon Generals' reports of 1972) had overcome common sense (cf. Howitt and Cumberbatch, 1975). Greer et al. (1982) conclude that there are just two models of television effect, modelling or 'arousal'. They suggest that the latter implies that behaviour which is aroused can be *different* from that shown by the model, so that the medium is a secondary rather than primary model for change (cf. Emery, 1976). But while this widens the idea of imitation, it does not fundamentally change it.

Models of effect can be interesting but an understanding of the nature of television must go beyond a simple hypothesis of imitation. Children reveal that there are some clear ground rules of response, a series of attitudes that belie the notion of high arousal or modelling. The term 'effect' itself has not proved helpful since it implies one act of response, an aspect that leaves out what the subject himself brings to the circumstances. The German word 'Wirkung', which combines both 'effect' and 'response', would be more useful, although the very word 'response' itself implies a richer indication of the complexity of what takes place. It is clear that much depends on the attitudes that children bring to television, expressed in their tastes and expectations. Obviously they adapt to what is offered so that there is a complete circle of expectations, but this does not imply that television is a general collective creation of the cultural desires of the audience, or a monument to such tastes. The connection is much closer; 'effects' lie not only in isolated parts of the content but in the actual conditions of viewing. Children form attitudes towards the experience of watching television which then inform their subsequent patterns of response. The relationship between expected content and subsequent attitude is itself important; all kinds of perception must be seen as a two-way influence (Kausler, 1974). 'Effect' lies in the nature of response itself.

Far from a simple relationship between the stimulus and the audience, going in one direction, the attitudes brought to bear by the audience both inform and transform what is seen. The onlooker is aware of what he is doing and of his own levels of attention. For just as the television image is a mixture of the main message and the incidental, so is the response a balance between a conscious, even self-conscious, awareness of what is being watched and subconscious responses. All these different aspects relate to each other so that in any view of response we must take into account at least six different relationships.

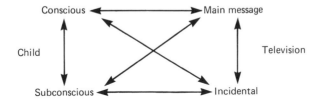

It is possible to concentrate upon the incidental, as it is possible to allow the main message of a programme to be imbibed without attention. Subconscious responses include personal associations and imaging as well as the associations created by the incidental imagery of programmes. The response of a child is more complex than a matter of ordering, learning and recalling distinct items of information. The complexity lies in children's awareness of the designs that television programmes have on them and the use they make of them, in children's ability to be critical, to have preferences, to make associations, as well as the varying levels of attention. Their attitudes are not a matter of constant 'set' but the way this 'set' is applied to television. For there are a whole range of possible levels of attention, from close critical awareness to an almost complete distraction.

In a child's response to television we need to take into account at least two levels. The first is a conscious relationship between content and understanding, through sophisticated expectations of entertainment or instruction together with critical interest in, and awareness of, the ideas to be learned and the satisfaction to be gained. The second underlies 'normal' levels of awareness. It is the relationship between the recognition of whatever satisfies expectations, the sense of the familiar, and the pleasures that derive from weak emotional responses through the associations that form the 'hidden curriculum' of the programme. The attitude of watching, including some expectations and a lack of concentration, can affect subsequent behaviour through the application of such attitudes to other events, but this is a far cry from simple modelling. Habits can affect performance and children assimilate habits of learning that are acquired in watching television and can be transferred to hobbies or lessons in school. But even such attitudes do not remain constant, even if children's expectations seem to. Any simple notion that children are subliminally manipulated is undermined by children's invariable capacity to learn, just as the simple models of effect that assume careful modelling or imitation of a particular event are undermined by the hidden complexities. As James said:

> No doubt it is often *convenient* to formulate the mental facts in an atomistic sort of way, and to treat the higher states of consciousness as if they were all built out of unchanging simple ideas . . . But . . . A permanently existing 'idea' or 'Vorstellung' which makes its appearance before the footlights of consciousness at periodical intervals, is as mythological an entity as the Jack of Spades. (1890, p.236)

There are certain principles about the relationship between children and television that need to be borne in mind. The first is the importance of what a child brings with him when he watches television. The second is the constant flow between the analysable, the definable, the memorable, and the incidental, the tone, the half recognised. All aspects of the state of viewing constantly inform each other, the moods and the images, the verbal style and the message, the content as archetypes as well as definition, the critical awareness and the subconscious. Thus when we find that children are influenced by television it is through a process of learning that is a far cry from the traditional notions of being filled up with information as if children were 'empty vessels'. The habits that children acquire in watching television are themselves important, even although learning is itself habitually thought of as a series of facts to be learned or models to be imitated. The myth that learning takes place through conscious attention to the wisdom, or the violence, being displayed still pervades discussions about the mass media. Television's crucial part in the formation of styles of attention, or inattention, is too often ignored. The acquisition of the habit of subconscious inattentive viewing, half-hearted attention sustained over long periods, an indifference to information and the casualness of boredom are all part of children's response to television. The effect itself lies in the act of watching.

Conclusions

'We live from hand to mouth, most of us, with a small family of immediate desires.'

G. Eliot, *Mill on the Floss,* Chapter 3.

'I like watching the television. If we did not have one I would be bored stiff.'   (boy, 11)

Children are capable of intense appreciation and the closest critical scrutiny. They can be absorbed in a story and learn new information rapidly and efficiently. No account of children's responses should ignore this fact by being trapped into an over-simple generalisation. While there are some clear findings about the ways in which children respond to television, these are always in contrast to children's capacities. This is one of the reasons why there is such a large gap between the critics of television and the producers of programmes. The latter accept payment for their belief that the programmes they make do good. They place their sensitivity and intelligence into the most careful thought about the quality of what they produce. And they have enough evidence, through questionnaires and letters, to show that in every programme they make for children there is a lot of 'feedback' showing just such discrimination and interest they intend to create. This proof of children's ability to attend to the intended message of the programme contrasts with some of the research evidence that gives an impression that children are being moulded into imitators of violence or into passive and inarticulate zombies. Given the terms of reference of those who are looking for interesting responses to particular programmes by supportive mothers and their children (like, for example, an analysis of *You and Me* (Hobsbaum and Ghikas, 1979) carried out for the BBC) it is not surprising that the findings suggest the programme to be successful in what it sets out to do. Once the task is to compare one programme to another, it is almost inevitable that what will be discovered will be the extent to which the producers' intentions are met. What is left out of such a survey is the more complex lasting question of response, not in terms of showing interest or learning information, but in terms of attitudes.

Those who do not take into account children's ability to discriminate enthusiastically and those who only look at this ability therefore miss out one or other end of the complete spectrum. It is not surprising that there should be difficulties in coming to a clear view, just as there are temptations in arriving at a partial one. It is important to remember that the positive and negative views of television are both, in a sense, correct, but that they only make sense when they are taken together. Underlying those moments of intense interest and concern lie hours of negligent indifference. Surrounding the sudden surprise into fear, shock or excitement, are a host of images half-forgotten and fully scorned. The nature of children's response is such that those layers of the mind more prone to associate than to analyse are as important as those that are attuned to certain tasks. Although the ability to recall information depends upon close attention, changes in opinion or attitude are actually inhibited by the same closeness of attention. Most of what is learned from television contrasts to the conditions of schools or experiments.

The literature in such an important subject is disappointing because of the temptation not so much to arrive at simplistic conclusions, as to use conclusions as a starting point. The hypothesis that children all imitate what they see, or that they model their behaviour on that of their favourite heroes, or that they see the world as a collection of stereotypes provided by television, or that the producers of television shows are all wickedly engaged in manipulating their viewers into distinct political action; none of these can be borne out. Each has been disproved on many occasions, and yet the fascination with attempts to prove such hypotheses seems to remain. But the real problem with the generalisations made about television is that they have generalised in a peculiar way. Instead of trying to make sense of the complex nature of children's response most of the generalisations have assumed that response is simple, and that television is complex. Once it is taken for granted that children pay attention at one level all the time, there is an excuse to assume that the connection between the intentions of programme makers and their audience is a close one. Obviously it is infinitely easier to analyse a programme than try to understand how people learn, and how they become what they are. By treating a complex thing, like attention, as if it were simple, many researchers have ignored a comparatively simple matter, like inattention.

No outline of the storage of information can explain those levels of response children reveal in their experience of television. Their engagement with the auditory and visual stimuli of television includes a habit of inattention. Unlike their verbal performance the learning that takes place as a result of television is far more generalised; not so full of details, despite the details of the imagery, and far more inclined to make sense of the complex stimuli by simplifying them mentally. Children need to make sense of television in their own way even more than other experiences of perception, for they find it difficult to make distinctions between memory and the products of their own fantasy, between perceptual images and their own imagination (Kolers, 1968; Miller, Galanter and Pribram, 1960). Children learn to adapt, but they learn to adapt to what they expect to see more easily than to the complex surfaces of programmes. The 'hidden' message contained implicitly in all that they watch is that they should be amused, and that television is dedicated to the art of entertainment. For this reason children find it difficult to take television as seriously as critics, and difficult to attend to in the same way as a lesson in school.

Adaptation to television is both a matter of expecting entertainment and a matter of avoiding any threats to this expectation. It is not the medium itself which imposes social norms as much as the individuals responding to the medium. The 'routine' response derives from the knowledge of what to seek out and what to ignore, not in terms of the type of content, but in terms of the ease of pleasure. Thus the 'ritual' of television is a matter of the audience's ability to make categorisations of their experience. They use strategies to seek out and deal with material that demands minimal attention and little reliance on memory; avoiding any great load on their inner resources (Kintsch, 1977). In terms of content analysis it is the insignificant that is associated with a kind of subliminal persuasion, a persuasion not deliberately imposed but undeliberately extracted. Thus the effects of television lie not simply in the nature of the content shown, but in the attitudes, and the levels of consciousness that are involved. Television creates a base for a general attitude which, for all the varieties of activity in which it can express itself, remains an underlying constant that is difficult to change. Thus television is no threat, cannot easily be manipulated to bend its audience in directions of action or depravity. But at another level, television can be a subtle threat through the means it provides to an audience intent *not* to learn from or to respond to what it sees.

Naturally the relationship between the desire for entertainment and the programmes that are offered is a close one. The audience shows clear preferences to which the programmers respond. But underlying the levels of entertainment offered is the fact that the audience will make out of what it sees whatever it will. The way in which children respond depends more on the amount that they see than on the nature of individual programmes. The distinctions between programmes and advertisements are not perceived as being essentially significant, even though their intentions could hardly be more different. For the styles of programmes are more important than their subjects; matters of pace and visual change, with high levels of movement or contrast, all suggest to the audience what they see as an appropriate style of attention (Huston et al. 1981). On the one hand each programme, carefully presented by skilled technicians and gifted producers, represents a unique experience; on the other hand the audience takes out just a part of it and blends it into the general experience of watching television.

What, then, are the effects of television? To some extent this is a misleading question. The nature of children's response is such that 'effect' is no simple matter that can be transferred from one medium to the respondent. Television is, after all, a 'medium' through which a complex variety of stimuli are transferred. Children's capacity for idiosyncratic interpretation is almost infinite. It is therefore a dangerous process to try to answer what seems like a simple question, but is in fact not only a complex one but one which demands an answer implying an interpretation of the nature of human learning. Nevertheless there are enough signs in the evidence we have for it to be done, even if the answer is not the crude banner that those who seek to have their prejudices confirmed would like to see unfurled. There are enough consistencies in the style of children's television viewing to show that underlying the individual interpretations of content, the 'effects' of television lie in the formation of general attitudes and in styles of interpretation. There is no evidence that consistently supports the notion that children copy what they see, mirroring the violence, seduced into the love of particular products, terrified by horror and manipulated into certain beliefs. The real effect lies below such lurid speculations.

Children show consistent expectations of television. Their tastes are akin to those of adults, with a pervasive desire for entertainment that fulfils familiar norms. They resent those shows that make demands on them, even if, having seen one, they afterwards recollect it more completely. Their favourite programmes, to which they show strong loyalty, and to which they look forward, leave little impression behind. Children neither remember what they have seen of a familiar ritual nor do they wish to remember. Even educational television which has palpable designs upon them is surprisingly unsuccessful in imparting information. But educational television is not popular compared to those programmes that children watch later in the evenings, even though most children watch television for several hours, from the moment they come home from school to late at night. The more children watch, the less they manage to recall or interpret. Their very styles of viewing show a laconic indifference to what is offered that makes television seem like a consistent background to other events. The part that television plays in their lives is a minor if pervasive one; fitting in to other events, knowing its place and rarely of such high salience that children approach it with awed anticipation. On the contrary, children do not expect much from television apart from the fulfilment of a need for entertainment without demands.

Children, therefore, approach television in a fairly sophisticated, adult way. They do not believe everything they see. They know that heroes are those characters that survive from thriller to thriller, and they expect the news to be either entertaining or irrelevant to their own circumstances. Thus they learn to adapt to the amount that is constantly offered to them; discriminating not between programmes but between different levels of interest. The recognition value of their favourite stars lies in their actions as well as looks; they are expected, without any sense of awe, to do certain stunts. They are known to earn a great deal of money. But few are taken very seriously. The generally friendly tone, the immediate intimacy of television, means that it is received casually, and not as some portentous public statement. To make children respond in a serious manner entails the presence of some other authority, cajoling them into interest. For children otherwise see that television is not to be taken seriously, that the murders are there as stunts, that shooting is a part of entertainment. Thus the violence on television passes them by; instead of responding to it as if it were real, they do not notice that it gives a picture of the world that is singularly brutal. The research on violence is actually concerned with obedience to justifying authorities and does not explore the response to the fantasies which are ill-attended.

Children's recall of programmes gets worse the more that they watch, for they achieve a plateau of inattention and stay there. The information, serious or trivial, only stays in their consciousness if there is some personal association that makes it interesting. Only those items or images oft repeated become remembered through recognition. Thus the advertisements, admired for their entertainment, provide a disproportionate amount of material that they recall, not in terms of the quality of the product, but in the jingles, songs or catch-phrases that they promote. Television becomes for children propaganda for itself, for ease of entertainment, for the fulfilment of the same expectations in a variety of different ways. In a parody of their elders children censure what other people would like to see, and berate the violence contained in their favourite programmes, but being all exceptions to the general rule go on relishing just those programmes that they berate. Far from analysing the meaning of the plot, or the significance of the information, children respond to the repeated images that they associate with the world of television.

Children do not expect television to present an image of the real world. The likeness is at times uncanny, but the ways in which television, especially through the fantasies of serials, cuts up, and orders, juxtaposes and controls a picture of the world, suggests different kinds of auditory and visual perception. Television images are not ordered by the recipient; the subconscious associations are more important. Thus the fact of children's inattention is itself significant in forming their own attitudes to the world. One of the most significant complexities of children's response to television is the relationship between the real and the fantastic. For television, while viewed as entertainment, attempts to present interpretations of a real world. Sometimes the serials themselves seem to parody the most ordinary of domestic circumstances, and sometimes the soap operas actually build in to their stories some public, some almost real event, like a royal wedding, to coincide with the private dramas (Hobson, 1982). Thus the public and the private, always in tension in the face of any event, are deliberately juxtaposed, are put into another dimension.

Some of the most obvious cases when the real and the fantastic have seemed to merge have been those in which a public event has been mitigated or changed by the element of the unreal. The two most oft-cited examples are the mistaking a real person for a fictional one or vice versa, or the use of a fictional action in normal life. Neither of these are, in fact, new phenomena, and neither explains the problem of fantasy and reality created by television. Obviously the association of an actor with his role will make him more recognisable as the latter; doctors in television series can be taken for real doctors, just as a famous public man is recognised as if he were a familiar friend, before the puzzlement of placing him sets in, and just as Sir Arthur Conan Doyle used to complain that he was addressed as Sherlock Holmes. Some actions appear to belong to the world of fiction before the realities of the horror strike the onlooker, like a murder of a foreign diplomat in full daylight; but this shock of puzzlement at the event does not necessarily depend on a slowness of response induced by television shows as well as in seeing them. Thus some bank robbers have had difficulty in persuading their victims that they are not taking part in a television programme (Letkemann, 1973). American soldiers in the Vietnam war began to act as if they were in a conventional war movie the moment that television cameras arrived (Knightley, 1975).

The transference of fantasy into real life is actually more a matter of using materials for imaginative personal extensions (cf. Opie and Opie, 1969). Television is naturally an important source of material for those

182

who wish to use it. Those who seek ideas and those who seek publicity all find in television a most useful tool (Schmid and Graaf, 1980), just as books and magazines or hearsay have also been useful conveyers of ideas. A film which showed a particular means of extorting money through the threat of blowing up an aircraft has often been blamed for giving rise to several similar incidents, just as hijacking, earlier not thought of, has now spread into a fashion. Television in these cases is merely the instrument of communication, like any other. But television is also blamed for giving children the idea that they too are as invulnerable as their heroes; both in terms of action and effects. The more subtle charge on television is that a young child might imitate Batman and fling himself out of a window assuming he could fly, or that a real loaded gun would have no more consequences than those used in Westerns. But in these examples television is the instrument used in a particular way; the pathology of individual cases are involved rather than the nature of 'effect'.

And yet there is a less crude way in which television enters the distortions of the real and the fantastic. Children obviously know the difference, and are not easily deceived. They know that the advertiser's job is to sell; they know that the deaths in a Western are all simulated. But the significant fact is that they do not care. They become indifferent to the juxtaposition. The fantasy wishes of children have been recognised as significant insights into their inner thoughts; both for psychiatrists' reasons (Winkley, 1982; Simmonds, 1969) and for the understanding of recurrent response patterns (Kanner, 1972). When asked to state their three wishes it is interesting to note how often children mix up the world that is offered by television with the real one. Television not only becomes a part of their fantasies, providing material for their natural tendency to have fantasies, but seems to suggest an attitude in which the pragmatic and the glamorous are very closely related. Some aspects of children's wishes are obviously not only influenced by television. When girls are asked to say what they would like to have, nearly all of them mention animals, mostly horses. Boys, on the other hand, give almost equal weight to transport in some form or another. There is no point in assuming that television creates these sexual stereotypes. But apart from these examples it is clear that television has become an important part of children's worlds.

There are very few children who state in their three wishes what would be deemed to be 'normal' desires, for a dog, a cat and a horse, to work hard, go to school and learn mathematics.

'A baby, luxury bedroom, a horse. Trip in Concorde, cruise round the world; get married.' (girls, 10)

'PVC or leather jacket; Digital watch; schoolboy scrambler.
Drive a Seddon Atkinson artic; go on back of Barry Sheene's
cycle; play football with Manchester United.' (boys, 10)

There are a very few whose desires are very single-minded, like a nine-
year-old girl:

'I want horses, a saddle, a bridle; to go riding, enter a gym-
khana, win the Grand National.'

But even here there is a touch of fantasy. The majority of children
show an imagination in which television, with its stars, its glamour and
its advertisements, are part of their world:

'Good education; good life, good looks. Be a star; write
a book, go out with Mick.' (girl, 9)
'Horse, skateboard; lots of money. Meet Liver birds, meet
Starsky and Hutch; Pass my award 1 and 2.' (boy, 10)
'Skateboard; long dress; lots of money. Go abroad, live in
Scotland with Aunt Kelly; be bionic.' (girl, 11)

The desire to be 'bionic' is mentioned by about a third of the children.
The desire to appear on television in some capacity or other is mentioned by even more. Those who do not necessarily wish to appear on
television nevertheless wish to 'meet' the stars, whether they be Starsky
and Hutch or the Honey Monster. The realistic and the fantastic are
constantly juxtaposed — 'be bionic; work in the bar with Dad' (boy, 9);
'be on TV; work in a factory' (girl, 10).

The entry of television into their wishes is on a variety of levels, from
the qualities like 'bionics' that are pure fantasy to the chance for fame
and money. In the centre of their wishes, for they seem to combine all
the elements, are the advertisements. The desire to appear on television
includes the desire to take part in advertisements:

'Play with the Honey Monster; paint a palace on a Crown
paint advert; go into the jungle from Cadbury's chocolate.'
(girl, 8)
'Do adverts with Fawcett Majors; live at Hollywood; see the
stars.' (girl, 11)

Advertisements are seen as part of the glamour and the reward of television. There is no doubt in children's minds that television has a great
deal to do with money as well as fame. Many children say that they
would like to be rich — 'I want to be rich and famous' — and most
associate fame with riches:

184

'I want posh clothes, money and a car. So everybody would say isn't she rich and praise me.' (girl, 11)

As children become older their replies become increasingly mercenary on the one hand and fanciful on the other, combining a love of money, fame, and super-human qualities such as bionics. Children show a curious mixture of the subjective with the objective; a knowledge that television is a fantasy world of entertainment and awareness that it provides an equally glossy world for its stars. On television the public world easily becomes personal, as easily as the compère pretends familiarity with the anonymous single individuals behind the television cameras. We can see how simple it is for children to picture themselves in a world in which the real and the fantastic are interconnected, as in the world of entertainment:

'Air hostess; I would like to be an air hostess because I would like the money and you get tips on the side off millionaires and royalty.' (girl, 11)
'I would like to be a nurse when I leave school but if I can't I would like to be a movie star and then I would be very famous and I would make thousands of pounds.' (girl, 12)

Children's views of the qualities of their favourite television stars were equally mixed. About a third mentioned the super-human strength, or other supernatural power like bionics that is purely the result of a particular kind of American thriller material. Others wanted the more pragmatic elements, like money. Girls desired the 'good looks' and boys the 'big car'. Their answers again showed that they were not viewing television as an example of the real world from which they could learn. The exceptions show by contrast how far children are from relating the style of their heroes realistically to themselves: 'A very good polite voice, and sense of humour and a good voice' (boy, 11) or 'Tony Hart's drawings' (girl, 10) stand out from the general desire for strength, slim figures, or invisibility. The qualities that children cited were not so much associated with the personalities of their heroes but the types of roles that they play.

Children obviously know the difference between the real and the fantastic; but their view of television makes this distinction insignificant in their eyes. They are accustomed to being entertained, and actually learn to resent the demands made in documentaries that contain truths they deem irrelevant to them. Children are being nurtured into the future mass audiences, prepared at an early stage for all the forms of mass entertainment from pop music to magazines. But this arises out of the attitudes brought to bear, rather than an automatic reflection of those who desire to manipulate them. The important point is that the more the distinctions between the real and the fantastic are broken down in entertainment, the more of a contrast there is between the actually real and the fantastic in normal circumstances. The fantasy world of entertainment, by absorbing the real, contrasts the more with the world of work, with its responsibilities and its demands. Given the fitful glimpses of the real, in the parody of excitement contained in programmes, and received calmly by their audiences, the actuality of everyday events, like the job of the real policeman, seems dull by comparison. But it is the fact that the spurious excitement of the thriller does not arouse strong reactions that matters. The sophistication children learn is that of being able to ignore the stimulation offered. The indifference to demands is subtly encouraged. The distinction between work and play is ironically maintained through the audience's response to a medium which ostensibly attempts to service both.

One of the most difficult parts of the evidence to sum up is the air of general boredom expressed by so many children. Correlations between them and the time spent watching television, like all such correlations, prove nothing. But the air of indifference is consistently expressed by children towards television, together with the consumer loyalty to their favourite programmes and to the act of viewing. A large proportion of children link television with being tired or bored, not surprisingly, considering the amount of time spent watching. But just as the entertainment offered by television is a state of mind consistently achieved whatever programme is being shown, and just as little is subsequently recalled, so there seems to be a general expectation of such pleasures which depend on outside stimulation in many teenagers.

> 'The most thing that interests me (being frank) is cigarettes, money, drink and lads; they are the only pleasures in life to me.' (girl, 14)
>
> 'Interests mean something what on Telly like *Top of the Pops.* Cigarettes and drink also interest me and also going out places and getting drunk. These things interest me because I am young and you only live your life once.' (girl, 13)
>
> 'What interest me is drink, cigs and money and lads and going out like the tow-bar and the disco. What interests me the most is cigs, drink and that because you might as well enjoy yourself now because you only live your life once.' (girl, 13)

186

'What interests me is watching football and drinking,
money, girls, Discos, reading the papers, watching television,
and the Fair travel, cigarettes, camping out. (boy, 14)

In many of the statements given by teenagers this air of weariness is
pervasive, as if the greatest pleasures in a meaningless life were those of
boredom, and the tired stimulations which might have caused the boredom in the first place required to overcome it. There is far greater
interest expressed in being drunk, a subsequent state, than in drinking.
Like 'watching the telly' it is not a means but an end in itself.

'I think that's all that interests me. It really isn't much.'
(girl, 9)

For many children television is another way of passing the time, it is
'something to do when there is nothing to do' (girl, 10) or 'it gives you
something to do from 4 o'clock' (girl, 8). Far from being an exciting
new medium, television is seen in the pattern of boredom; both a cause
and an effect.

The statements that children make illuminate particular attitudes to
their lives that could be caused by unemployment, depressing living
conditions, a lack of hope, little parental concern or education, or any
number of factors. It is impossible to isolate a medium like television in
this cycle of indifference, but it is clear that television is a natural part
of it. That there are certain attitudes learned in the act of watching
television is as clear as the fact that television, like drink or cigarettes,
can be used to alleviate boredom. But to say simply that television
causes the indifference is to oversimplify. For the effect of television
cannot be summed up in a single phrase. The answer to the question of
what is the effect of television lies throughout this book. It lies in the
attitudes children bring to watching television, in their adaptation to its
offerings, and in their shared cynicism that reflects the constant cheerfulness of the compères. Throughout the book are pervasive themes
which show how subtle is the response of children, and how the distinction between capacity and actual performance constantly operates.
Children do not respond to television in the classical simplicity of
operant conditioning, or in the computer based analogy of information
processing. Their ability to recognise rather than recall, to image rather
than analyse and associate rather than criticise means that they enter
the world of television in a subtle, almost deliberately subconscious
way.

Underlying all the responses is the fact that, as in state-dependent
learning, children learn to associate a 'set' with watching television.
They find their own clues to the programmes as well as their own
expectations. The amount of information presented, both aural and

visual, demands a selective attention which children employ not in terms of plot or ratiocination but in terms of associations. Thus the constant state of half-hearted attention is more important than the distinctions between programmes. Children can make what they wish out of any programme they see; to understand response we need to look further at the nature of learning rather than the content presented. Television, while different from any other type of medium, is an archetype of all kinds of stimulation, information and entertainment. The understanding of the nature of children's attitudes towards, and the effects of, television is a crucial means of exploring how children learn and how they form their awareness of the world. And yet, as the literature on 'effect' makes clear, the nature of response is rarely explored, as rarely as are children's capacities to learn fully exploited. The findings and the answers to them both point out the importance of making more of children's capacity to respond at different levels. A blanket attack on all television is no answer, even if some of the findings are rather depressing. Much more to the point is a greater concern and attention to the possibilities children show of applying their minds with that alertness of attention and discrimination that the majority of producers like to think takes place anyway.

Appendix

Table 1
Percentage of children watching television
during the previous evening

	Age	Per cent		Age	Per cent
Girls	7	100	Boys	7	100
	8	87		8	83
	9	91		9	92
	10	95		10	97
	11	100		11	97
	12	96		12	89

Table 2
Average number of programmes seen by
children on a typical evening

	Age	Programmes		Age	Programmes
Girls	7	3	Boys	7	3
	8	3		8	3
	9	4		9	4
	10	5		10	5
	11	6		11	6
	12	6		12	5

Table 3
Average expressing preference for different
types of programmes

	Age	Drama	Comedy	Others
Girls	8	44	31	25
	9	64	25	11
	10	61	30	9
	11	59	33	8
	12	68	32	—
Boys	8	59	31	10
	9	66	27	6
	10	74	22	4
	11	65	20	15
	12	85	5	10

Table 4
Percentage of children able to recall any episode that
they have seen of *Dr Who*

	Age	Per cent		Age	Per cent
Girls	7	100	Boys	7	100
	8	92		8	100
	9	81		9	69
	10	50		10	58
	11	62		11	57
	12	38		12	41

Table 5
Percentage of children able to recall one programme seen the previous evening

	Age	Full description Per cent	Essential points Per cent	One detail Per cent	Cannot Per cent
Girls	7	—	100	—	—
	8	—	100	—	—
	9	8	82	10	—
	10	13	74	13	—
	11	9	65	19	7
	12	20	52	23	5
Boys	7	—	100	—	—
	8	—	90	10	—
	9	19	58	23	—
	10	20	48	32	—
	11	16	43	38	3
	12	6	29	59	6

Table 6
Average number of television programmes seen by those able to give

	Programmes
Full description	3.1
Essential points	4.2
One detail	5.9
Nothing	5.2

Table 7
Percentage giving as their favourite character a real personality or a fictional hero

	Age	Real Per cent	Fictional Per cent
Girls	7	50	50
	8	38	62
	9	32	68
	10	47	53
	11	37	63
	12	20	80
Boys	7	61	39
	8	50	50
	9	48	52
	10	56	44
	11	32	68
	12	38	62

Table 8
Percentage of children citing their favourite character as part of their favourite programmes

	Age	Per cent		Age	Per cent
Girls	8	59	Boys	8	68
	9	63		9	67
	10	53		10	36
	11	30		11	34

Table 9
Types of product within the advertisements cited by children as their favourites

	Age	Sweets/toys Per cent	Household goods/others Per cent
Girls	8	38	62
	9	28	72
	10	9	81
	11	3	97
Boys	8	33	67
	9	49	51
	10	41	59
	11	38	62

Table 10
Reasons given for liking a particular advertisement

	Age	The product Per cent	The advertisement Per cent
Girls	7	60	40
	8	60	40
	9	28	72
	10	16	84
	11	18	82
	12	20	80
Boys	7	100	—
	8	40	60
	9	20	80
	10	21	79
	11	17	83
	12	9	91

Table 11
Percentage of children saying that they believe their favourite advertisements

	Age	Per cent		Age	Per cent
Girls	7	82	Boys	7	94
	8	71		8	69
	9	62		9	56
	10	43		10	51
	11	40		11	43
	12	27		12	25

Table 12
Percentage of children who have watched television after midnight

	Age	Per cent		Age	Per cent
Girls	8	50	Boys	8	51
	9	71		9	82
	10	100		10	93
	11	100		11	100

Bibliography

Abelson, R.P., 'Are Attitudes Necessary?' in King, B.T., and McGinnies, E. (eds), *Attitudes, Conflict and Social Change*, Academic Press, New York 1972, pp.19—32.

Abrams, M., 'Child Audiences for Television in Great Britain', *Journalism Quarterly*, vol. 33, 1956, pp.35—41.

Adams, J.A., *Human Memory*, McGraw-Hill, New York 1967.

Adler, R., and Cater, D. (eds), *Television As a Cultural Force*, Praeger, New York 1976.

Adler, R., Lesser, G., Meringoff, L., Robertson, T., Rossiter, J.R., and Ward, S., *The Effects of Television Advertising on Children: Review and Recommendations*, Lexington Books, Massachusetts 1980.

Adorno, T.W., 'Television and the Patterns of Mass Culture', in Schramm, W. (ed.), *Mass Communications*, Urbana, University of Illinois Press, Illinois 1972, pp.594—612.

Advertising Standards Authority, *British Code of Advertising Practice*, London 1976.

Agassi, J., 'The Worker and the Media', *Archives Européenes de Sociologie*, vol. 11, no. 1, 1970, pp.26—68.

Albert, R.S., 'The Role of Mass Media and the Effect of Aggressive Film Content upon Children's Aggressive Responses and Identification Choices', *Genetic Psychology Monographs*, no. 55, 1957, pp.221-285.

Allport, G.W., and Postman, L.P., *The Psychology of Rumor*, Holt, Rinehart, New York 1947.

Allyn, J., and Festinger, L., 'The Effectiveness of Unanticipated Persuasive Communications', *Journal of Abnormal and Social Psychology*, vol. 62, no. 1, 1961, pp.35–40.

Altheide, D.L., *Creating Reality: How T.V. News Distorts Events*, Sage, Beverley Hills, California 1976.

Altick, R.D., *The English Common Reader: A Social History of the Mass Reading Public 1800-1900*, University Press, Chicago 1957.

Ames, L.B., 'Children's Stories', *Genetic Psychological Monographs*, no. 73, 1966, pp.337–96.

Anderson, J.R., and Bower, G.H., *Human Associative Memory*, Winston and Sons, Washington DC 1973

Anisfeld, M., and Knapp, M., 'Association, Synonymity and Directionality in False Recognition', *Journal of Experimental Psychology*, vol. 77, no. 2. 1968, pp.171–9.

Annan, N. (Chairman), *Report of the Committee on the Future of Broadcasting*, HMSO, London 1977.

Annis, P.M., 'Mass Media and Young Children', MA Thesis, University of Leicester 1973.

Applebee, A.N., *The Child's Concept of Story: Ages 2 to 17*, University Press, Chicago 1978.

Argyle, M., *The Psychology of Interpersonal Behaviour*, Penguin, Harmondsworth 1967.

Arless, M.J., *Thirty Seconds*, Farras, Straus and Giroux, New York 1980.

Arnheim, R., *Visual Thinking*, Faber and Faber, London 1970.

Arnheim, R., 'The World of the Daytime Serial', in Schramm, W. (ed.), *Mass Communications*, University of Illinois Press, Urbana, Illinois, 1972, pp.392–411.

Asch, J.E., 'Effects of Group Pressure upon the Modification and Distortion of Judgement', in Guelzkow, H. (ed.), *Groups, Leadership and Men*, Carnegie Press, Pittsburgh 1951.

Atkin, C.K., Murray, J.P., and Nayman, O.B., 'The Surgeon General's Research Program on Television and Social Behaviour: A Review of Empirical Findings', *Journal of Broadcasting*, no. 16, Winter 1971-2, pp.21–35.

Atkinson, R.C., and Shiffrin, R.M., 'Human Memory: A Proposed System and its Control Processes', in Spence, K.W., and Spence, J.T. (eds), *The Psychology of Learning and Motivation: Advances in Research and Theory*, Academic Press, New York 1968, pp.89–195. Reprinted (in part) in Gardiner, J.M., *Readings in Human Memory*, Methuen, London 1976, pp.25–57.

Atkinson, R.C., and Shiffrin, R.M., 'The Control of Short-term Memory', *Scientific American*, no. 225, 1971, pp.82–90.

Ausubel, D.P., *Education Psychology: A Cognitive View*, Holt, Rine-hart, New York 1968.

Averill, J.R., Malmstrom, E.J., Koriat, A., and Lazarus, R.S., 'Habituation to Complex Emotional Stimuli', *Journal of Abnormal Psychology*, no. 80, 1972, pp.20—28.

Baddeley, A.D., *The Psychology of Memory*, Basic Books, New York 1976.

Baddeley, A.D., 'Short-term Memory for Word Sequences as a Function of Acoustic, Semantic and Formal Similarity', *Quarterly Journal of Experimental Psychology*, no. 18, 1966, pp.362—5.

Baggeley, J., and Duck, S., *Dynamics of Television*, Saxon House, Farnborough 1976.

Bailyn, L., 'Mass Media and Children: A Study of Exposure Habits and Cognitive Effects', *Psychological Monographs: General and Applied*, no. 471, vol. 73, no. 1, 1959, pp.1—48.

Balázs, B., *Theory of the Film* (trans. E. Bone), Dover, New York 1970.

Ball, S., and Bogatz, G., *The First Year of Sesame Street: An Evaluation*, Educational Testing Service, Princeton, New Jersey 1970.

Ball-Rokeach, S., and De Fleur, M., 'A Dependency Model of Mass Media Effects', *Communication Research*, no. 3, 1976, pp.3—21.

Bandura, A., *Aggression: A Social Learning Analysis*, Prentice Hall, New Jersey 1973.

Bandura, A., 'A Social-learning Theory of Identificatory Processes', in Goslin, D.A. (ed.), *Handbook of Socialisation Theory and Research*, Rand McNally, Chicago 1969, pp. 213-262.

Bandura, A., and Huston, A.C., 'Identification as a Process of Incidental Learning', *Journal of Abnormal and Social Psychology*, vol. 63, no. 2, 1961, pp.311—8.

Bandura, A., Ross, D., and Ross, S.A., 'Transmission of Aggression through Imitation of Aggressive Models', *Journal of Abnormal and Social Psychology*, no. 63, no. 3, 1961, pp.575—82.

Bandura, A., Ross, D., and Ross, S.A., 'Imitation of Film-Mediated Aggressive Models', *Journal of Abnormal and Social Psychology*, vol. 66, 1963, pp.3—11.

Bandura, A., and Walters, R.H., *Social Learning and Personality Development*, Holt, New York 1963

Barclay, A.M., and Haber, R.N., 'The Relation of Aggressive to Sexual Motivation', *Journal of Personality*, vol. 33, 1965, pp.462—75.

Barcus, F.E., with Wolkin, R., *Children's Television: An Analysis of Programming and Advertising*, Praeger, New York 1977.

Bartlett, F.C., *Remembering: A Study in Experimental and Social Psychology*, University Press, Cambridge 1932.

Bartlett, F.C., *Political Propaganda*, University Press, Cambridge 1940.

Bates, A., 'Towards a Better Research Framework for Evaluating the Effectiveness of Educational Media', *British Journal of Educational Technology*, no. 3, vol.12, October 1981, pp.215–33.

Bates, E., *Language and Context: The Acquisition of Pragmatics*, Academic Press, New York 1976.

Bauer, R., 'Limits of Persuasion', *Harvard Business Review*, vol. 36, no. 5, 1958, pp.105–10.

Bauer, R., and Greyser, S., *Advertising in America: The Consumer View*, Harvard Business School, Boston 1968.

Bechtel, R.B., Achelpohl, C., and Akers, R., 'Correlates between Observed Behaviour and Questionnaire Responses on Television Viewing', in Rubinstein, E., Comstock, G., and Murray, J. (eds), *Television and Social Behaviour, Vol. IV: Television in Day-to-Day Life: Patterns of Use*, United States Government Printing Office, Washington DC, 1972, pp.274–344.

Belbin, E., 'The Effects of Propaganda on Recall, Recognition and Behaviour', *British Journal of Psychology*, vol. 47, no. 3, 1956.

Belson, W.A., *The Impact of Television: Methods and Findings in Programme Research*, Crosby Lockwood, London 1967.

Belson, W.A., *Television Violence and the Adolescent Boy*, Saxon House, Farnborough 1978.

Belson, W.A., 'The Effects of Television on Family Life', *Discovery*, vol. 21, no. 19, 1960, pp.426–30.

Bennett, N., *Teaching Style and Pupil Progress*, Open Books, London 1976.

Berelson, B., 'Communications and Public Opinion', in Schramm, W. (ed.) *Mass Communications*, University of Illinois Press, Urbana 1960, pp.527–43. (Second edition, 1972, with new preface and articles.)

Berelson, B., and Steiner, G. (eds), *Human Behaviour: An Inventory of Scientific Findings*, Harcourt Brace, New York 1964.

Berelson, B., and Janowitz, M. (eds), *Reader in Public Opinion and Communication*, second edition, Free Press, New York 1966.

Berger, S.M., 'Conditioning through Vicarious Instigation', *Psychological Review*, vol. 69, 1962, pp.450–66.

Berkowitz, L., *Aggression: A Social Psychological Analysis*, McGraw-Hill, New York 1962.

Berkowitz, L. (ed.), *Advances in Experimental Social Psychology*, vol. 1, Academic Press, New York 1964.

Berkowitz, L., 'The Contagion of Violence: an S-R Mediational Analysis of Some Effects of Observed Aggression', in Arnold, W.J., and Page, M.M. (eds), *Nebraska Symposium on Motivation*, vol. 18, University Press, Nebraska 1970, pp.95–135.

Berkowitz, L., 'Sex and Violence: We Can't have it Both Ways', *Psychology Today*, vol. 5, no. 7, pp.14—23.

Berkowitz, L., and Rawlings, E., 'Effects of Film Violence on Inhibitions against Subsequent Aggression', *Journal of Abnormal and Social Psychology*, vol. 66, 1963, pp.405—15.

Berlyne, D.E., *Conflict, Arousal and Curiosity*, McGraw-Hill, New York 1960.

Berlyne, D.E., 'The Influence of Complexity and Novelty in Visual Figures on Orienting Responses', *Journal of Experimental Psychology*, vol. 55, 1958, pp.289—96.

Bernstein, B., *Class, Codes and Control, Vol. 3: Towards a Theory of Educational Transmissions,* second edition, Primary Socialization, Language and Education, Routledge and Kegan Paul, London 1977.

Bernstein, B., 'Aspects of Language and Learning in the Genesis of the Social Process', *Journal of Child Psychology and Psychiatry*, vol. 1, 1961, pp.313—24.

Berry, R., *Communication through the Mass Media: A Reader in Communications*, Arnold, London 1971.

Bettinghaus, E.P., and Preston, I.L., 'Dogmatism and Performance of the Communicator under Cognitive Stress', *Journalism Quarterly*, vol.41, 1964, pp.399—402.

Bever, T.G., Smith, M.L., Bengen, B., and Johnson, T.G., 'Young Viewer's Troubling Responses to T.V. Ads', *Harvard Business Review*, vol. 53, no. 6, 1975, pp.109—19.

Bigsby, C.W.C. (ed.), *Approaches to Popular Culture*, Arnold, London 1976.

Birnbaum, N., *The Crisis in Industrial Society*, Oxford University Press, New York 1969.

Blair, E. (George Orwell), 'Boy's Weeklies', *Horizon*, March 1940. Reprinted in Orwell, S., and Angus, I. (eds), *Collected Essays, Journalism and Letters*, vol. 1, Secker and Warburg, London 1968, pp.505—31.

Blair, E., 'The Sporting Spirit', *Tribune*, December 1945. Reprinted in *Collected Essays, Journalism and Letters*, vol. 4, pp.61—4.

Bloomfield, T.M., 'Single Channel Theory and Dichotic Listening', *Nature*, vol. 236, 1972, pp.465—6.

Blumler, J., 'Producers' Attitudes towards Television Coverage of an Election Campaign: A Case Study', *Sociological Review Monograph No. 13*, 1969.

Bogart, L., *The Age of Television*, Crosby, Lockwood and Son, London, second edition, revised and enlarged, 1958.

Bogart, L., 'Warning: The Surgeon General has Determined that T.V. Violence is Moderately Dangerous to Your Child's Mental Health', *Public Opinion Quarterly*, vol. 36, 1973, pp.491—521.

Bogatz, G., and Ball, S., *The Second Year of Sesame Street: A Continuing Evaluation*, Educational Testing Service, Princeton, New Jersey 1971.

Bonjeau, C.M., Hill, R.J., and Martin, H.W., 'Reactions to the Assassination in Dallas', in Greenberg, B., and Parker, E. (eds), *The Kennedy Assassination and the American Public*, University Press, Stanford 1965, pp.178—98.

Bonsfield, W.A., 'The Occurrence of Clustering in the Recall of Randomly Arranged Associates', *Journal of General Psychology*, vol. 49, 1953, pp.229—40.

Bower, G.H., 'Mental Imagery and Associative Learning', in Gregg, L.W. (ed.), *Cognition in Learning and Memory*, Wiley, New York 1972, pp.51—88.

Bower, R.T., *Television and the Public*, Holt, Rinehart and Winston, New York 1973.

Bower, T.G.R., *The Perceptual World of the Child*, Open Books, London 1977.

Bower, T.G.R., 'The Visual World of Infants', *Scientific American*, vol. 215, no. 6, 1966, pp.80—92.

Bransford, J.D., and Franks, J.I., 'The Abstraction of Linguistic Ideas', *Cognitive Psychology*, vol. 2, 1971, pp.331—50.

Brecht, B., *Collected Plays*, vol. 1, edited by Willett, J., and Manheim, R., Methuen, London 1970.

Breed, W., 'Social Control in the News Room', *Social Forces*, vol. 33, 1955, pp.326—35.

Breed, W., 'Mass Communication and Social Integration', *Social Forces*, vol. 37, 1958, pp.109—16.

Brehm, J.W., 'Motivational Effects of Cognitive Dissonance', in Jones, M.R. (ed.), *Nebraska Symposium on Motivation*, vol. 10, Lincoln University Press, Nebraska 1962, pp.51—77.

Brinson, P. (Chairman), *Broadcasting and Youth*, a study commissioned by the BBC, the Calouste Gulbenkian Foundation, the IBA, and the Manpower Services Commission, London 1979.

British Broadcasting Corporation, *Violence on Television: Programme Content and Viewer Perception*, projects carried out by Irene S. Shaw and David Newell under the direction of B.P. Emmett, head of Audience Research, and with the advice and assistance of Elihu Katz, London 1972 (ref. Shaw and Newell, 1972).

British Broadcasting Corporation, Audience Research Department, *Children as Viewers and Listeners*, London 1974.

British Broadcasting Corporation, Audience Research Department, *Annual Review of BBC Research Findings*, London 1977.

British Broadcasting Corporation, General Advisory Council, *The BBC's Programme Responsibilities towards Adolescents and Young Adults*, London 1978.

British Broadcasting Corporation, with the Gulbenkian Foundation, Independent Broadcasting Authority and the Manpower Services Commission, *Broadcasting and Youth*, London 1979 (ref. Brinson, P., 1979).

Broadbent, D.E., *Perception and Communication*, Pergamon, Oxford 1958.

Broadbent, D.E., 'The Well-Ordered Mind', *American Educational Research Journal*, vol. 3, no. 4, 1966, pp.281—95.

Bronfenbrenner, U., with the assistance of Condy, J.C. Jnr., *Two Worlds of Childhood; U.S. and U.S.S.R*, Allen and Unwin, London 1971.

Brown, J. (ed.), *Recall and Recognition*, J. Wiley, London 1976.

Brown, R. (ed.), *Children and Television*, Collier MacMillan, London 1976.

Bruce, D., and Crowley, J., 'Acoustic Similarity Effects on Retrieval from Secondary Memory', *Journal of Verbal Learning and Verbal Behaviour*, vol. 9, 1970, pp.190—6.

Bruner, J.S., *The Process of Education*, Harvard University Press, Cambridge, Massachusetts 1960.

Bruner, J.S., *Towards a Theory of Instruction*, Belknap, Harvard University Press, Cambridge, Massachusetts 1967.

Bruner, J.S., and Anglia, J.M. (eds), *Beyond the Information Given: Studies in the Psychology of Knowing*, Allen and Unwin, London 1974.

Bruner, J.S., 'Organisation of Early Skilled Action', *Child Development*, vol. 44, 1973, pp.1—11.

Bruner, J.S., Goodnow, J.J., and Austin, G.A., *A Study of Thinking*, Wiley, New York 1956.

Bruner, J.S., and Goodman, C.C., 'Value and Need as Organising Factors in Perception', *Journal of Abnormal and Social Psychology*, vol. 42, no. 1, 1947, pp.33—44.

Bruner, J.S., and Postman, L., 'Emotional Selectivity in Perception and Reaction', *Journal of Personality*, vol. 16, 1947, pp.69—77.

Bursk, E.L., 'Opportunities for Persuasion', *Harvard Business Review*, vol. 36, no. 5, 1958, pp.111—19.

Busby, L.J., 'Sex-role Research on the Mass Media', *Journal of Communication*, vol. 25, no.4, 1975, pp.107—131.

Buss, A.H., *The Psychology of Aggression*, Wiley, New York 1961.

Buss, A.H., 'Aggression Pays', in Singer, J.L. (ed.), *The Control of Aggression and Violence: Cognitive and Physiological Factors*, Academic Press, New York 1971, pp.7—18.

Calfree, R.C., Chapman, R.S., and Venezky, R.L., *How a Child Needs to Think to Learn to Read*, Technical Report, No. 131, Wisconsin Research and Development Centre for Cognitive Learning, 1970.

Calvert, S., Huston, A., Watkins, B., and Wright, J.C., 'The Relation between Selective Attention to Televison Forms and Children's Comprehension of Content, *Child Development*, vol. 53, no. 3, June 1982, pp.601–10.

Cantril, H.H., Gandet, H., and Herzog, G., *The Invasion from Mars*, Princeton University Press, New Jersey 1940.

Carpenter, E., *Oh, What a Blow that Phantom Gave Me!*, Paladin, St Albans 1976.

Carrick James Market Research Ltd, *A National Survey Amongst 7–17 year olds*, Pye Ltd, Cambridge 1978.

Chaffee, S.H., 'Television and Adolescents' Aggressiveness' (Overview), Comstock, G.A., and Rubinstein, E.A., (eds), *Television and Social Behaviour, Vol. 3: Television and Adolescent Aggressiveness*, United States Government Printing Office, Washington DC 1972, pp.1–34.

Chaffee, S.H., and MacLeod, J.M., 'Adolescent Television Use in the Family Context', in Comstock, G.A., and Rubenstein, E.A. (eds), *Television and Social Behaviour Vol. 3: Television and Adolescent Aggressiveness*, United States Government Printing Office, Washington DC 1972, pp.114–72.

Chaffee, S.H., and Petrick, M.J., *Using the Mass Media: Communication Problems in American Society*, McGraw-Hill, New York 1975.

Chase, S., *Men and Machines*, Cape, London 1929.

Chatman, S., 'The Semantics of Style', in Kristeva, J., *Essays in Semiotics*, Mouton, The Hague 1971, pp.399–422.

Cisin, I.H., Coffin, T.E., Janis, I.L., Klapper, J.T., Mendelsohn, H., Omwake, E., Pinderhughes, C.A., Pool, I de Sola, Seigel, A.E., Wallace, A.P.C., Watson, A.S., and Wiebe, G.D., *Television and Growing Up: The Impact of Televised Violence*, United States Government Printing Office, Washington DC 1972.

Clark, C., 'Race, Identification and Television Violence', in Comstock, G.A., Rubinstein, E.A., and Murray, J.P. (eds), *Further Explorations: Television and Social Behaviour Vol. 5*, United States Government Printing Office, Washington DC 1972, pp.120–84.

Clarke, P. (ed.), *New Models of Mass Communication Research*, Sage, Beverly Hills, California 1973.

Cline, V.B., Croft, R.G., and Courrier, S., 'Desensitization of Children to Television Violence', *Journal of Personality and Social Psychology*, vol. 27, 1973, pp.360–5.

Coates, B., and Hartup, W., 'Age and Verbalisation in Observational Learning', *Developmental Psychology*, vol. 1, 1969, pp.556–62.

Cochrane, P., 'Sex Crimes and Pornography Revisited', *International Journal of Criminology and Penology*, vol. 6, 1978, pp.307–17.

Cofer, C.N., 'On Some Factors in the Organisational Characteristics of Free Recall', *American Psychologist*, vol. 20, 1965, pp.261–72.

Cohen, S., and Young, J. (eds), *The Manufacture of News: Social Problems, Deviance and the Mass Media*, Constable, London 1973.

Collins, A.M., and Quillian, M.R., 'Retrieval Time from Semantic Memory', *Journal of Verbal Learning and Verbal Behaviour*, vol. 8, 1969, pp.240—7.

Collins, A.M., 'Facilitating Retrieval from Semantic Memory: The Effect of Repeating Part of an Inference', in Saunders, A.F. (ed.), Attention and Performance, vol. 3, *Acta Psychologica*, vol. 33, 1970, pp.304—14.

Collins, W.A., 'Children's Comprehension of Television Content', in Wartella, E. (ed.), *Children Communicating: Media and Development of Thought, Speech, Understanding*, Sage, Beverly Hills, California 1979, pp.21—52.

Collins, W.A., Wellman, H., Keniston, A.H., and Westley, S.D., 'Age-related Aspects of Comprehension and Influence from a Televised Dramatic Narrative', *Child Development*, no. 49, 1978, pp.389—99.

Comstock, G., Chaffee, S., Katzman, N., McCombs, M., and Roberts, D., *Television and Human Behaviour*, Columbia University Press, New York 1978.

Conrad, P., *Television: The Medium and its Manners*, Routledge and Kegan Paul, London 1982.

Conrad, R., 'Acoustic Confusions in Immediate Memory', *British Journal of Psychology*, vol. 55, 1964, pp.75—84.

Cook, T.D., Appleton, H., Conner, R.F., Shaffer, A., Tamkin, G., and Weber, S.J., *Sesame Street Revisited*, Russell, Sage, New York 1975.

Corkindale, D.R., and Kennedy, S.A., *Measuring the Effect of Advertising*, Saxon House, Farnborough 1975.

Court, J.H., 'Pornography and Sex Crimes: A Re-Evaluation in the Light of Recent Trends Around the World', *International Journal of Penology and Criminology*, vol. 5, 1977, pp.129—57.

Coward, R., and Ellis, J., *Language and Materialism: Developments in Semiology and the Theory of the Subject*, Routledge and Kegan Paul, London 1977.

Cox, D.F., 'Clues for Advertising Strategists', *Harvard Business Review*, 1961. Reprinted in Dexter, L.A., and White, D.A. (eds), *People, Society and Mass Communications*, Free Press, New York 1964, pp.359—74.

Craik, F.I.M., 'The Fate of Primary Memory Items in Free Recall', *Journal of Verbal Learning and Verbal Behaviour*, vol. 9, 1970, pp.143—8.

Craik, F.I.M., 'A "Levels of Analysis" View of Memory', in Pliner, P., Krames, L., and Alloway, T. (eds), *Communication and Affect: Language and Thought*, Academic Press, New York 1973.

Craik, F.I.M., and Lockhart, R.S., 'Levels of Processing: A Framework for Memory Research', *Journal of Verbal Learning and Verbal Behaviour*, vol. 11, 1972, pp.671–84.

Cronbach, L.J., and Snow, R.E., *Aptitudes and Instructional Methods: A Handbook for Research on Interactions*, Irvington, New York 1977.

Crowder, R.G., and Raeburn, V.P., 'The Stimulus Suffix Effect with Reversed Speech', *Journal of Verbal Learning and Verbal Behaviour*, vol. 9, 1970, pp.342–5.

Crystal, D., and Davy, D., *Investigating English Style*, Longmans, London 1969.

Cullingford, C., 'Comics and Children', *Education 3–13*, vol. 5, no. 1, 1977, pp.40–2.

Cullingford, C., 'Listen with Humour', *Times Educational Supplement*, 22 October 1982, p.22.

Cullingford, C., 'Children and Poetry', *English in Education*, vol. 13, no. 2, 1972, pp.56–61.

Cullingford C., 'Why Children Like Enid Blyton', *New Society*, vol. 49, no. 879, 1979, pp.290–1.

Cullingford, C., 'The Message in the Music', *Guardian*, 28 December 1982, p.10.

Curran, J., Gurewitch, M., and Woollacott, J. (eds), *Mass Communication and Society*, Arnold, London 1977.

Darwin, C., Turvey, M., and Crowder, R., 'An Auditory Analogue of the Sperling Partial Report Procedure: Evidence for Brief Auditory Storage', *Cognitive Psychology*, vol. 3, 1972, pp.255–67.

Davis, J.C., and Smith, M.C., 'Memory for Unattended Input', *Journal of Experimental Psychology*, vol. 96, 1972, pp.380–8.

Davison, P., Meyersohn, R., and Shils, E. (eds), *Literary Taste, Culture and Mass Communication, Vol. 9: Uses of Literacy; Media*, Chadwyck-Healey, Cambridge 1978.

Davitz, J.R., 'The Effects of Previous Training on Post Frustration Behaviour', *Journal of Abnormal Social Psychology*, vol. 47, 1952, pp.309–15.

Deese, J., *The Structure of Associations in Language and Thought*, Johns Hopkins Press, Baltimore 1965.

Deese, J., 'Influence of Inter-Item Associative Strength upon Immediate Free Recall', *Psychological Review*, vol. 5, 1959, pp.305–12.

De Fleur, M.L., 'Occupational Roles as Portrayed on Television', *Public Opinion Quarterly*, vol. 28, 1964, pp.57–74.

De Fleur, M.L., and Ball-Rokeach, S., *Theories of Mass Communication*, McKay, New York 1975.

De Fleur, M.L., and De Fleur, L.B., 'The Relative Contribution of Television as a Learning Source for Children's Occupational Knowledge', *American Sociological Review*, vol. 32, no. 5, 1969, pp.777–89.

Dembo, R., and McCron, R., 'Social Factors in Media Use', in Brown, R. (ed.), *Characteristics of Local Media Audiences*, Teakfield, London 1978.

Derrida, J., *Of Grammatology* (trans. G. Spivak), Johns Hopkins University Press, Baltimore 1977.

De Sola Pool, I., and Shulman, I., 'Newsmen's Fantasies, Audiences, and Newswriting', in Dexter, L.A., and White, D.M. (eds), *People, Society and Mass Communications*, Free Press, New York 1964, pp.141–59.

Dexter, L.A., and White, D.M. (eds), *People, Society and Mass Communications*, Free Press, New York 1964.

Diamond, E., *The Tin Kazoo: Television, Politics and the News*, MIT Press, Cambridge, Massachusetts 1975.

Dichter, F., *Effective Advertising*, McGraw-Hill, New York 1941.

Dollard, J., Doob, L., Miller, N., Mowrer, O., and Sears, R., *Frustration and Aggression*, Yale University Press, New Haven 1939.

Dominick, J.R., and Greenberg, B.S., 'Attitudes Towards Violence: The Interaction of Television Exposure, Family Attitudes and Social Class', in Comstock, G.A., and Rubenstein, E.A. (eds), *Television and Adolescent Aggressiveness; Vol. 3 of Television and Social Behaviour*, United States Government Printing Office, Washington DC 1972, pp.314–35.

Dominick, J.R., and Rauch, G.E., 'The Image of Women in Network T.V. Commercials', *Journal of Broadcasting*, vol. 16, no. 3, 1972, pp.259–65.

Drabman, R., and Thomas, M., 'Does Media Violence Increase Children's Toleration of Real-Life Aggression?', *Developmental Psychology*, vol. 10, 1974, pp.418–21.

Dunn, G., *The Box in the Corner: Television and the Under Fives*, Macmillan, London 1977.

Duncker, K., 'Experimental Modifications of Children's Food Preferences Through Social Suggestion', *Journal of Abnormal and Social Psychology*, vol. 33, 1938, pp.489–507.

Dyer, G., *Advertising as Communication*, Methuen, London 1982.

Ebbinghans, H., *Grundzuge der Psychologie*, Veit GmbH, Leipzig 1902.

Edgar, R., *Children and Screen Violence*, University Press, Brisbane 1977.

Edwards, A.D., 'Social Class and Linguistic Choice', *Sociology*, vol. 10, 1976, pp.101–10.

Efron, E., *The News Twisters*, Nash Publishing, New York 1971.

Ehrenberg, A.S.C., 'Repetitive Advertising and the Consumer', *Journal of Advertising Research*, vol. 14, no. 2, 1974, pp.25–34.

Ekman, P., Liebert, R.M., Friesen, M.V., Harrison, R., Zlatchin, C., Malstrom, E.J., and Baron, R.A., 'Facial Expression of Emotion While Watching Televised Violence as Predictors of Subsequent Aggression', in Comstock, G.A., Rubinstein, E.A., and Murray, J.P. (eds), *Television and Social Behaviour, Vol. 5: Television's Effects: Further Explorations*, United States Government Printing Office, Washington DC 1972.

Elias, C.S., and Perfetti, C.A., 'Encoding Task and Recognition Memory: The Importance of Semantic Encoding', *Journal of Experimental Psychology*, vol. 99, no. 2, 1973, pp.151–6.

Eliot, T.S., *Notes Towards the Definition of Culture*, Faber and Faber, London 1948.

Ellingson, R.J., 'Studies of Electrical Activity of the Developing Human Brain', in Himwich, H.E., and Himwich, W.E., *The Developing Brain*, Elsevier, Barking, Essex 1964.

Ellul, J., *The Technological Society* (translated from French), Vintage Books, New York 1964.

Emery, F., and Emery, M., *A Choice of Futures*, Mastmus Nyhoff, Leiden 1976.

Emery, F., and Martin, D., *Psychological Effects of the 'Western' Film — A Study in Television Viewing: Studies in Mass Communication*, University Department of Audio Visual Aids, Melbourne 1957.

Epstein, E.L., *Language and Style*, Methuen, London 1978.

Eron, L.D., 'Relationship of T.V. Viewing Habits and Aggressive Behaviour in Children', *Journal of Abnormal and Social Psychology*, vol. 67, 1963, pp.193–6.

Eron, L.D., Walder, L.O., and Lefkowitz, M.M., *Learning of Agression in Children*, Little, Brown and Co., Boston 1971.

Eron, L.D., Huesman, L.R., Lefkowitz, M.M., and Walder, L.O., 'Does Television Violence Cause Aggression?', *American Psychologist*, vol. 27, no. 4, 1972, pp.253–63.

Estes, W.K. (ed.), *Handbook of Learning and Cognitive Processes, Attention and Memory*, Lawrence Erlbaum Associates, New Jersey 1976.

Eysenck, H.J., 'Television and the Problem of Violence', *New Scientist*, vol. 12, 1961, pp.606–7.

Eysenck, H.J., and Eysenck, S., *Manual: Eysenck Personality Inventory*, University Press, London 1964.

Eysenck, H.J., and Nias, D.K.B., *Sex, Violence and the Media*, Maurice Temple Smith, London 1978.

Faber, R.J., Brown, J.D., and McLeod, J.M., 'Coming of Age in the Global Village: Television and Adolescence', in Wartella, E. (ed.), *Children Communicating: Media and Development of Thought, Speech, Understanding*, Sage, Beverly Hills 1979, pp.215–50.

Farina, A., Allen, J., and Saul, B., 'The Role of the Stigmatized Person in Affecting Social Relationships', *Journal of Personality*, vol. 36, 1968.

Fearing, F., 'A Word of Caution for the Intelligent Consumer of Motion Pictures', *Quarterly of Film, Radio and Television*, vol. 6, 1964, pp.139—40.

Feilitzen, C. von, 'The Functions Served by the Media', in Brown, R. (ed.), *Children and Television*, Collier Macmillan, London 1976, pp.90—115.

Feshbach, S., and Singer, J.L., *Television and Aggression: An Experimental Field Study*, Josey-Bass, San Francisco 1971.

Feshbach, S., 'The Drive-reducing Function of Fantasy Behaviour', *Journal of Abnormal and Social Psychology*, vol. 50, no. 1, 1955, pp.3—11.

Feshbach, S., 'The Catharsis Hypothesis and Some Consequences of Interaction with Aggressive and Neutral Play Objects', *Journal of Personality*, vol. 24, 1956, pp.449—62.

Feshbach, S., 'The Stimulating versus Cathartic Effect of a Vicarious Aggressive Activity', *Journal of Abnormal and Social Psychology*, vol. 63, no. 2, 1961, pp.381—5.

Feshbach, S., 'Aggression', in Mussen, P.H. (ed.), *Carmichael's Manual of Child Psychology*, third edition, vol. 2, Wiley, New York 1970, pp.159—259.

Feshbach, S., 'Reality and Fantasy in Filmed Violence', in Murray, J.P., Rubinstein, E.A., and Comstock, G.A. (eds), *Television and Social Behaviour: Vol. 2: Television and Social Learning*, United States Government Printing Office, Washington DC 1972, pp.318—45.

Festinger, L., *A Theory of Cognitive Dissonance*, Row, Peterson, Evanston, Illinois 1957.

Festinger, L., 'Behavioural Support for Attitude Change', *Public Opinion Quarterly*, vol. 28, 1964, pp.404—17.

Festinger, L., and Maccoby, N., 'On Resistance to Persuasive Communications', *Journal of Abnormal and Social Psychology*, vol. 68, no. 4, 1964, pp.359—66.

Fisher, R., and Bruss, W., 'The Viewing on T.V.: Perception Passivity and Reading', *Colorado Journal of Educational Research*, vol. 15, 1976, pp.33—7.

Fiske, J., and Hartley, J., *Reading Television*, Methuen, London 1978.

Fitzgerald, D., and Ausubel, D., 'Cognitive versus Affective Factors in the Learning and Retention of Controversial Material', *Journal of Educational Psychology*, vol. 54, 1963, pp.73—84.

Foulkes, D., Belvedere, E., and Brubacker, T., 'Televised Violence and Dream Content', in Comstock, G.A., Rubinstein, E.A., and Murray, J.P. (eds), *Television and Social Behaviour: Vol. 5: Television's Effects: Further Explorations*, United States Government Printing Office, Washington DC 1972.

Freedman, L.A., 'Daydream in a Vacuum Tube: A Psychiatrist's Comments on the Effects of Television', in Schramm, W., Lyle, J., and Parker, E.B., *Television in the Lives of our Children: The Effects of Television on American Children*, University Press, Stanford, California 1961, pp.189–94.

Freud, S., *Civilization and Its Discontents* (translated by Riviere, J., and revised by Strachay, J.), Hogarth Press, London 1972, first published 1930.

Friedman, H.L., and Johnson, R.L., 'Mass Media Use and Aggression: A Pilot Study', in Comstock, G.A., and Rubinstein, E.A. (eds), *Television and Social Behaviour: Vol. 3: Television and Adolescent Aggressiveness*, United States Government Printing Office, Washington DC 1972.

Friedrich, L., and Stein, A., *Aggressive and Pro-Social Television Programmes and the Natural Behaviour of Pre-School Children*, Monographs of the Society for Research in Child Development, no. 38 (4, serial no. 151), 1973.

Friedrich, L., and Stein, A., 'Pro-Social Television and Young Children: The Effects of Verbal Labeling and Role Playing on Learning and Behaviour', *Child Development*, vol. 46, 1975, pp.27–38.

Fruch, T., and McGhee, P.E., 'Traditional Sex Role Development and Amount of Time Spent Watching Television', *Developmental Psychology*, vol. 11, no. 109, 1975.

Furu, T., in collaboration with Nakamo, I., Furuhata, K., Akutsu, J., Hirata, U., and Ikuta, T., *The Function of Television for Children and Adolescents*, Monumenta Nipponica, Sophia University, Tokyo 1971.

Furu, T., and Ino, K., 'Children's Viewing Patterns and Factors Influencing Their Program Choices', *Annual Bulletin of Radio and T.V.* Culture Research Institute of Japan 1961, pp.223–61.

Gagné, R.A., *The Conditions of Learning*, Holt, Rinehart and Winston, New York 1965.

Geen, R., 'Observing Violence in the Mass Media: Implications of Basic Research', in Geen, B., and O'Neal, E., *Perspectives on Aggression*, Academic Press, New York 1976, pp.193–234.

Gerbner, G., 'Toward a General Model of Communication', *Audio-Visual Communications Review*, 4, 1956, pp.171–99.

Gerbner, G., 'Cultural Indicators: The Case of Violence in Television Drama', *Annals of the American Association of Political and Social Science*, vol. 338, 1970, pp.69–81.

Gerbner, G., 'Violence in Television Drama: Trends and Symbolic Functions', in Comstock, G.A., and Rubinstein, E.A. (ed.), *Television and Social Behaviour: Vol. 1: Media Content and Control*, United States Government Printing Office, Washington DC 1972.

Gerbner, G., 'The Dynamics of Cultural Resistance', in Tuckman, G., Daniels, A.K., and Benét, J., *Hearth and Home: Images of Women in the Mass Media*, Oxford University Press, New York 1978, pp.46—50.

Gerbner, G., Holsti, O.R., Krippendorff, K., Paisley, J., and Stone, P. (eds), *The Analysis of Communication Content: Development in Scientific Theories and Computer Techniques*, Wiley, New York 1969.

Gesell, A., Ilg, F., and Ames, L.B. (in collaboration with Bullis, G.), *The Child from Five to Ten*, Harper and Row, new edition, New York 1977, first published 1946.

Gibson, E.J., *Principles of Perceptual Learning and Development*, Prentice-Hall, Englewood Cliffs, New Jersey 1969.

Gibson, E.J., 'The Development of Perception as an Adaptive Process', *American Scientist*, vol. 58, 1970, pp.103—7.

Giddens, A., *New Rules of Sociological Method*, Hutchinson, London 1976.

Giner, S., *Mass Society*, Martin Robertson, London 1976.

Glasgow University Media Group, *Bad News*, Routledge and Kegan Paul, London 1976.

Glasgow University Media Group, *More Bad News*, Routledge and Kegan Paul, London 1980.

Glucksberg, S., and Cowen, G.N., 'Memory for Non-Attended Auditory Material', *Cognitive Psychology*, vol. 1, 1970, pp.149—56.

Glynn, S.M., Britton, B.K., Muth, D., and Dogan, N., 'Writing and Revising Persuasive Documents: Cognitive Demands', *Journal on Educational Psychology*, vol. 74, no. 4, 1982, pp.557—67.

Golding, P., *The Mass Media*, Longmans, London 1974.

Goldstein, A.G., and Chance, J.E., 'Recognition of Complex Visual Stimuli', *Perception and Psychophysics*, vol. 9, 1971, pp.237—41.

Gomberg, A.W., 'The Four Year Old Child and Television: The Effects on his Play at School', PhD. Dissertation, Teachers College, Columbia University 1961.

Goodhardt, G.J., Ehrenberg, A.S.C., and Collins, M.A., *The Television Audience: Patterns of Viewing*, Saxon House, Farnborough 1975.

Goodwin, D.W., Powell, B., Bremer, D., Home, H., and Stern, J., 'Alcohol and Recall: State Dependent Effects in Man', *Science*, vol. 1, no. 963, 1969, p.1358.

Gordon, G.S., *Persuasion: The Theory and Practice of Manipulative Communication*, Hastings House, New York 1971.

Greenberg, B.S., 'Viewing and Listening Parameters Among British Youngsters', in Brown, R. (ed.), *Children and Television*, Collier Macmillan, London 1976, pp.29—44.

Greenberg, B.S., and Tannenbaum, P.H., 'Communicator Performance Under Cognitive Stress', *Journalism Quarterly*, vol. 39, 1962, pp.169—78.

208

Greenberg, B.S., and Dervin, B., 'Mass Communication Among the Urban Poor', *Public Opinion Quarterly*, vol. 34, no. 2, 1970, pp.224–35.

Greenwald, A., 'Cognitive Learning, Cognitive Response to Persuasion and Attitude Change', in Greenwald, A., Brock, T., and Ostrom, T. (eds), *Psychological Foundations of Attitudes*, Academic Press, New York 1968, pp.147–70.

Greer, D., Potts, R., Wright, J.C., and Huston, A.C., 'The Effects of Television Commercial Form and Commercial Placement on Children's Social Behaviour and Attention', *Child Development*, vol. 53, no. 3, 1982, pp.611–9.

Gregory, R.L., *Eye and Brain: The Psychology of Seeing*, Weidenfeld and Nicholson, London 1966.

Gregory, R.L., *The Intelligent Eye*, Weidenfeld and Nicholson, London 1970.

Gregory, R.L., *Concepts and Mechanisms of Perception*, Duckworth, London 1974.

Groombridge, B., *Television and the People: A Programme for Democratic Participation*, Penguin, Harmondsworth 1972.

Grusec, J.E., and Brinker, D.B., Jnr, 'Reinforcement for Imitation as a Social Learning Determinant with Implications for Sex-Role Development', *Journal of Personality and Social Psychology*, vol. 21, pp.149–58.

Hale, G.A., Miller, L.K., and Stevenson, H.W., 'Incidental Learning of Film Content: A Development Study', *Child Development*, vol. 39, 1968, pp.69–77.

Hall, S., Hobson, D., Lowe, A., and Willis, P., *Culture, Media, Language: Working Papers in Cultural Studies*, 1972–79, Hutchinson, London 1980.

Hall, S., and Whannel, P., *The Popular Arts*, Hutchinson, London 1964.

Halloran, J.D., *Control or Consent?: A Study of the Challenge of Mass Communication*, Sheed and Ward, London 1963.

Halloran, J.D., *The Effects of Mass Communication: With Special Reference to Television*, University Press, Leicester 1964.

Halloran, J.D. (ed.), *Findings and Cognition on the Television Perception of Children and Young People*, Internationales Zentralinstitut für das Jugend-und-Bildungs-Fernsehen, Munich 1969.

Halloran, J.D., Brown, R., and Chaney, D.C., *Television and Delinquency: T.V. Research Committee Working Paper No. 3*, University Press, Leicester 1970.

Halloran, J.D., 'Television and Violence', *Twentieth Century*, Winter, 1964, pp.61–72.

Halloran, J.D., 'Volkschulkinder und Fernsehen', in Hömberg, E. (ed.), *Volkschulkinder und Fernsehen: Empirische Untersuchungen in Drei Ländern*, Stiftung Prix Jennesse, Munich 1978 (whole volume).

Halmos, P. (ed.), 'The Sociology of Mass Media Communicators', *Sociological Review*, Monograph 13, 1969.

Hamer, C.F., and Brown, P.A., 'Clarification of the Instigation to Action Concept in the Frustration-Aggression Hypothesis', *Journal of Abnormal and Social Psychology*, vol. 51, 1955, pp.204–6. 204-206.

Hanratty, M.A., Liebert, R.M., Morris, L.W., and Fernandez, L.E., 'Imitation of Film-Mediated Aggression Against Live and Inanimate Victims', *Proceedings of the 77th Annual Convention of the American Psychological Association*, 1969, pp.457–8.

Hanratty, M.A., O'Neal, E., and Sultzer, J.L., 'Effect of Frustration upon Imitation of Aggression', *Journal of Personality and Social Psychology*, vol. 21, 1972, pp.30–4.

Hapkiewitz, W., and Roden, A., 'The Effect of Aggressive Cartoons on Children's Inter-Personal Play', *Child Development*, vol. 42, 1971, pp.1583–5.

Harless, J.D., 'An Experimental Investigation into the Impact of Adventure-Mystery Novels on Attitudes of Readers', PhD Thesis, University of Iowa 1969.

Harless, J.D., 'The Impact of Adventure Fiction on Readers: The Tough-Guy Type', *Journalism Quarterly*, vol. 49, 1972, pp.65–73.

Hartley, E.L., 'The Influence of Repetition and Familiarisation on Consumer Preferences', paper presented to American Psychological Association 1961.

Hartley, R., *The Impact of Viewing Aggression*, Office of Social Research, CBS, New York 1964.

Hartmann, P., and Husband, C., *Racism and Mass Media,* Davis-Poynter, London 1974.

Head, S.W., 'Content Analysis of Television Programmes', *Quarterly of Film, Radio and Television*, vol. 1, 1954, pp.178–82.

Hebb, D.O., 'Drives and the C.N.S. (Conceptual Nervous System)', *Psychological Review*, vol. 62, no. 4, 1955, pp.243–54.

Helitzer, M., and Heyel, C., *The Youth Market: Its Dimensions, Influence and Opportunities for You*, Media Books, New York 1970.

Helmreich, R., 'Stress, Self-Esteem and Attitudes', in King, B., and McGinnies, E., *Attitudes, Conflict and Social Change*, Academic Press, New York 1972, pp.33–48.

Henry, J., *Culture Against Man,* Random House, New York 1963.

Hepner, A., *Effective Advertising*, McGraw-Hill, New York 1941.

Herriot, P. *Attributes of Memory*, Methuen, London 1974.

Herzog, H., 'What do we Really Know about Daytime Serial Listeners?', in Lazarsfeld, P., and Stanton, F. (eds), *Radio Research New York, 1942-3,* Academic Press, New York 1944, pp.3–31.

Hicks, D.J., 'Effects of Co-Observer's Sanctions and Adult Presence on Imitative Aggression', *Child Development*, vol. 39, 1968, pp.303–9.

Hilgard, E., *Theories of Learning and Instruction: 63rd Year Book of the National Society for the Study of Education*, University Press, Chicago 1964.

Himmelweit, H.T., Oppenheim, A.N., and Vince, P., *Television and the Child: An Empirical Study of the Effect of Television on the Young*, Nuffield Foundation with Oxford University Press, London 1958.

Hoban, C.F., 'The Usable Residue of Educational Film Research', in Schramm, W. (ed.), *New Teaching Aids for the American Classroom*, Stanford University Press 1960, pp.65—115.

Hobsbaum, A., and Chikas, C., *Watching 'You and Me': A Report on Young Viewers at Home and in School,* BBC, London 1979.

Hobson, D., *Crossroads: The Drama of Soap-Opera*, Methuen, London 1982.

Hockey, G.R.J., and Hamilton, P., 'Arousal and Information Selection in Short-Term Memory', *Nature*, vol. 226, 1970, pp.866—7.

Holland, N.N., *The Dynamics of Literary Response*, Academic Press, New York 1968.

Holland, N.N., *Five Readers Reading*, Yale University Press, New Haven, Connecticut 1975.

Home Office, *Research Study No. 40: Screen Violence and Film Censorship — A Review of Research*, by Brody, S., HMSO, London 1977.

Hood, S., *The Mass Media*, Macmillan, London 1972.

Hornik, R., 'Out-of-School Television and Schooling: Hypothesis and Methods', *Review on Educational Research*, vol. 51, no. 2, 1981, pp.193—214.

Horowitz, L.M., Lampel, A.K., and Takanishi, R.N., 'The Child's Memory for Utilized Scenes', *Journal of Experimental Child Psychology*, vol. 8, 1969, pp.375—88.

Horowitz, M.J., *Image Formation and Cognition*, Appleton Century Crofts, New York, second edition, 1978.

Horton, D., Manksch, H., and Lang, K., *Chicago Summer Television, July 30th—August 5th, 1951*, National Association of Educational Broadcasters, Urbana, Illinois 1951.

Horton, D., and Wohl, R.R., 'Mass Communication and Para Social Interaction', *Psychiatry*, vol. 19, 1956, pp.215—29.

Hovland, C.I. (ed.), *The Order of Presentation in Persuasion*, Yale University Press, New Haven, Connecticut 1957.

Hovland, C.I., Harvey, D.J., Sherif, M., 'Assimilation and Contrast Effects in Reaction to Communication and Attitude Change', *Journal of Abnormal and Normal Psychology*, no. 57, 1957, pp.244—52.

Hovland, C.I., Lumsdaine, A.A., and Sheffield, F.D., *Experiments on Mass Communications: Studies in Social Psychology in World War Two*, vol. 3, University Press, Princeton 1949.

Hovland, C.I., Janis, I.L., and Kelley, H., *Communication and Persuasion: Psychological Studies of Opinion Change*, Yale University Press, New Haven, Connecticut 1953.

Hovland, C.I., and Weiss, W., 'The Influence of Source Credibility on Communication Effectiveness', *Public Opinion Quarterly*, vol. 15, 1951, pp.635—50.

Hovland, C.I., Lumsdaine, A.A., and Sheffield, F.D., 'Changing Opinions on a Controversial Subject', in Schramm, W. (ed.), *The Process and Effects of Mass Communications*, University Press, Urbana, Illinois 1955, pp.261—74.

Hovland, C.I., *Television and Children*, New University Education, London 1977.

Howe, M.J.A., 'Repeated Presentation and Recall of Meaningful Prose', *Journal of Educational Psychology*, vol. 61, 1970, pp.214—9.

Howitt, D., and Cumberbatch, G., *Mass Media, Violence and Society*, Elek Science, London 1975.

Hoyt, J.L., 'Effects of Media Violence "Justification" on Agression', *Journal of Broadcasting*, vol. 14, no. 4, 1970, pp.455—64.

Hudson, L., *Frames of Mind: Ability, Perception and Self-Perception in the Arts and Sciences*, Methuen, London 1968.

Hull, C.L., *Principles of Behaviour*, New York 1949.

Hull, C.L. Felsinger, J., Gladstone, A., and Yamagachi, H., 'A Proposed Quantification of Habit Strength', *Psychological Review*, vol. 54, no. 5, 1947, pp.237—54.

Huston, A.C., Wright, J.C., Wartella, E., Rice, M.L., Watkins, B.A., Campbell, T., and Potts, R., 'Communication More Than Contents: Formal Features of Children's Television Programmes', *Journal of Communication*, vol. 31, no. 3, 1981, pp.32—48.

Independent Broadcasting Authority, Working Party, *Second Interim Report: The Portrayal of Violence on Television*, London 1975.

Independent Broadcasting Authority, Audience Research Department, *Children and Television*, London 1974.

Iser, W., *The Act of Reading: A Theory of Aesthetic Response*, Routledge and Kegan Paul, London 1976.

James, W., *The Principles of Psychology*, Henry Holt, New York 1890.

Janis, I.L., *Victims of Groupthink: A Psychological Study of Foreign Policy Decisions and Fiascoes*, Houghton Mifflin, Boston 1972.

Janis, I.L., 'Personality as a Factor in Susceptibility to Persuasion', in Schramm, W. (ed.), *Science of Human Communication*, Basic Books, New York 1963, pp.53—64.

Janis, I.L., and Feshbach, S., 'Effects of Fear-Arousing Communications', *Journal of Abnormal and Social Psychology*, vol. 48, no. 1, 1953, pp.78—92.

Kanner, L., *Child Psychiatry*, Thomas, Springfield, Massachusetts 1972.

Katona, G., *Organising and Memorizing: Studies in the Psychology of Learning and Teaching*, Columbia University Press, New York 1940.

Katz, D., 'The Functional Approach to the Study of Attitudes', *Public Opinion Quarterly*, vol. 24, 1960, pp.163—204.

Katz, E., 'The Two-Step Flow of Communication', *Public Opinion Quarterly*, vol. 21, 1957, pp.346—5.

Katz, E., and Lazarsfeld, P.F., *Personal Influence: The Part Played by People in the Flow of Mass Communications*, Free Press, Glencoe, Illinois 1955.

Kausler, D.H., *The Psychology of Verbal Learning and Memory*, Academic Press, London 1974.

Kay, H., 'Toward an Understanding of News Reading Behaviour', *Journalism Quarterly*, vol. 33, 1954, pp.15—31.

King, B.T., and McGinnies, E. (eds), *Attitudes, Conflict and Social Change*, Academic Press, New York 1972.

Kintsch, W., *Memory and Cognition*, Wiley, New York 1977.

Kintsch, W., 'Models of Free Recall and Recognition', in Norman, D.A. (ed.), *Models for Human Memory*, Academic Press, New York 1970, pp.333—73.

Kiss, G.R., 'Steps Towards a Model of Word Selection', in Meltzer, B., and Michie, D. (eds), *Machine Intelligence 4*, University Press, Edinburgh 1969, pp.315—36.

Klapper, J.L., *Effects of the Mass Media*, Bureau of Applied Social Research, Columbia University Press, New York 1948.

Klapper, J.L., *The Effects of Mass Communication*, Glencoe Press, New York 1960.

Klapper, J.L., 'The Comparative Effects of the Various Media', in Schramm, W. (ed.), *The Process and Effects of Mass Communication*, University of Illinois Press, Urbana, Illinois 1955.

Kleinsmith, L.J., and Kaplan, S., 'Interaction of Arousal and Recall Interval in Nonsense Syllable Paved-Associative Learning', *Journal of Experimental Psychology*, vol. 67, 1964, pp.124—6.

Kline, F.G., and Tichenor, P.J. (eds), *Current Perspectives in Mass Communication Research*, Sage, Beverly Hills, California 1972.

Knightley, P., *The First Casualty*, André Deutsch, London 1975.

Kniveton, B.H., and Stephenson, G.M., 'The Effect of Social Class on Imitation in a Pre-Experience Situation', *British Journal of Social and Clinical Psychology*, vol. 11, 1972, pp.225—34.

Kohlberg, L., 'A Cognitive-Developmental Analysis of Children's Sex-role Concepts and Attitudes', in Maccoby, E. (ed.), *The Development of Sex Differences*, University Press, Stanford, California 1966.

Kolers, P.A., 'Some Psychological Aspects of Pattern Recognition', in Kolers, P.A., and Eden, M. (eds), *Recognizing Patterns: Studies in Living and Automatic Systems*, Massachusetts Institute of Technology Press, Boston 1968, pp.4—63.

Krugman, H.E., 'An Application of Learning Theory to T.V. Copy Testing', *Public Opinion Quarterly*, vol. 26, 1962, pp.626–34.

Krugman, H.E., 'The Impact of Television Advertising: Learning with Involvement', *Public Opinion Quarterly*, vol. 29, 1965, pp.349–56.

Krugman, H.E., 'The Measurement of Advertising Involvement', *Public Opinion Quarterly*, vol. 39, 1966, pp.583–96.

Krugman, H.E., 'Brain Wave Measures of Media Involvement', *Journal of Advertising Research*, February 1971, pp.3–9.

Krugman, H.E. and Hartley, E.L., 'The Learning of Tastes', *Public Opinion Quarterly*, vol. 24, pp.621–31.

Krugman, H.E., and Hartley, E.L., 'Passive Learning from Television', *Public Opinion Quarterly*, vol. 34, 1970, pp.184–90.

Krull, R., and Husson, W., 'Children's Attention: The Case of T.V. Viewing', in Wartella, E. (ed.), *Children Communicating: Media and Development of Thought, Speech, Understanding*, Sage Annual Reviews of Communication Research, Beverly Hills, California, vol. 7, 1979, pp.83–114.

Labov, W., Cohen, P., Robins, C., and Lewis, J., *A Study of the Non-Standard English of Negro and Puerto-Rican Speakers in New York City, Vol. 2: The Use of Language in the Speech Community*, Final Report of Co-operative Research Project No. 3288, Columbia University, New York 1968.

Lang, K., and Lang, G., *Politics and Television*, Quadrangle Books, Chicago 1968.

Lang, K., and Lang, G., 'The Unique Perspective of T.V. and its Effects: A Pilot Study', *American Sociological Review*, vol. 18, no. 1, 1953, pp.3–12.

Lange, D.L., Baker, R.K., and Ball, S.J., *Mass Media and Violence: A Report to the National Commission on the Causes and Prevention of Violence*, United States Government Printing Office, Washington DC 1969.

Langholtz, L.V., *The Hidden Myth*, Heinemann, London 1975.

Larrabee, E., and Meyersohn, R. (eds), *Mass Leisure*, Free Press, Glencoe, Illinois 1958.

Lasswell, H., 'The Structure and Function of Communication in Society', in Bryson, L.B. (ed.), *The Communication of Ideas*, Harper and Row, New York 1948.

Latané, B., and Darley, J.M., *The Unresponsive Bystander: Why Doesn't He Help?*, Appleton, New York 1970.

Latané, B., and Darley, J., 'Determinants of Bystander Intervention', in Macauley, M.E., and Berkowitz, L. (eds), *Altruism and Helping Behaviour*, Academic Press, New York 1970.

Lawler, J.G., *Celestial Pantomine: Poetic Structures of Transcendence*, Yale University Press, New Haven 1979.

Lazarsfeld, P.F., Berelson, B., and Gandet, H., *The People's Choice: How the Voter Makes Up His Mind in a Presidential Campaign*, Duell, Sloan and Pearce, New York 1944, third edition, Columbia Press, New York 1968.

Lazarsfeld, P.F., and Kendall, P., *Radio Listening in America*, Prentice-Hall, New York 1948.

Lazarsfeld, P.F., 'Why is so Little Known About the Effects of Television on Children and What can be Done? Testimony before the Kefanver Committee of Juvenile Delinquency', *Public Opinion Quarterly*, vol. 19, 1955, pp.243–51.

Lazarsfeld, P.F., and Merton, R.K., 'Mass Communication, Popular Taste and Organised Social Action', in Bryson, L. (ed.), *The Communication of Ideas*, Harper and Row, New York 1948. Reprinted in Rosenberg, B., and White, D.M. (eds), *Mass Culture: The Popular Arts in America*, Free Press, New York 1957, pp.457–73.

Lazarus, R.S., and McCleary, R.A., 'Autonomic Discrimination without Awareness: A Study of Subception', *Psychological Review*, vol. 58, 1951, pp.113–22.

Lazarus, R.S., Speisman, J., Mordkoff, A., and Davison, L., 'A Laboratory Study of Psychological Stress Produced by a Motion Picture Film', *Psychological Monographs*, no. 76 (whole no. 553), 1962.

Leavis, F.R., *The Common Pursuit*, Chatto and Windus, London 1958.

Leavis, F.R., and Thompson, D., *Culture and Environment: The Training of Critical Awareness*, Chatto and Windus, London 1933.

Leavis, Q.D., *Fiction and the Reading Public*, Chatto and Windus, London 1932.

Leavis, Q.D., 'A Middleman of Ideas', *Scrutiny*, vol. 1, no. 1, 1932, pp.69–73.

Le Bon, G., *The Crowd*, Larlin Corporation, New York 1977. Reprint of 1958 edition.

Leech, G., *English in Advertising: A Linguistic Study of Advertising in Great Britain*, Longmans, London 1966.

Lefkowitz, M., Eron, L.D., Walder, L.O., and Huesmann, L.P., *Growing up to be Violent: A Longitutional Study of the Development of Aggression*, Pergamon Press, New York 1977.

Lefkowitz, M., Eron, L.D., Walder, L.O., and Huesmann, L.P., 'Television Violence and Child Aggression: A Follow-up Study', in Comstock, G.A., and Rubinstein, E.A. (eds), *Television and Social Behaviour, Vol. 3: Television and Adolescent Aggressiveness*, United States Government Printing Office, Washington DC 1972, pp.35–135.

Leifer, A.D., Collins, W.A., Gross, B.M., Taylor, P.H., Andrews, L., and Blackmer, E.R., 'Developmental Aspects of Variables Relevant to Observational Learning', *Child Development*, vol. 42, 1970, pp.1509–16.

Leifer, A.D., and Roberts, D., 'Children's Responses to Television Violence', in Murray, J.P., Rubinstein, E.A., and Comstock, G.A. (eds), *Television and Social Behaviour: Vol. 2: Television and Social Learning*, United States Government Printing Office, Washington DC 1972, pp.43—180.

Lemon, J., 'Dominant or Dominated? Women on Prime-Time Television', in Tuchman, G., Daniels, A.K., and Benét, J., *Hearth and Home: Images of Women in the Mass Media*, Oxford University Press, New York 1978, pp.51—68.

Lesser, G.S., *Children and Television: Lessons from Sesame Street*, Vintage Books, New York 1974.

Lesser, G.S., 'Learning, Teaching and Television Production for Children: The Experience of Sesame Street', *Harvard Educational Review*, vol. 42, no. 2, 1972, pp.232—72.

Lesser, H., *Television and the Pre-School Child: A Psychological Theory of Instruction and Curriculum Development*, Academic Press, New York 1977.

Lesser, L.N., 'An Experimental Investigation of Children's Behaviour as a Function of Interpolated Activities and Individual Differences in Imaginative Behaviour', *Dissertation Abstract*, vol. 24, no. 2, 1963, pp.836—7.

Lesser, S.O., *Fiction and the Unconscious*, Vintage Books, New York 1962.

Letkemann, P., *Crime as Work*, Prentice-Hall, Englewood Cliffs, New York 1973.

Lewis, G.H., 'The Sociology of Popular Culture', *Current Sociology*, vol. 26, no. 3, Sage, New York 1978.

Levine, J.M., and Murphy, G., 'The Learning and Forgetting of Controversial Material', *Journal of Abnormal and Social Psychology*, vol. 38, 1943, pp.507—17.

Levi-Strauss, C., *Structural Anthropology*, Basic Books, New York 1963.

Leyens, J.P., Camino, L., Parke, R.D., and Berkowitz, L., 'The Effects of Movie Violence on Aggression in a Field Setting as a Function of Group Dominance and Cohesion', *Journal of Personality and Social Psychology*, vol. 32, 1975, pp.346—60.

Liebert, R.M., Neale, J.M., and Davidson, E.S., *The Early Window: Effects of Television on Children and Youth*, Pergamon Press, New York 1973.

Liebert, R.M., 'Television and Social Learning: Some Relationships between Viewing and Behaving Aggressively (Overview)', in Murray, J.P., Rubinstein, E.A., and Comstock, G.A., *Television and Social Behaviour: Vol. 2: Television and Social Learning*, United States Printing Office, Washington DC 1972, pp.1—42.

Liebert, R.M., and Baron, R.A., 'Short Term Effects of Televised Aggression on Children and Youth', in Murray, J.P., Rubinstein, E.A., and Comstock, G.A., *Television and Social Behaviour: Vol. 2: Television and Social Learning*, United States Printing Office, Washington DC 1972, pp.181—201.

Lloyd, K.E., Lyne, S.R., and Feallock, J.B., 'Short-Term Retention as a Function of the Average Number of Items Presented', *Journal of Experimental Psychology*, vol. 60, no. 4, 1960, pp.201—7.

Lock, A., 'The Emergence of Language', in Lock, A. (ed.), *Action, Gesture and Symbol: The Emergence of Language*, Academic Press, London 1978, pp.3—18.

Lockhart, R.S., Craik, F.I.M., and Jacoby, L., 'Depth of Processing, Recognition and Recall', in Brown, J.R. (ed.), *Recall and Recognition*, Wiley, London 1976, pp.75—102.

Lohisse, J., *Anonymous Communication: Mass Media in the Modern World*, translated from the French by Corrin, S., Allen and Unwin, London 1973 (La Communication Anonyme 1969).

Lorch, E.P., Anderson, D.R., and Levin, S.R., 'The Relationship of Visual Attention to Children's Comprehension of Television', *Child Development*, vol. 50, 1979, pp.722—7.

Lovibond, S.H., 'The Effect of Media Stressing Crime and Violence upon Children's Attitudes', *Social Problems*, vol. 15, 1967, pp.91—100.

Lyle, J., and Hoffman, H., 'Exploration in Patterns of Television Viewing by Pre-School-Age Children', in Rubinstein, E.A., Comstock, G.A., and Murray, J.P. (eds), *Television and Social Behaviour: Vol. 4: Television in Day-to-Day Life: Patterns of Use*, United States Printing Office, Washington DC 1972, pp.45—61.

Lyle, J., and Hoffman, H., 'Television Viewing by Pre-School-Age Children', in Brown, R. (ed.), *Children and Television*, Collier, Macmillan, London 1976, pp.45—61.

Maccoby, E.E., 'Television: Its Impact on School Children', *Public Opinion Quarterly*, vol. 15, 1951, pp.421—44.

Maccoby, E.E., 'Why do Children Watch Television?', *Public Opinion Quarterly*, vol. 18, 1954, pp.239—44.

Maccoby, E.E., 'The Effects of Television', in Schramm, W. (ed.), *The Science of Human Communication: New Directions and New Findings in Communication Research*, Basic Books, New York 1963, pp.116—27.

Maccoby, E.E., Matthews, R.E., and Morton, A.S., 'Youth and Political Change', *Public Opinion Quarterly*, vol. 18, 1954, pp.23—39.

Maccoby, E.E., Levin, H., and Selyor, B.M., 'The Effects of Emotional Arousal on the Retention of Film Content: A Failure to Replicate', *Journal of Abnormal and Social Psychology*, vol. 53, 1956, pp.373—4.

Maccoby, E.E., and Wilson, W., 'Identification and Observational Learning from Films', *Journal of Abnormal and Social Psychology*, vol. 55, 1957, pp.76–87.

Maccoby, E.E., Wilson, W., and Burton, R., 'Differential Movie-Viewing Behaviour of Male and Female Viewers', *Journal of Personality*, vol. 26, 1958, pp.259–67.

Maccoby, E.E., and Hagen, J.W., 'Effects of Distraction upon Central versus Incidental Recall: Development Trends', *Journal of Experimental Child Psychology*, vol. 2, 1965, pp.280–9.

MacMenamin, M.J., 'Effect of Instructional Television on Personality Perception', *Audio-Visual Communication Review*, vol. 22, 1974.

McCombs, M.E., 'Role of Television in the Acquisition of Language', PhD Dissertation, University of Stanford 1966.

McGinnies, E., 'Emotionally and Perceptual Defense', *Psychological Review*, vol. 56, 1949, pp.244–51.

McGuire, W.J., 'Inducing Resistance to Persuasion', in Berkowitz, L. (ed.), *Advances in Experimental Social Psychology, Vol. 1*, Prentice-Hall, New York 1964, pp.191–229.

McIntyre, J.J., and Teevan, J.J., Jnr, 'Television Violence and Deviant Behaviour', in Comstock, G.A., and Rubinstein, E.A. (eds), *Television and Social Behaviour: Vol. 3: Television and Adolescent Aggressiveness*, United States Government Printing Office, Washington DC 1972, pp.383–435.

McLeod, J., Ward, S., and Tancill, K., 'Alienation and Uses of the Mass Media', *Public Opinion Quarterly*, vol. 29, 1966, pp.583–94.

McLeod, J., Atkin, C.K., and Chaffee, S.A., 'Adolescents, Parents and Television Use: Adolescent Self-report Measures from Maryland and Wisconsin Samples', in Comstock, G.A., and Rubinstein, E.A. (eds), *Television and Social Behaviour: Vol. 3: Television and Social Aggressiveness*, United States Government Printing Office, Washington DC 1972, pp.173–238.

McLeod, J., Atkin, C.K., and Chaffee, S.H., 'Adolescents, Parents and Television Use: Self-report and Other-report Measures from the Wisconsin Sample', in Comstock, G.A., and Rubinstein, E.A. (eds), *Television and Social Behaviour: Vol. 3: Television and Social Aggressiveness*, United States Government Printing Office, Washington DC 1972, pp.239–313.

McLuhan, M., *The Mechanical Bride: The Folklore of Industrial Man*, Vanguard, New York 1951.

McLuhan, M., *The Gutenberg Galaxy*, University Press, Toronto 1962.

McLuhan, M., *Understanding Media: The Extensions of Man*, McGraw-Hill, New York 1964.

McLuhan, M., *In Personal Communications*, 1967.

McQuail, D., *Towards a Sociology of Mass Communications*, Collier, Macmillan, London 1969.

McQuail, D., *Mass Communications Theory: An Introduction*, Sage, London 1983.

McQuail, D., and Windahl, S., *Communication: Models for the Study of Mass Communications*, Longmans, London 1981.

Mannheim, K., *Ideology and Utopia*, Harcourt Brace, New York 1936.

Mannheim, K., *Man and Society in an Age of Reconstruction*, Harcourt Brace, New York 1940.

Manstead, T., and McCullogh, C., 'Sex-role Stereotyping in British Advertisements', *British Journal of Social Psychology*, no. 20, 1981, pp.171–80.

Marcuse, H., *One Dimensional Man*, Routledge and Kegan Paul, London 1964.

Marks, M.R., and Jack, O., 'Verbal Context and Memory Span for Meaningful Material', *American Journal of Psychology*, vol. 65, 1952, pp.298–300.

Marsh, P., *Aggro: The Illusion of Violence*, Dent, London 1978.

Mednick, S.A., 'The Associative Basis of the Creative Process', *Psychological Review*, vol. 69, 1962, pp.220–32.

Melody, W., *Children's Television: The Economics of Exploitation*, Yale University Press, New Haven, Connecticut 1973.

Meltzer, L.L., 'Visual Perception: Stage One of a Long-term Investigation into Cognitive Components on Achievement', *British Journal of Educational Psychology*, vol. 52, no. 2, 1982, pp.144–54.

Mendelsohn, H., 'Measuring a Process of Communications Effect', *Public Opinion Quarterly*, vol. 26, 1962, pp.411–6.

Mendelsohn, H., 'Sociological Perspectives on the Study of Mass Communications', in Dexter, L.A., and White, D.M. (eds), *People, Society and Mass Communications*, Free Press, New York 1964.

Meringoff, L.K., 'Influence of the Medium on Children's Story Apprehension', *Journal of Educational Psychology*, no. 72, 1980, pp.240–9.

Merton, R.K., *Social Theory and Social Structure*, Free Press, Glencoe, Illinois 1957.

Meyer, T.P., 'Some Effects of Real Newsfilm Violence on the Behaviour of Viewers', *Journal of Broadcasting*, vol. 15, no. 3, 1971, pp.275–85.

Mialeret, G., and Melies, M.G., 'Expériences sur la Compréhension du Langage Cinématographique', *Revue Internationale de Filmolgie*, vol. 5, 1954, pp.221–8.

Milgram, S., *Obedience to Authority: An Experimental View*, Tavistock, London 1974.

Milgram, S., 'Behavioural Study of Obedience', *Journal of Abnormal and Social Psychology*, vol. 67, 1963, pp.371–8.

Milgram, S., 'Group Pressure and Action against a Person', *Journal of Abnormal and Social Psychology*, vol. 69, 1964, pp.371—8.

Milgram, S., and Shotland, R.L., *Television and Anti-Social Behaviour: Field Experiments*, Academic Press, New York 1973.

Miller, G.A., *Spontaneous Apprentices: Children and Language*, Seabury Press, New York 1977.

Miller, G.A., 'The Magical Number Seven, Plus or Minus Two: Some Limits on our Capacity for Processing Information', *Psychological Review*, vol. 63, no. 2, 1956, pp.81—97.

Miller, G.A., Galanter, E., and Pribram, K.H., *Plans and the Structure of Behaviour*, Holt, New York 1960.

Miller, G.A., and Selfridge, J.A., 'Verbal Context and the Recall of Meaningful Material', *American Journal of Psychology*, vol. 63, 1950, pp.176—85.

Mills, C.W., *The Power Elite*, Oxford University Press, New York 1959.

Moray, N., 'Attention in Dichotic Listening: Affective cues and the Influence of Instructions', *Quarterly Journal of Experimental Psychology*, vol. 11, 1959, pp.56—60.

Morin, *L'Espirit du Temps*, Paris 1962.

Murdock, G., and Phelps, G., *Mass Media and the Secondary School*, Macmillan, London 1973.

Mussen, P., and Rutherford, E., 'Effects of Aggressive Cartoons on Children's Aggressive Play', *Journal of Abnormal and Social Psychology*, vol. 66, 1962, pp.461—4.

Neisser, U., *Cognitive Psychology*, Appleton-Century Crofts, New York 1967.

Nelson, K.J., 'The Organisation of Free Recall by Young Children', *Journal of Experimental Child Psychology*, vol. 8, no. 2, 1969, pp.284—95.

Newcomb, T.M., 'An Approach to the Study of Communication Acts', *Psychological Review*, vol. 60, 1953, pp.393—404.

Newell, A., and Simon, H.A., *Human Problem Solving*, Prentice-Hall, New Jersey 1972.

Noble, G., *Children in Front of the Small Screen*, Constable, London 1975.

Noble, G., 'Young Children and Television: Some Selected Hypotheses and Findings', *Screen*, vol. 11, part 4/5, 1970, pp.31—47.

Noble, G., 'Concepts of Order and Balance in a Children's T.V. Programme', in Brown, R. (ed.), *Children and Television*, Collier Macmillan, London 1976, pp.62—74.

Norman, D.A., 'Memory While Shadowing', *Quarterly Journal of Experimental Psychology*, vol. 21, 1969, pp.85—93.

Norman, D.A., 'The Role of Memory in the Understanding of Language', in Kavanagh, J.F., and Mattingly, I.G. (eds), *Language by Ear and by Eye: The Relationship between Speech and Reading*, MIT Press, Cambridge, Massachusetts 1972, pp.277—88.

Nunnally, J., and Bobren, H., *Journal of Personality*, vol. 27, 1959, pp.38—46.

Opie, I., and Opie, P., *The Lore and Language of School Children*, Routledge and Kegan Paul, London 1959.

Opie, I., and Opie, P., *Children's Games in Street and Playground*, Clarendon Press, Oxford 1969.

Orne, M., and Scheibe, K., 'The Contribution of Non-deprivation Factors in the Production of Sensory-Deprivation Effects: The Psychology of the "Panic Button"', *Journal of Abnormal and Social Psychology*, vol. 68, 1964.

Ornstein, R.E., *The Psychology of Consciousness*, Harcourt Brace, Jovanovich, New York 1977.

Ortega y Gasset, *Dehumanization of Art, and Other Essays on Art, Culture and Literature,* University Press, Princeton 1969.

Orwell, G., See Blair, E.

Osborn, D.K., and Endsley, R.C., 'Emotional Reactions of Young Children to T.V. Violence', *Child Development*, vol. 42, 1971, pp.321—31.

Packard, V., *The Hidden Persuaders,* Longmans, London 1957.

Paivio, A., *Imagery and Verbal Processes,* Holt, Rinehart and Winston, New York 1971.

Paivio, A., 'On the Functional Significance of Imagery', *Psychological Bulletin*, no. 78, 1970, p.385.

Paivio, A., 'Mental Imagery in Associative Learning and Memory', *Psychological Review,* vol. 76, 1969, pp.241—62.

Palmer, E.L., and Dorr, A., *Children and the Faces of Television: Teaching, Violence, Selling,* Academic Press, New York 1980.

Park, R.E., 'News as a Form of Knowledge', in Steinberg, C.S. (ed.), *Mass Media and Communication,* second edition, revised and enlarged, Hastings House, New York 1972, pp.123—41.

Parke, R., Berkowitz, L., Leyers, J., West, S., and Sebastian, R., 'Some Effects of Violent and Non-Violent Movies on the Behaviour of Juvenile Delinquents', in Berkowitz, L. (ed.), *Advances in Experimental Social Psychology, Vol. 10*, Academic Press, New York 1977.

Parkin, F., *Class Inequality and Political Order,* McGibbon and Kee, London 1971.

Pask, G., 'Strategy, Competence and Conversation as Determinants of Learning', *Programmed Learning and Educational Technology,* vol. 6, 1972, pp.250—67.

Patterson, G.R., Littman, R.A., and Bricker, W., 'Assertive Behaviour in Children: A Step towards a Theory of Aggression', *Monographs of Social Research in Child Development*, no. 32, 1967.

Pearlin, L.I., 'Social and Personal Stress and Escape Television Viewing', *Public Opinion Quarterly*, vol. 23, 1959, pp.255—9.

Philo, G., Hewitt, J., Bekarrell, P., and Davis, H., *Really Bad News*, Writers and Readers, London 1982.

Piaget, J., *La Langue et La Pensée chez l'Enfant*, Neuchatel, Paris 1923.

Piaget, J., *Plays, Dreams and Imitation in Childhood*, translated by Gattegno, C., and Hodgson, F.M., Routledge and Kegan Paul, London 1962.

Piaget, J., and Inhelder, B., *Mental Imagery in the Child: A Study of the Development of Imaginal Representation*, Routledge and Kegan Paul, London 1971.

Piepe, A., Miles, E., and Lannon, J., *Television and the Working Class*, Saxon House, Farnborough 1975.

Pilkington, H. (Chairman), *The Future of Broadcasting in the United Kingdom*, Command 1753, HMSO, London 1962.

Posner, M.I., 'Abstraction and the Process of Recognition', in Bower, G.H., and Spence, J.T. (eds), *The Psychology of Learning and Motivation, vol 3*, Academic Press, New York 1969, pp.43—100.

Postman, L., and Egan, J.P., *Experimental Psychology*, Harper and Row, New York 1949.

Powers, P.C., and Geen, R.G., 'Effects of the Behaviour and the Perceived Arousal of a Model on Instrumental Aggression', *Journal of Personality and Social Psychology*, vol. 23, no. 2, 1972, pp.175—83.

Preston, M.I., 'Children's Reactions to Movie Horrors and Radio Crime', *Journal of Pediatrics*, vol. 19, no. 2, 1941, pp.147—68.

Pribram, K.H., 'Neurological Notes on the Art of Educating', in Hilgard, E. (ed.), *Theories of Learning and Instruction*, University Press, Chicago, 1964, pp.78—110.

Rabinovitch, M.S., McLean, M.S. Jnr, Markham, J.W., and Talbott, A.D., 'Children's Violence Perception as a Function of Television Violence', in Comstock, G.A., Rubinstein, E.A., and Murray, J.P. (eds), *Television and Social Behaviour: Vol. 5: Television's Effects: Further Explorations*, United States Government Printing Office, Washington DC 1972, pp.231—51.

Ray, M., 'Marketing Research', in Clarke, P., *New Models of Mass Communications Research*, Sage, Beverly Hills, California 1973.

Read, H., 'The Necessity of Art', *Saturday Review*, 6 December 1969, pp.24—7.

Richards, I.A., *Principles of Literary Criticism*, Routledge and Kegan Paul, London 1925.

Richardson, A., *Mental Imagery*, Routledge and Kegan Paul, London 1969.

Riesman, D., with Glazer, N., and Denney, R., *The Lonely Crowd*, Yale University Press, New Haven, Connecticut 1950.

Riley, J.W., Cantwell, F.V., and Ruttinger, K.F., 'Some Observations on the Social Effects of Television', *Public Opinion Quarterly*, 1949, vol. 13, pp.223–34.

Riley, J.W., and Riley, M.W., 'Mass Communications and the Social System', in Merton, R.K., et al. (eds), *Sociology Today*, Basic Books, New York 1959.

Riley, M.W., and Riley, J.W., 'A Sociological Approach to Communication Research', *Public Opinion Quarterly*, vol. 15, 1951, pp. 445-460.

Robinson, J.P., 'Television and Leisure Time: Yesterday, Today and (Maybe) Tomorrow', *Public Opinion Quarterly*, vol. 32, 1969, pp. 211-222.

Robinson, J.P., 'Mass Communications and Information Diffusion', in Kline, F.G., and Tichenor, P.J. (eds), *Current Perspectives in Mass Communication Research*, Sage, Beverly Hills, California 1972, pp.71–93.

Robinson, J.P., and Hirsch, P., 'It's the Sound that Does It', *Psychology Today*, vol. 15, 1969, pp.42–95.

Robinson, J.P., and Bachman, J.G., 'Television Viewing Habits and Aggression', in Comstock, G.A., and Rubinstein, E.A. (eds), *Television and Social Behaviour: Vol. 3: Television and Adolescent Aggressiveness*, United States Government Printing Office, Washington DC 1972, pp.372–82.

Rosenberg, B., and White, D.M. (eds), *Mass Culture: The Popular Arts in America*, Free Press, New York 1957.

Rosnow, A., 'A Spread of Effect in Attitude Formation', in Greenwald, A., Brock, T., and Ostrom, T. (eds), *Psychological Foundations of Attitude*, Academic Press, New York 1968, pp.89–107.

Rotman, B., *Jean Piaget: Psychologist of the Real*, Harvester Press, Hassocks, Sussex 1977.

Rubinstein, E.A., 'The T.V. Violence Report: What's Next?', *Journal of Communication*, vol. 24, no. 1, 1974, pp.80–8.

Ruble, D.N., Balaban, T., and Cooper, J., 'Gender Constancy and the Effects of Sex-Typed Television Toy Commercials', *Child Development*, vol. 52, 1981, pp.667–73.

Rundus, D., 'Analysis of Rehearsal Processes in Free Recall', *Journal of Experimental Psychology*, vol. 89, no. 1, 1971, pp.63–77.

Rutter, M., Maugham, B., Mortimore, P., Ouston, J., with Smith, A., *Fifteen Thousand Hours: Secondary Schools and their Effects on Children*, Open Books, London 1979.

Sabini, J., and Silver, M., *Moralities on Everyday Life*, Oxford University Press, New York 1982.

Salomon, G., 'Shape, Not Only Content: How Media Symbols Partake in the Development of Abilities', in Wartella, E. (ed.), *Children Communicating: Media and Development of Thought, Speech, Understanding*, Sage, Beverly Hills, California 1979, pp.53–82.

Salomon, G., Eglstein, S., Finkelstein, R., Finkelstein, I., Mintzberg, E., Malve, D., and Velner, L., 'Educational Effects of "Sesame Street" on Israel's Children', Hebrew University of Jerusalem: School of Education 1972.

Samuelson, M., Carter, R.F., and Ruggels, L., 'Education, Available Time and Use of Mass Media', *Journalism Quarterly*, vol. 40, 1963, pp.491–6.

Sandell, R., *Linguistic Style and Persuasion*, European Monographs in Social Psychology, 11, Academic Press, London 1977.

Sargant, W., *Battle for the Mind: A Physiology of Conversion and Brain-washing*, Heinemann, London 1957.

Sargent, L.W., and Stempel, G.H. III, 'Poverty, Alienation and Mass Media Use', *Journalism Quarterly*, vol. 45, 1968, pp.324–6.

Schachter, S., 'The Interaction of Cognitive and Physiological Determinants of Emotional State', in Berkowitz, L. (ed.), *Advances in Experimental Social Psychology, Vol. 1*, Academic Press, New York 1964, pp.49–80.

Schmid, A., and de Graaf, J., 'Insurgent Terrorism and the Western News Media', Centre for the Study of Social Conflicts, Leiden, 1980.

Schneller, R., 'Training for Critical T.V. Viewing', *Educational Research*, vol. 24, no. 2, 1982, pp.99–106.

Schramm, W. (ed.), *The Process and Effects of Mass Communication*, University Press, Urbana, Illinois 1955.

Schramm, W. (ed.), *The Impact of Educational Television*, University Press, Urbana, Illinois 1960.

Schramm, W. (ed.), *Mass Communications*, University Press, Urbana, Illinois, second edition, 1960.

Schramm, W. (ed.), *The Science of Human Communication: New Directions and New Findings in Communication Research*, Basic Books, New York 1963.

Schramm, W. (ed.), *The Research on Programmed Instruction: An Annotated Bibliography*, United States Office of Education, Washington DC 1964.

Schramm, W. (ed.), *Big Media, Little Media: Tools and Technologies for Instruction*, Stage Publications, London 1971.

Schramm, W., Lyle, J., and Parker, E.G., *Television in the Lives of Our Children*, University Press, Stanford, California 1961.

Schrank, J. (ed.), *Understanding Mass Media,* National Text Book Library, Stokie, Illinois 1975.

Searle, J.R., *Speech Acts,* University Press, Cambridge 1969.

Seeman, M., 'On the Meaning of Alienation', *American Sociological Review,* vol. 24, 1959, pp.783–91.

Seggar, J., and Wheeler, P., 'The World of Work on Television: Ethnic and Sex Representation in T.V. Drama', *Journal of Broadcasting,* vol. 17, 1973, pp.201–14.

Shannon, C., and Weaver, W., *The Mathematical Theory of Communication,* University of Illinois Press, Urbana 1949.

Sharp, R., and Green, A., *Education and Social Control: A Study in Progressive Primary Education,* Routledge and Kegan Paul, London 1975.

Shaw, I.S., and Newell, D.S., *Violence on Television: Programme Content and Viewer Perception,* BBC, London 1972.

Sheehah, P.W., 'The Functional Similarity of Imaging to Perceiving: Individual Differences in Vividness of Imagery', *Perceptual and Motor Skills,* vol. 23, 1966, pp.1011–33.

Shepherd, R.N., 'Recognition Memory for Words, Sentences and Pictures', *Journal of Verbal Learning and Verbal Behaviour,* vol. 6, 1967, pp.156–63.

Shils, E.A., 'The Study of the Primary Group', in Jacobs, N. (ed.), *Culture for the Millions? Mass Media in Modern Society,* Norstrand, Princeton 1959.

Short, J., Williams, E., and Christie, B., *The Social Psychology of Telecommunications,* Wiley, London 1976.

Shotter, J., 'The Cultural Context of Communication Studies: Theoretical and Methodological Issues', in Lock, A. (ed.), *Action, Gesture, and Symbol,* Academic Press, London 1978, pp.43–48.

Shulman, M., *The Ravenous Eye: The Impact of the Fifth Factor,* Cassell and Coronet, London 1973.

Shute, H., *Underlying Factors in Reading Success and Failure,* Educational Enquiry Monograph, Aston, Birmingham, no. 3, 1976.

Siegel, A.E., 'Film-mediated Fantasy Aggression and Strength of Aggressive Drive', *Child Development,* vol. 27, 1956, pp.365–78.

Siegel, A.E., 'The Influence of Violence in the Mass Media upon Children's Role Expectations', *Child Development,* vol. 29, 1958, pp.35–56.

Siegel, A.E., and Kohn, L., 'Permissiveness, Permission and Aggression: The Effect of Adult Presence or Absence on Aggression in Children's Play', *Child Development,* vol. 30, 1959, pp.131–41.

Siegel, A.W., and Stevenson, H.W., 'Incidental Learning: A Developmental Study', *Child Development,* vol. 37, 1966, pp.811–17.

Sigelman, L., 'Reporting the News: An Organisational Analysis', *American Journal of Sociology*, no. 79, 1973, pp.132—51.

Simmel, G., *Die Grosstädte und das Geisleben*, Dresden 1903.

Simmons, J., *Psychiatric Examination of Children*, Lenard Febiger, Philadelphia 1969.

Singer, B.D., 'Mass Media and Communication Processes in the Detroit Riot of 1967', *Public Opinion Quarterly*, vol. 34, 1970, pp.236—45.

Singer, J.L. (ed.), *The Control of Aggression and Violence: Cognitive and Physiological Factors*, Academic Press, New York 1971.

Singer, J.L., and Singer, D.G., *Television, Imagination and Aggression: A Study of Pre-Schoolers* , Lawrence Erlbaum, Hillsdale, New Jersey 1981.

Singer, J.L., and Tower, R., Singer, D.G., and Biggs, A., 'Pre-Schoolers' Comprehension and Play Behaviour Following Viewing of "Mr Rogers" and "Sesame Street"', paper presented at the American Psychological Association, San Francisco 1977.

Skinner, B.F., *Verbal Behaviour*, Prentice-Hall, Englewood Cliffs, New Jersey 1957.

Smith, A., *The Shadow in the Cave: The Broadcaster, the Audience, and the State*, Allen and Unwin, London 1973.

Smith, G.J.W., and Henrikson, M., 'The Effect on an Established Percept of a Perceptual Process beyond Awareness', *Acta Psychologica*, vol. 11, 1955, pp.346—55.

Smith, M.B., Bruner, J.S., and White, R.W., *Opinions and Personality*, Wiley, New York 1956.

Smythe, D.W., 'Some Observations on Communications Theory', *Audio-Visual Communication Review*, vol. 2, 1954, pp.24—37.

Smythe, D.W., *Three Years of New York Television: Jan 4—10, 1951, 2,3*, National Association of Educational Broadcasters, Urbana, Illinois 1953.

Smythe, D.W., and Campbell, A., *Los Angeles Television: May 23—29, 1951*, National Association of Educational Broadcasters, Urbana, Illinois 1951.

Sokolov, J.M., *Perception and the Conditioned Reflex*, translated from the Russian by Waydenfeld, S.W., Pergamon Press, Oxford 1963.

Sonnenschein, S., 'The Effects of Redundant Communications on Listeners: When More is Less', *Child Development*, vol. 53, no. 3, pp.717—29.

Spengemann, W.C., *The Forms of Autobiography: Episodes in the History of a Literary Genre*, Yale University Press, New Haven, Connecticut 1980.

Sperling, G., 'The Information Available in Brief Visual Presentations', *Psychological Monographs*, vol. 74 (whole no. 498), 1960.

Sperling, G., 'A Model for Visual Memory Tasks', *Human Factors*, vol. 5, 1963, pp.19—31.

Sprafkin, J.N., Liebert, R.M., and Poulos, R., 'Effects of a Pro-social Televised Example on Children's Helpings', *Journal of Experimental Child Psychology*, vol. 20, 1975, pp.119—26.

Sprafkin, J.N., and Liebert, R.M., 'Sex-Typing and Children's Television Preferences', in Tuchman, G., Daniels, A.K., and Benét, J., *Hearth and Home: Images of Women in the Mass Media*, Oxford University Press, New York 1978, pp.228—39.

Staats, A.W., 'Learning Behaviour Theory Contributions to Attitude Theory', in Greenwald, A., Brock, T., and Ostrom, T. (eds), *Psychological Foundations of Attitudes*, Academic Press, New York 1968, pp.33—66.

Star, S., and Hughes, H., 'Report on an Educational Campaign: The Cincinnati Plan for the United Nations', *American Journal of Sociology*, vol. 50, pp.389—400.

Stearn, G.E. (ed.), *McLuhan Hot and Cool*, Penguin, Harmondsworth 1968.

Stein, A.H., and Friedrich, L.K., *Impact of Television on Children and Youth*, University Press, Chicago 1975.

Stein, A.H., and Friedrich, L.K., 'Television Content and Young Children's Behaviour', in Murray, J.P., Rubinstein, E.A., and Comstock, G.A. (eds), *Television and Social Behaviour: Vol. 2: Television and Social Learning*, United States Government Printing Office, Washington DC 1972, pp.202—317.

Steinberg, C.S. (ed.), *Mass Media and Communication*, second edition, revised and enlarged, Hastings House, New York 1972.

Steuer, F., Applefield, J., and Smith, R., 'Televised Aggression and the Interpersonal Aggression of Pre-School Children', *Journal of Experimental Child Psychology*, vol. 11, 1971, pp.442—7.

Stevenson, H.W., 'Television and the Behaviour of Pre-School Children', in Murray, J.P., Rubinstein, E.A., and Comstock, G.A. (eds), *Television and Social Behaviour: Vol. 2: Television and Social Learning*, United States Government Printing Office, Washington DC 1972, pp.346—71.

Storr, A., *Human Aggression*, Allen Lane, London 1968.

Stroop, J.R., 'Studies of Interference in Serial Verbal Reactions', *Journal of Experimental Psychology*, vol. 18, 1935, pp.643—62.

Swartz, J.A., 'The Anatomy of the Comic Strip and the Value World of Kids', PhD Dissertation, Ohio State University 1978.

Swinehart, J.W., and McLeod, J.M., 'News about Science: Channels, Audiences and Effects', *Public Opinion Quarterly*, vol. 29, 1961, pp.583—9.

Swingewood, A., *The Myth of Mass Culture*, Macmillan, London 1977.

Tarde, G., *Gabriel Tarde on Communication and Social Influence*, edited by Clark, T., University Press, Chicago 1969.

Thomas, M.H., Horton, R.W., Lippincott, E.C., and Drabman, R.S., 'De-sensitization to Portrayals of Real-Life Aggression as a Function of Exposure to Television Violence', *Journal of Personality and Social Psychology*, vol. 35, 1977, pp.450–8.

Thomson, O., *Mass Persuasion in History: A Historical Analysis of the Development of Propaganda Techniques*, Paul Harris, Edinburgh 1977.

Thompson, D., 'A Cure of Amnesia', *Scrutiny*, vol. 2, 1933, pp.2-11.

Thompson, R.J., *Television Crime — Drama: Its Impact on Children and Adolescents*, F.W. Cheshire, Melbourne 1959.

Thorndyke, P.W., 'Cognitive Structures in Comprehension and Memory of Narrative Discourse', *Cognitive Psychology*, vol. 9, 1977, pp.77–110.

Tichenor, J.P., Donohue, G.A., and Olien, C.N., 'Mass Media Flow and Differential Growth in Knowledge', *Public Opinion Quarterly*, vol. 34, 1970, pp.159–70.

Tichenor, J.P., Donohue, G.A., and Olien, C.N., 'Community Issues/Conflicts', in Clarke, P. (ed.), *New Models of Communications Research*, Sage, Beverly Hills, California 1973.

Tiegler, T., 'On the Biological Basis of Sex Differences in Aggression', *Child Development*, vol. 51, no. 4, 1980, pp.943–63.

Tracey, M., *The Production of Political Television*, Routledge and Kegan Paul, London 1977.

Trenaman, J.M., and McQuail, D., *Television and the Political Image: A Study of the Impact of Television on the 1959 General Election*, Methuen, London 1961.

Tuchman, G., Daniels, A.K., and Benét, J., *Hearth and Home: Images of Women in the Mass Media*, Oxford University Press, New York 1978.

Tulving, E., 'Subjective Organisation in Free Recall of "Unrelated" Words', *Psychological Review*, vol. 69, 1962, pp.344–54.

Tulving, E., 'Subjective Organisation and Effects of Repetition in Multi-Trial Free-Recall Learning', *Journal of Verbal Learning and Verbal Behaviour*, vol. 5, 1966, pp.193–7.

Tulving, E., 'Episodic and Semantic Memory', in Tulving, E., and Donalstone, D. (eds), *Organisation of Memory*, New York 1972, pp.381–403.

Tulving, E., 'Ecphoric Processes in Recall and Recognition', in Brown, R. (ed.), *Children and Television*, Collier Macmillan, London 1976, pp.37–73.

Tulving, E., and Pearstone, Z., 'Availability versus Accessibility of Information in Memory for Words', *Journal of Verbal Learning and Verbal Behaviour*, vol. 5, 1966, pp.381—91.

Tulving, E., and Madigan, S.A., 'Memory and Verbal Learning', *Annual Review of Psychology*, vol. 21, 1970, pp.437—84.

Turner, E.A., and Rommetveit, R., 'Focus of Attention in Recall of Active and Passive Sentences', *Journal of Verbal Learning and Verbal Behaviour*, vol. 7, 1968, pp.543—8.

Tversky, A., and Kahneman, D., 'Availability: a Heuristic for Judging Frequency and Probability', *Cognitive Psychology*, vol. 5, 1973, pp.207—32.

Tversky, B., 'Pictorial and Verbal Encoding is a Short Term Memory Task', *Perceptual Psychophysics*, vol. 6, 1969, p.225.

Ullman, S., *Meaning and Style: Collected Papers*, Blackwell, Oxford 1973.

Underwood, B.J., and Schulz, R.W., *Meaningfulness and Verbal Learning*, Lippincott, Chicago 1960.

Underwood, B.J., 'Interference and Forgetting', *Psychological Review*, vol. 64, 1957, pp.49—60.

Underwood, G., *Attention and Memory*, Pergamon Press, Oxford 1976.

United States Surgeon General's Scientific Advisory Committee on Television and Social Behaviour, vol. 1, Comstock, G.A., and Rubinstein, E.A. (eds), *Media Content and Control;* vol. 2, Murray, J.P., Rubinstein, E.A., and Comstock, G.A. (eds), *Television and Social Learning;* vol. 3, Comstock, G.A., and Rubinstein, E.A. (eds), *Television and Adolescent Aggressiveness;* vol. 4, Rubinstein, E.A., Comstock, G.A., and Murray, J.P. (eds), *Television in Day-to-Day Life: Patterns of Use;* vol. 5, Comstock, G.A., Rubinstein, E.A. and Murray, J.P. (eds), *Television's Effects: Further Explorations*, United States Government Printing Office, Washington DC 1972.

Usherwood, B., 'Sound Commentary: Pop Music', *Library Association Record*, vol. 81, 1979, pp.16—19.

Valentine, C.W., *The Experimental Psychology of Beauty*, Camelot Press, London 1962.

Veblen, T., *The Theory of the Leisure Class*, Macmillan, New York 1899.

Vernon, M.D., *The Psychology of Perception*, Penguin, Harmondsworth 1962 (note: first edition used).

Vernon, M.D., 'Perception and Understanding of Instructional Television Programmes', *British Journal of Psychology*, vol. 44, 1953, pp.116—26.

Vygotsky, L.S., *Thought and Language*, Massachusetts Institute of Technology Press, Cambridge, Mass. 1962.

Vygotsky, L.S., *Mind in Society: The Development of Higher Psychological Processes*, edited by Cole, M., John-Steuner, V., Scribner, E., and Sanderman, E., Harvard University Press, Cambridge, Mass. 1978.

Wade, S., and Schramm, W., 'The Mass Media as Sources of Public Affairs, Science and Health Knowledge', *Public Opinion Quarterly*, vol. 33, 1969, pp.196—209.

Wakshlag, J.J., Day, K.O., and Zillman, D., 'Selective Exposure to Educational Television Programs as a Function of Differently Paced Humorous Inserts', *Journal of Educational Psychology*, vol. 73, no. 1, 1981, pp.27—32.

Wakshlag, J.J., Reitz, R.J., and Zillman, D., 'Selective Exposure to an Acquisition of Information from Educational Television Programs as a Function of Appeal and Tempo of Background Music', *Journal of Educational Psychology*, vol. 74, no. 5, 1982, pp.666—77.

Walster, E., and Festinger, L., 'The Effectiveness of "Overheard" Persuasive Communications', *Journal of Abnormal and Social Psychology*, vol. 65, 1962, pp.395—402.

Walters, R.H., and Brown, M., 'Studies of Reinforcement of Aggression: Transfer of Responses to an Interpersonal Situation', *Child Development*, vol. 34, 1963, pp.563—71.

Walters, R.H., and Thomas, E.L., 'Enhancement of Punitiveness by Visual and Audio-visual Displays', *Canadian Journal of Psychology*, vol. 16, 1963, pp.244—55.

Ward, S., 'Effects of T.V. Advertising on Children and Adolescents', in Brown, R. (ed.), *Children and Television*, Collier Macmillan, London 1976, pp.297—319.

Ward, S., Levinson, D., and Wackmann, D., 'Children's Attention to Television Advertising', in Rubinstein, E.A., Comstock, G.A., and Murray, J.P. (eds), *Television and Social Behaviour: Vol. 4: Television in Day-to-Day Life: Patterns of Use*, United States Government Printing Office, Washington DC 1972, pp.491—515.

Ward, S., and Wackmann, D., 'Television Advertising and Intrafamily Influence: Children's Purchase Influence Attempts and Parental Yielding', in Rubinstein, E.A., Comstock, G.A., and Murray, J.P. (eds), *Television and Social Behaviour: Vol. 4: Television in Day-to-Day Life: Patterns of Use*, United States Government Printing Office, Washington DC 1972, pp.516—25.

Ward, S., and Wackmann, D., 'Children's Information Processing', in Clarke, P. (ed.), *New Models for Mass Communications Research*, Sage, Beverly Hills, California 1973, pp.126—46.

Ward, S., Wackmann, D., and Wartella, E., *How Children Learn to Buy*, Sage, Beverly Hills, California 1977.

Wartella, E. (ed.), *Children Communicating: Media and Development of Thought, Speech, Understanding*, Sage, Beverly Hills, California 1979.

Waugh, N.C., and Norman, D.A., 'Primary Memory', *Psychological Review*, vol. 72, 1965, pp.89—104.

Weber, M., *Die Grosstadt*, Glencoe Press, Chicago 1958. (Originally published 1921.)

Wells, W.D., *Television and Aggression: Replication of an Experimental Field Study*, Graduate School of Business, Chicago 1973.

Wertham, F.C., *Seduction of the Innocent*, Rinehart, Holt, New York 1954.

West, S.G., 'Mainlining Soaps: The Allure of Daytime Television Drama', in Schrank, J., *Understanding Mass Media*, National Text Book Library, Stokie, Illinois 1975.

Whale, J.H., *The Politics of the Media*, University Press, Manchester 1977.

Whitehead, A.N., *An Enquiry Concerning the Principles of Natural Knowledge*, University Press, Cambridge 1925.

Wilensky, H.L., 'Mass Society and Mass Culture: Inter-dependence or Independence?', *American Sociological Review*, vol. 19, 1964, pp.173—97. Reprinted in Berelson, B., and Janowitz, M. (eds), *Reader in Public Opinion and Communication*, Free Press, New York 1966.

Williams, B. (Chairman), *Report of the Committee on Obscenity and Film Censorship*, HMSO, London 1979.

Williams, R., *Culture and Society 1780—1950*, Chatto and Windus, London 1958.

Williams, R., *The Long Revolution*, Chatto and Windus, London 1961.

Williams, R., *Television, Technology and Cultural Form*, Fontana/Collins, London 1974.

Williams, R., *Culture*, Fontana, London 1981.

Williamson, D., 'Pilot Study at Fossdene School, Charlton, on 36 8—11 year olds', larger study being developed for Mrs S. Oppenheimer, Consumer Affairs Minister and the Advertising Standards Authority 1980.

Winick, C. (ed.), *Deviance and the Mass Media*, Sage, Beverly Hills, California 1978.

Winick, C., Williamson, L.G., Chuzmir, S., and Winick, M.P., *Children's T.V. Commercials: A Content Analysis*, Praeger, New York 1973.

Winick, M.P., and Winick, C., *The Television Experience: What Children See*, Sage, Beverly Hills, California 1979.

Winkley, D., 'Children's Response to Stories', DPhil Thesis, Oxford 1975.

Winkley, L., 'The Implications of Children's Wishes — Research Note', *Journal of Child Psychology and Psychiatry*, vol. 23, no. 4, 1982, pp.477—83.

Winn, M., *The Plug-in Drug: Television, Children and the Family*, Viking Press, New York 1977.

Wittgenstein, L. von, *Philosophical Investigations*, translated by Anscombe, G.E.M., Blackwell, Oxford 1967.

Wober, M., 'Children and Television', *Independent Broadcasting*, vol. 2, 1974, pp.4–7.

Woodrick, C., Chisson, B., and Smith, D., 'Television Viewing Habits and Parents – Observed Behaviours of Third-Grade Children', *Psychological Reports*, vol. 40, 1977, p.830.

Woodring, P., 'Reform Movements from the Point of View of Psychological Theory', in Hilgard, E. (ed.), *Theories of Learning and Instruction*, University Press, Chicago, 1964, pp.286–305.

Wright, C.R., *Mass Communication: A Sociological Perspective*, Random House, New York 1959.

Wright, C.R., 'Functional Analysis in Mass Communication', in Dexter, L.A., and White, D.M. (eds), *People, Society and Mass Communications*, Free Press, New York 1964, pp.91–109.

Wright, J.C., and Huston, A.C., 'The Forms of Television: Nature and Development of Television Literacy in Children', in Gardner, H., and Kelly, H. (eds) *Children and the Words of Television*, Josey-Bass, San Francisco 1981.

Wright, J.C., and Vlietstra, A., 'The Development of Selective Attention: From Perceptual Exploration to Logical Search', in Reese, H.W. (ed.), *Advances in Child Development and Behaviour, Vol. 10*, Academic Press, New York 1975.

Wright, J.M. von, 'Selection in Visual Immediate Memory', *Quarterly Journal of Experimental Psychology*, vol. 20, 1968, pp.62–8.

Yaffe, M., 'Pornography: An Updated Review (1972–1977)', in Williams, B. (Chairman), *Report of the Committee on Obscenity and Film Censorship*, HMSO, London 1979, pp.235–44.

Yntema, D.B., and Muesner, G.E., 'Remembering the Present States of a Number of Variables', *Journal of Experimental Psychology*, vol. 60, 1960, pp.18–22.

Yung, C.G., *Studies in Word Association*, Heinemann, London 1918.

Yussen, S.R., 'Determinants of Visual Attention and Recall in Observational Learning by Pre-Schoolers and Second Graders', *Development Psychology*, vol. 10, 1974, pp.93–110.

Zajonc, R.B., 'Some Effects of the "Space" Serials', *Public Opinion Quarterly*, vol. 18, 1954, pp.367–74.

Zeiler, M.D., and Kelley, C.A., 'Fixed-Ratio and Fixed-Interval Schedules of Cartoon Presentation', *Journal of Experimental Child Psychology*, vol. 8, 1969, pp.306–13.

Zielske, H.A., 'The Remembering and Forgetting of Advertising', *Journal of Marketing*, January 1959, pp.239–43.

Zillman, D., Williams, B.R., Bryant, J., Boynton, E.R., and Wolf, M.A., 'Acquisition of Information for Educational Television Programs as a Function of Differently Paced Humorous Inserts', *Journal of Educational Psychology*, vol. 72, 1980, pp.170—80.

Zuekerman, M., 'The Effects of Subliminal and Supraliminal Suggestion on Verbal Productivity', *Journal of Abnormal and Social Psychology*, vol. 60, 1960, pp.404—11.

Index

Television:
subliminal world of (cont.)
visual elements 159; responses and previous associations 159; subconscious reception of attitudes 161–2, 179;
use of TV images in children's play 140
See also Educational television
Thatcher, Margaret 8, 111, 161
That's Life 57
Tom and Jerry 5, 9, 70
Tomorrow's World 5, 78: childrens recall of 93
Top of the Pops 4, 5, 6, 9, 13, 78, 186
Two Ronnies 5

University Challenge 13

Viewing habits of children: 'heavy' viewing 13; interaction between programmes and other events 16–17; knowledge of schedules 13–14, 17, 20–1, 87; late night viewing 14–15; parental wishes and 15–16; prevalence of TV sets 11, 12; serial watching 14; time spent watching 11, 12, 180
See also Recall and recognition

Viewing styles of children: combining viewing with other activities 18, 19; pleasure and boredom in TV 22–4, 186–8; reactions to TV 22–3, 148–9; selective attention 19–20, 28–30; TV contrasted with classroom 20–21
Violence: and fantasy 76–7; as programme texture 68–70; children's blind eye for 75, 77, 81, 168, 181; obedient aggression 74; seen as ritual only 69, 77; studies into effects of 70–7; theoretical approaches to 173–4

Wagner, Lindsay 52, 136
Wayne, John 46
Wilson, Harold 8
Winkler, Henry 47
Wogan, Terry 45
Wonder Woman 14, 40, 41, 52: children's recall of 88, 90; heroine's characteristics 41, 42, 80
Words and Pictures 17
World in Action, The 13

You and Me 177

Zavaroni, Lena 48